Research Methods for the

lewis levenberg · Tai Neilson
David Rheams
Editors

Research Methods for the Digital Humanities

palgrave
macmillan

Editors
lewis levenberg
Levenberg Services, Inc.
Bloomingburg, NY, USA

David Rheams
The University of Texas at Dallas
Richardson, TX, USA

Tai Neilson
Macquarie University
Sydney, NSW, Australia

ISBN 978-3-319-96712-7   ISBN 978-3-319-96713-4   (eBook)
https://doi.org/10.1007/978-3-319-96713-4

Library of Congress Control Number: 2018950497

Cover credit: Photoco

This Palgrave Macmillan imprint is published by the registered company Springer Nature Switzerland AG
The registered company address is: Gewerbestrasse 11, 6330 Cham, Switzerland

CONTENTS

NOTES ON CONTRIBUTORS

Mark Alfano's work in moral psychology encompasses subfields in both philosophy (ethics, epistemology, philosophy of science, philosophy of mind) and social science (social psychology, personality psychology). He is ecumenical about methods, having used modal logic, questionnaires, tests of implicit cognition, incentivizing techniques borrowed from behavioral economics, neuroimaging, textual interpretation (especially of Nietzsche), and Digital Humanities techniques (text-mining, archive analysis, visualization). He has experience working with R, Tableau, and Gephi.

David Arditi is an Associate Professor of Sociology and Director of the Center for Theory at the University of Texas at Arlington. His research addresses the impact of digital technology on society and culture with a specific focus on music. Arditi is author of *iTake-Over: The Recording Industry in the Digital Era* and his essays have appeared in *Critical Sociology, Popular Music & Society*, the *Journal of Popular Music Studies, Civilisations, Media Fields Journal* and several edited volumes. He also serves as Co-Editor of *Fast Capitalism*.

Federica Bressan (1981) is a post-doctoral researcher at Ghent University, where she leads a research project on multimedia cultural heritage under the Marie Curie funding programme H2020-MSCA-IF-2015. She holds an M.D. in Musicology and a Ph.D. in Computer Science. From 2012 to 2016 she held a post-doctoral research position at the Department of Information Engineering, University of

Padova, Italy, where she coordinated the laboratory for sound preservation and restoration. The vision underlying her research revolves around technology and culture, creativity and identity. Her main expertise is in the field of multimedia preservation, with a special attention for interactive systems.

Erin Brock Carlson is a Ph.D. candidate at Purdue University in Rhetoric and Composition, where she has taught advanced professional writing courses and mentored graduate students teaching in the introductory composition program. Her research interests include public rhetorics, professional-technical writing, and participatory research methods. Her work has appeared in *Kairos: A Journal of Rhetoric, Technology, and Pedagogy* and *Reflections: A Journal of Writing, Service-Learning, and Community Literacy*, and is forthcoming in the print version of *Computers and Composition*.

Andrea Copeland is the Chair of Library and Information Science and Associate Professor at Indiana University—Purdue University Indianapolis. Her research focus is public libraries and their relationship with communities. She is the co-editor of a recent volume, *Participatory Heritage*, which explores the many ways that people participate in cultural heritage activities outside of formal institutions. It also examines the possibility of making connections to those institutions to increase access and the chance of preservation for the tangible outputs that result from those activities.

Robert W. Gehl is an Associate Professor of Communication at the University of Utah. He is the author of *Weaving the Dark Web: Legitimacy on Freenet, Tor, and I2p* (MIT Press, 2018) and *Reverse Engineering Social Media* (Temple University Press, 2014). His research focuses on alternative social media, software studies, and Internet cultures.

Natalia Grincheva holder of several prestigious academic awards, including Fulbright (2007–2009), Quebec Fund (2011–2013), Australian Endeavour (2012–2013) and other fellowships, Dr. Natalia Grincheva has traveled around the world to conduct research for her doctoral dissertation on digital diplomacy. Focusing on new "Museology and Social Media Technologies", she has successfully implemented a number of research projects on the "diplomatic" uses of new media by the largest museums in North America, Europe, and Asia. Combining digital media studies, international relations and new museology, her research provides an analysis of non-state forms of contemporary cultural diplomacy, implemented online within a museum context. A frequent speaker, panel participant or a session chair in various international conferences, Natalia is also an author of numerous articles published in *International Academic Journals*, including *Global Media and Communication Journal*, *Hague Journal of Diplomacy*, *Critical Cultural Studies*, the *International Journal of Arts Management, Law and Society*, and many others.

E. B. Hunter formerly the artistic director of an immersive Shakespeare project at a restored blast furnace in Birmingham, Alabama, E. B. Hunter is finishing her Ph.D. in theatre at Northwestern University. Hunter researches live cultural contexts—theatre, museums, and theme parks—to find the production choices that create authenticity and meaningful interactivity. To test her findings in a digital environment, Hunter launched the startup lab Fabula(b) at Northwestern's innovation incubator. She is currently leading the build of Bitter Wind, a HoloLens adaptation of Agememnon, which has been featured by Microsoft and SH// FT Media's Women in Mixed Reality initiative.

lewis levenberg lives and works in New York State.

Tai Neilson is a lecturer in Media at Macquarie University, Sydney. His areas of expertise include the "Political Economy of Digital Media and Critical Cultural Theory". Dr. Neilson has published work on journalism and digital media in *Journalism, Fast Capitalism*, and *Global Media Journal*. His current research focuses on the reorganization of journalists labour through the use of digital media. Dr. Neilson teaches classes in news and current affairs, and digital media. He received his Ph.D. in Cultural Studies from George Mason University in Virginia and his M.A. in Sociology from the New School for Social Research in New York.

Trinity Overmyer is a Ph.D. candidate in Rhetoric and Composition at Purdue University, where she serves as Assistant Director. In her current research at Los Alamos National Laboratory, Trinity explores the knowledge-making practices of data scientists and engages critically with large-scale data as a medium of inscription and a rhetorical mode of inquiry. She has worked extensively in "Technical Writing and Design, Community Engagement, and Qualitative Research Methods", both within and outside the university. She teaches multimedia and technical writing courses in the Professional Writing program at Purdue.

David Rheams is a recent Ph.D. graduate from George Mason University's Cultural Studies program. His research interests include topics on environmental communications, science and technology studies, and the Digital Humanities. David has been in the software industry for over 15 years leading support and product teams.

Roopika Risam is an Assistant Professor of English at Salem State University. She is the author of *New Digital Worlds: Postcolonial Digital Humanities in Theory, Praxis, and Pedagogy* (Northwestern University Press, 2018). Her research focuses on Digital Humanities and African diaspora studies. Risam is director of several projects including The Harlem Shadows Project, Social Justice and the Digital Humanities, Digital Salem, and the NEH and IMLS-funded Networking the Regional Comprehensives.

Henriette Roued-Cunliffe is an Associate Professor in Digital Humanities at the Department of Information Studies, University of Copenhagen, Denmark. She has worked extensively within the field of archaeological computing with subjects such as open heritage data and heritage dissemination. As a part of her D.Phil. at the University of Oxford she specialized in collaborative digitisation and online dissemination of heritage documents through XML and APIs. Her current research project has taken a turn towards participatory collaborations between DIY culture (genealogists, local historians, amateur archaeologists, etc.) and cultural institutions, particularly on the Internet.

J. J. Sylvia IV is an Assistant Professor in Communications Media at Fitchburg State University. His research focuses on understanding the impact of big data, algorithms, and other new media on processes of subjectivation. Using the framework of posthumanism, he explores how the media we use contribute to our construction as subjects. By developing a feminist approach to information, he aims to bring an affirmative and activist approach to contemporary data studies that highlights the potential for big data to offer new experimental approaches to our own processes of subjectivation. He lives in Worcester, M.A. with his wife and two daughters.

Assoc. Prof. Nick Thieberger is a linguist who has worked with Australian languages and wrote a grammar of Nafsan from Efate, Vanuatu. He is developing methods for creation of reusable datasets from fieldwork on previously unrecorded languages. He is the editor of the journal *Language Documentation & Conservation*. He taught in the Department of Linguistics at the University of Hawai'i at Mānoa and is an Australian Research Council Future Fellow at the University of Melbourne, Australia where he is a CI in the ARC Centre of Excellence for the Dynamics of Language.

Albert William is a Lecturer, Media Arts and Science at Indiana University—Purdue University Indianapolis. William specializes in three-dimensional design and animation of scientific and medical content. He has been involved in project management and production for numerous projects with SOIC for organizations. William teaches a range of 3-D courses at SOIC. He's received the 2003 Silicon Graphics Inc. Award for excellence in "Computational Sciences and Visualization" at Indiana University, and the 2016 award for Excellence in the Scholarship of Teaching.

Tarrin Wills was Lecturer/Senior Lecturer at the University of Aberdeen from 2007–2018 and is now Editor at the Dictionary of Old Norse Prose, University of Copenhagen. He is involved in a number of DH projects, including the Skaldic Project, Menota and Pre-Christian Religions of the North, and leads the Lexicon Poeticum project. Tarrin has worked extensively with XML and database-based DH projects, including building complex web applications.

Zebulun M. Wood is a Lecturer and Co-Director of Media Arts and Science undergraduate program. He works in emerging media, focusing in 3-D design integrated formats. He works with students on projects that improve lives and disrupt industries, and instructs in all areas of 3-D production, including augmented and virtual reality.

Ayoung Yoon is an Assistant Professor of Library and Information Science, and Data Science at Indiana University—Purdue University Indianapolis. Dr. Yoon's research focuses on data curation, data sharing and reuse, and open data. She has worked for multiple cultural institutions in South Korea and the United States where she established a background in digital preservation. Dr. Yoon's work is published in *International Journal of Digital Curation*, and *Library and Information Science Research* among other journals.

LIST OF FIGURES

LIST OF TABLES

CHAPTER 1

Introduction: Research Methods for the Digital Humanities

Tai Neilson, lewis levenberg and David Rheams

This book introduces a range of digital research methods, locates each method within critical humanities approaches, presents examples from established and emerging practitioners, and provides guides for researchers. In each chapter, authors describe their pioneering work with an emphasis on the types of questions, methods, and projects open to digital humanists. Some methods, such as the translation of literary sources into digital games, are "native" to Digital Humanities and digital technologies. Others, such as digital ethnographies, are adopted and adapted from extensive traditions of humanities and social science research. All of the featured methods suggest future avenues for Digital Humanities research. They entail shifting ethical concerns related to

T. Neilson (✉)
Macquarie University, Sydney, NSW, Australia
e-mail: tai.neilson@mq.edu.au

l. levenberg
Levenberg Services, Inc., Bloomingburg, NY, USA
e-mail: work@lewislevenberg.com

D. Rheams
The University of Texas at Dallas, Richardson, TX, USA

© The Author(s) 2018   1
l. levenberg et al. (eds.), *Research Methods for the Digital Humanities*,
https://doi.org/10.1007/978-3-319-96713-4_1

online collaboration and participation, the storage and uses of data, and political and aesthetic interventions. They push against the boundaries of both technology and the academy. We hope the selection of projects in this volume will inspire new questions, and that their practical guidance will empower researchers to embark on their own projects.

Amidst the rapid growth of Digital Humanities, we identified the need for a guide to introduce interdisciplinary scholars and students to the methods employed by digital humanists. Rather than delimiting Digital Humanities, we want to keep the field open to a variety of scholars and students. The book was conceived after a panel on digital research methods at a Cultural Studies Association conference, rather than a Digital Humanities meeting. The brief emerged out of contributions from the audience for our panel, conversation between the panel presenters, and the broader conference that featured numerous presentations addressing digital methods through a range of interdisciplinary lenses and commitments. The guide is designed to build researchers' capacities for studying, interpreting, and presenting a range of cultural material and practices. It suggests practical and reflexive ways to understand software and digital devices. It explores ways to collaborate and contribute to scholarly communities and public discourse. The book is intended to further expand this field, rather than establish definitive boundaries.

We also hope to strengthen an international network of Digital Humanities institutions, publications, and funding sources. Some of the hubs in this network include the Alliance for Digital Humanities Organizations and the annual Digital Humanities conference, the journal *Digital Humanities Quarterly*, funding from sources like the National Endowment for Humanities' Office of Digital Humanities, and, of course, many university departments and research institutes. The editors are each affiliated with George Mason University (GMU), which houses the Roy Rosenzweig Center for History and New Media. GMU also neighbors other prominent institutes, such as the Maryland Institute for Technology in the Humanities, Advanced Technologies in the Humanities at University of Virginia, University of Richmond's Digital Scholarship Lab, and Carolina Digital Humanities Initiative. Because Digital Humanities is hardly an exclusively North American project, the contributions to this volume of authors and projects from Australia, Denmark, the Netherlands, and the United Kingdom illustrate the international reach of the field.

There are a number of other books that address the identity of Digital Humanities, its place in the university, or specific aspects of its practice. Willard McCarty's *Humanities Computing* is a canonical text, laying the philosophical groundwork and suggesting a trajectory for what, at the time of printing, was yet to be called Digital Humanities.[1] McCarty interrogates the "difference between cultural artifacts and the data derived from them." He argues that this meeting of the humanities and computation prompts new questions about reality and representation. Anne Burdick et al. position the field as a "generative enterprise," in which students and faculty make things, not just texts.[2] Like McCarty, they suggest that Digital Humanities is a practice involving prototyping, testing, and the generation of new problems. Further, *Debates in the Digital Humanities*, edited by Mathew Gold, aggregates essays and posts from a formidable cast and does a commendable job of assessing "the state of the field by articulating, shaping, and preserving some of the vigorous debates surrounding the rise of the Digital Humanities."[3] These debates concern disciplinarity, whether the field is about "making things" or asking questions, and what types of products can be counted as scholarly outputs. Other books cover specific areas of practice. For instance, the Topics in the Digital Humanities series published by University of Illinois Press includes manuscripts devoted to machine reading, archives, macroanalysis, and creating critical editions.[4] Digital Humanities is not only, or even primarily, defined by books on the subject; it is defined and redefined in online conversations, blog posts, in "about us" pages for institutions and departments, calls for papers, syllabi, conferences, and in the process of conducting and publishing research.

[1] Willard McCarty, *Humanities Computing* (New York, NY: Palgrave Macmillan, 2005), 5.

[2] Anne Burdick, Johanna Drucker, Peter Lunenfeld, Todd Presner, and Jeffrey Schnapp, *Digital_Humanities* (Cambridge, MA: The MIT Press, 2012), 5.

[3] Matthew K. Gold, *Debates in the Digital Humanities* (Minneapolis, MN: University of Minnesota Press, 2012), xi.

[4] Daniel Apollon, Claire Bélisle, and Philippe Régnier, *Digital Critical Editions* (Urbana-Champaign, IL: University of Illinois Press, 2014); Matthew Jockers, *Macroanalysis: Digital Methods and Literary History* (Urbana-Champaign, IL: University of Illinois Press, 2014); Stephen Ramsay, *Reading Machines: Toward an Algorithmic Criticism* (Urbana-Champaign, IL: University of Illinois Press, 2011); Christian Vandendorpe, *From Papyrus to Hypertext: Toward the Universal Digital Library* (Urbana-Champaign, IL: University of Illinois Press, 2009).

Digital Humanities also has its critics. For instance, Daniel Allington et al., authored a scathing critique titled "Neoliberal Tools (and Archives): A Political History of Digital Humanities" for the *Los Angeles Review of Books*. They insist that "despite the aggressive promotion of Digital Humanities as a radical insurgency, its institutional success has for the most part involved the displacement of politically progressive humanities scholarship and activism in favor of the manufacture of digital tools and archives."[5] They suggest that Digital Humanities appeal to university administrators, the state, and high-rolling funders because it facilitates the implementation of neoliberal policies: it values academic work that is "immediately usable by industry and that produces graduates trained for the current requirements of the commercial workplace."[6] Similarly, Alexander Galloway contends that these projects and institutions tend to resonate with "Silicon Valley" values such as "flexibility, play, creativity, and immaterial labor."[7] In response to Allington et al.'s polemic, *Digital Humanities Now* aggregated blog posts by scholars and students decrying the article and refuting its arguments. Rather than dismiss these criticisms outright, Patrick Jagoda encourages reflection on how some forms of Digital Humanities may elicit free or exploited labor and have a role in transforming the humanities and universities of which we are a part.[8] These are not reasons to give up on the name or the project of Digital Humanities, but they are questions with which a rigorous, critical, open, and politically active Digital Humanities must engage.

OUR APPROACH

We do not purport to make an intervention in definitional debates about Digital Humanities, although we acknowledge that we have our own epistemological, methodological, and even normative commitments. These proclivities are evident in our call for chapters, the self-selection of contributors, and our editorial decisions. Along with most humanists,

---

[5] Daniel Allington, Sara Brouillette, and David Golumbia, "Neoliberal Tools (and Archives): A Political History of Digital Humanities," *Los Angeles Review of Books*, May 1, 2016. https://lareviewofbooks.org/article/neoliberal-tools-archives-political-history-digital-humanities/.

[6] Ibid.

[7] Alexander R. Galloway, *The Interface Effect* (New York, NY: Polity Press, 2012), 27.

[8] Jagoda Macroanalysis, 359.

we are wary of positivist epistemologies and approaches to data collection and analysis. Hence, we adopt reflexive positions regarding the roles of research, interpretation, and critique. Our methodological commitments include, for example, the insistence on marrying theory and practice. As such we asked contributors to be explicit about how their work fits among or challenges existing projects and scholarship, and the questions their work poses and answers. The types of Digital Humanities we are interested in pursuing are also sensitive to the inclusion of underrepresented groups and challenging existing power relations. To do so, requires us to interrogate our own biases, the tools we use, and the products of our research. Each of these positions touches on significant tensions in the field and deserve elaboration.

One thing that unites humanists is our understanding that the texts we work with and the results of our research are not simply pre-existing data or truths ready to be found and reported. This anti-positivist epistemology suggests that the types of questions we ask shape the kinds of data we will produce. It is also an acknowledgment that the types of tools we employ determine the information we can access and, in turn, the types of conclusions we can draw. Johanna Drucker's work is instructive in this regard. In particular, she differentiates between *capta* and *data*. In her schema, "*capta* is 'taken' actively while *data* is assumed to be a 'given' able to be recorded and observed." She continues, "humanistic inquiry acknowledges the situated, partial, and constitutive character of knowledge production, the recognition that knowledge is constructed, *taken*, not simply given as a natural representation of pre-existing fact."[9] Digital humanists are exposing the fallacy that research involving quantitative or computational methods is necessarily positivist. Rather, there are productive tensions between interpretivist approaches and the quantitative characteristics of computing.

Digital Humanities often involves translating between different modes of expression. Humanities disciplines provide space to question cultural values and prioritize meaning-making over strict empiricism. Their methods are primarily heuristic, reflexive, and iterative. Texts are understood to change through consecutive readings and interpretations. They are always highly contextual and even subjective. Conversely, "computational environments are fundamentally resistant to qualitative

[9] Johanna Drucker, "Humanities Approaches to Graphical Display," *Digital Humanities Quarterly* 5, no. 1 (2011).

approaches."[10] Fundamentally, digital devices, operating systems, and software rely on denotative code, which has no room for ambiguity. This requires a translation between types of representation. To think about the translation between these different fields of human activity we can recall Walter Benjamin's argument in his essay "Task of the Translator."[11] He contends that translation is its own art form and like other art forms, it is a part of the technical standards of its time. Many digital humanists engage in the processes of translating texts into digital spaces and data, or translating digital and quantitative information into new texts and interpretations. Translating humanistic inquiry into digital processes can force humanists to make their assumptions and normative claims more explicit. At the same time, Digital Humanities practitioners might work to create computational protocols which are probabilistic, changeable, and performative based in critical and humanistic theory.[12]

Two concerns about theory have demanded attention in debates surrounding Digital Humanities. The first concerns whether there is a body of theory around which Digital Humanities work, curricula, and institutions can or should be organized. The second is a reprisal of debates about the distinctions between *logos* and *techne*, theory and practice. The Humanities consist of a huge diversity of disciplines and fields—adding the prefix "digital" seems only to compound this. The Digital Humanities community also tends to include people in different professional roles and from outside of the walls of the academy.[13] Digital humanists cannot claim a shared body of literature or theory that orients their work. As such, our insistence is that scholars (in the broadest sense) continue to consider the impacts of their work beyond the field of practice: to make explicit the positions from which they approach their work, the questions they intend to pose or answer, and how they contribute not just to the collection of cultural materials, but the development of knowledge.

---

[10] Johanna Drucker, quoted in Gold, *Debates in the Digital Humanities*, 86.

[11] Walter Benjamin, "The Task of the Translator," trans. Harry Zohn, in *Selected Writings*, ed. Marcus Bullock and Michael W. Jennings, 253–263 (Cambridge, MA: Harvard University Press, 1996 [1923]).

[12] Johanna Drucker, quoted in Gold, *Debates in the Digital Humanities*, 86.

[13] Lisa Spiro, quoted in Gold, *Debates in the Digital Humanities*, 16.

Some in Digital Humanities have signaled a "maker turn."[14] Among digital humanists, the distinction between theory and practice has been reframed as a debate "between those who suggest that digital humanities should always be about *making* (whether making archives, tools, or digital methods) and those who argue that it must expand to include *interpreting*" (italicization in original).[15] Among those who privilege making, Stephen Ramsay is often cited for his claim that Digital Humanities "involves moving from reading and critiquing to building and making."[16] The maker turn is in some respects a response to the problems with academic publishing, peer review, and promotion. Like other types of open access publishing, publicly available Digital Humanities projects are often part of the demand to retain ownership over one's work, disseminate information freely, and reach audiences outside of the university.

Approaches that shift the emphasis from contemplative and critical modes toward activities of design and making are not limited to Digital Humanities. They echo aspects of DIY culture, handicrafts, tinkering, modding, and hacking.[17] These values are also prominent among internet commentators and futurists who suggests that critique now takes place through the design and implementation of new systems.[18] Others caution that to privilege making may open the door to uncritical scholarship, which simply reproduces hegemonic values, leaves our assumptions unchecked, and fails to ask vital questions. There is room in Digital Humanities for those that are primarily interested in the development of new tools, platforms, and texts, and for those who are most interested in contributing to the critique of cultural material and technologies. In our development of this volume, we felt the need to theorize in order to render the practices, epistemologies and implications involved in digital methods, tools, archives, and software explicit.

---

[14]David Staley, "On the 'Maker Turn' in the Humanities," in *Making Things and Drawing Boundaries: Experiments in the Digital Humanities*, ed. Jentery Sayers (Minneapolis, MN: University of Minnesota, 2017).

[15]Kathleen Fitzpatrick, quoted in Gold, *Debates in the Digital Humanities*, 13–14.

[16]Stephen Ramsay, quoted in Gold, *Debates in the Digital Humanities*, x.

[17]Anne Balsamo, *Designing Culture: The Technological Imagination at Work* (Durham, NC: Duke University Press, 2011), 177.

[18]Terry Flew, *New Media: An Introduction*, 3rd ed. (Oxford, UK: Oxford University Press, 2008), 41.

If digital humanists cannot rally around a body of theory, and are critical of the notion that Digital Humanities should always or primarily be about making, then perhaps we can find commonality in our approach to methods. McCarty recalls his early experiences of teaching in the subject when the only concerns that his students from across the humanities and social sciences shared were related to methods.[19] As a result, McCarty sketched the idea of a "methodological commons," which scholars in a variety of fields can draw on at the intersection of the humanities and computing.[20] We should, however, exercise caution not to think about Digital Humanities as a set of digital tools, such as text markup and analysis software, natural language processors, and GIS (geographical information system), that can simply be applied to the appropriate data sets. These tools for storing, analyzing, and representing information are not neutral instruments. Rather, they bear the epistemological predispositions of their creators, and of the institutions and circumstances in which they are produced and used.[21] In short, digital humanists should avoid the instrumentalization of technologies and tools. Contributions to this volume represent a common, but contested and shifting, methodological outlook that focuses on the interrelationships between culture and digital technologies. In our view, the "digital" in Digital Humanities can refer to a tool, an object of study, a medium for presenting scholarly and aesthetic productions, a mode of communication and collaboration, a sphere of economic exchange and exploitation, and a site for activist and political intervention.

How To Use This Book

As the title indicates, this volume is intended as a reference guide to current practices in the Digital Humanities. The Digital Humanities field is one of experimentation both in practice and theory. Technological tools and techniques quickly change, as software is improved or falls into disuse. Research practices are also reevaluated and refined in the field. Therefore, experimentation is encouraged throughout these chapters. We hope that readers will turn to the chapters in this book for inspiration

---

[19] McCarty, *Humanities Computing*, 4.

[20] Ibid., 119.

[21] Svensson in Gold, *Debates in the Digital Humanities*, 41.

and guidance when starting new research projects. While technology has provided a bevy of new tools and toys to tinker with, technology itself is not the primary focus of Digital Humanities methods. The book contains technical discussions about computer code, visualization, and database queries, yet the tools are less notable than the practice. In other words, technology serves the methodology.

The broad scope of projects in this book should interest students, social scientists, humanists, and computer and data scientists alike. Each chapter relates to fields of expertise and skill sets with which individual readers will be more or less familiar. In some cases prior knowledge of theoretical frameworks in the humanities and social sciences will help the reader navigate chapters, but this knowledge is not a prerequisite for entry. Other chapters presuppose varying levels of technical knowledge, for instance, experience with spreadsheets or JS libraries. Here, there may be a steeper learning curve for readers who do not come from a technical or computer science background. Nonetheless, all of the chapters provide starting points from which readers with different skill sets can pose new questions or begin Digital Humanities projects.

Further, readers will find this book useful in their own ways. Programmers will find the discussions of database management, analytical software, and graphic interfaces useful when considering new software. Software design is not contained within any one specific section. Instead, it threads through many of the chapters. Programmers looking for ideas about how to create better tools for Digital Humanities projects will find the critiques and limitations of current software particularly useful. Digital archivists are presented with various ways to handle both large and small datasets. In some cases, storing data for ethnographic purposes requires a consumer application with the ability to take notes, as Tai Neilson's chapter discusses. Other archives require the secure access and storage practices described in Robert W. Gehl's chapter. There is an entire section devoted to the confluence of Digital Humanities methods and ethnographic research that we hope ethnographers will find illuminating. Ethnographers working on digital topics are breaking traditional boundaries between computational methods and qualitative research, and challenging the assumption that all quantitative practices are positivist. Graphic designers, those with an interest in user interfaces, and data visualization will find a range of methods and critical evaluations of data presentation. Like the software aspects of this book, concerns about data visualization and user interfaces are heard throughout many of the chapters. Rendering research visible is a critical component of Digital Humanities projects, as it affects the way we communicate findings, interact with our tools, and design our projects.

What Is In This Book

Each chapter in this volume presents a case study for a specific research project. While the case studies cover a wide range of topics, each contribution here discusses both the background and history of its research methods, and the reasons why a researcher might choose a particular Digital Humanities method. This allows the chapters to serve as both tutorials on specific research methods, and as concrete examples of those methods in action. In order to guide readers and to serve as a teaching resource, the volume includes definitions of key terms used. Each chapter will help readers navigate practical applications and develop critical understandings of Digital Humanities methods.

Presenting digital topics in the confines of print is difficult because digital objects are interactive by nature and tend to change rapidly. Therefore, considerations and instructions about specific consumer software are generally avoided in this text. Although helpful, instructions on software such as Microsoft Excel are better left to other, online, resources as instructions run the risk of being outdated upon publication. The same is true of fundamental web technologies. There are many online resources available for students to learn the basics of web design, database management, connection protocols, and other tools. Likewise, instructions on how to write code are not present because numerous resources are available to teach programming, user interface design, and other technical skills. Nor does this book attempt a complete history of Digital Humanities methods. Instead, we focus on current projects, with a nod to previous theorists' relevance to the case studies within this book.

We have arranged the chapters in this volume based on commonalities between the methods that each contributor uses in their research, generally categorizing each method as "analytical," "ethnographic," "representational," or "archival." The first few chapters of the volume, those in our "analytical" group, showcase computational approaches to the processing of large amounts of data (especially textual data). In "On Interdisciplinary Studies of Physical Information Infrastructure," lewis levenberg argues, through examples from a study of telecommunications networks in West Africa, for how a beginner researcher of information infrastructure—the physical and technical elements of how we move information around—can use a combination of practices and techniques from computer science, policy analysis, literary studies, sociology, and history, to collect, analyze, and draw conclusions from both computational and textual data sets. Similarly, in "Archives for the Dark Web," Robert W. Gehl argues that in order to study the cultures of Dark Web sites and users, the digital humanist must engage with these systems' technical infrastructures. This chapter provides a field guide for doing so, through data obtained from participant observation, digital archives, and the experience of running the routing software required to access the Dark Web itself. In a shift towards text-processing at larger scales, David Rheams's chapter, "Creating an Influencer-Relationship Model," shows how the creation and computational analysis of an original collection of news articles allows a researcher to realize patterns within texts. David Arditi's chapter, "MusicDetour," outlines the purpose and process of creating a digital archive of local music, ways to create research questions in the process of creating it, the process that he used while constructing such an the archive in the Dallas-Fort Worth area, and even some of the problems that copyright creates for the Digital Humanities. Mark Alfano's chapter, "Digital Humanities for History of Philosophy," shows the utility of text-processing techniques at a closer scale. He tracks changes in how Friedrich Nietzsche used specific terms throughout his body of work and then constructs arguments about how and why Nietzsche uses each concept. Importantly, these chapters do not only rely on technical apparatuses; indeed, they each also showcase humanists' analyses of technical structures.

In the following, "ethnographic" chapters, the authors highlight original uses of digital communications to facilitate interactive, interpersonal, social-scientific research. Natalia Grincheva's chapter "Digital Ethnography" explores how visitor studies methodologies, when specifically applied to museums as cultural institutions, significantly advanced those museums' cultural programming and social activities, especially through the development of digital media. Erin Brock Carlson and Trinity Overmeyer, in their chapter, "Photovoice Methods," captured otherwise-forgotten focus group data by asking participants in their community research project to take and discuss their own photographs in order to document the participants' experiences and to catalog their perceptions. And Tai Neilson, in his chapter "Digital Media,

Conventional Methods," offers a methodological treatise, and a guide to conducting online interviews in the Digital Humanities based on his study of digital journalism in New Zealand and the US. In their extensions of interview, participant observation and focus-group techniques, through innovative uses of multiple media, these contributions teach us how to use all the tools at our disposal to get more, and better data, while keeping a critical focus on the procedures of qualitative research.

The next several chapters concentrate on "representational" issues, through cases that challenge or address familiar questions from the humanities in the context of digital media. Elizabeth Hunter's chapter, "Building Videogame Adaptations of Dramatic and Literary Texts," traces the author's creation of an original video game, *Something Wicked*, based on Macbeth; this serves as a tutorial for how new researchers can ask interdisciplinary research questions through this creative process. Andrea Copeland, Ayoung Yoon, Albert Williams, and Zebulun Wood, in "Virtual Bethel," describe how a team of researchers are creating a digital model of the oldest black church in the city of Indianapolis, to create a virtual learning space that engages students in learning about the history of the church, local African American history, and how to use archives. And J. J. Sylvia's "Code/Art Approaches to Data Visualization" showcases the "Apperveillance" art project, in order to argue for how we might leverage the unique powers of generative data visualization to answer provocative questions in Digital Humanities. In each of these cases, the researchers' creativity and insight are as important to their contributions as are the sets of data with which they work.

Finally, the chapters grouped by their use of "archival" methods each provide us with fascinating improvements to existing techniques for historical media work, using digital tools and critical attention to detail. Nick Thieberger, in "Research Methods in Recording Oral Tradition," details the methods by which his research group in Australia set up a project to preserve records in the world's small languages. The case study demonstrates that these techniques are useful for archiving and re-using data sets across a range of humanities disciplines. "A Philological Approach to Sound Preservation," by Federica Bressan, provides a deep understanding of the challenges posed by audio media preservation from both a technical and an intellectual point of view, and argues for a rational systematization in the field of preservation work. Tarrin Wills's chapter, "User Interfaces for Creating Digital Research," provides a strong overview of how various applications and interfaces can be used to interact with information, using as its main case study the Skaldic Poetry Project (http://skaldic.org). In her chapter, "Developing Sustainable Open Heritage Datasets," Henriette Roued-Cunliffe investigates a collection of Danish photos to provide a practical overview of open data formats, and how they match up with different types of heritage datasets; she uses this case study to illustrate research issues with open heritage data, mass digitization, crowdsourcing, and the privileging of data over interfaces. Finally, Roopika Risam's chapter "Telling Untold Stories: Digital Textual Recovery Methods" uses structured markup languages to recover a digital critical edition of Claude McKay's poetry. The chapter demonstrates how digital works in the public domain can diversify and strengthen the cultural record. In each of these chapters, the contributors have broken new ground technically and methodologically, even as the conceptual roots of their work remain embedded in historical issues.

REFERENCES

Allington, Daniel, Sara Brouillette, and David Golumbia. "Neoliberal Tools (and Archives): A Political History of Digital Humanities." *Los Angeles Review of Books*, May 1, 2016. https://lareviewofbooks.org/article/neoliberal-tools-archives-political-history-digital-humanities/.

Apollon, Daniel, Claire Bélisle, and Philippe Régnier. *Digital Critical Editions*. Urbana-Champaign, IL: University of Illinois Press, 2014.

Balsamo, Anne. *Designing Culture: The Technological Imagination at Work*. Durham, NC: Duke University Press, 2011.

Benjamin, Walter. "The Task of the Translator," trans. Harry Zohn. In *Selected Writings*, edited by Marcus Bullock and Michael W. Jennings, 253–263. Cambridge, MA: Harvard University Press, 1996 [1923].

Burdick, Anne, Johanna Drucker, Peter Lunenfeld, Todd Presner, and Jeffrey Schnapp. *Digital_Humanities*. Cambridge, MA: The MIT Press, 2012.

Drucker, Johanna. "Humanities Approaches to Graphical Display." *Digital Humanities Quarterly* 5, no. 1 (2011). http://www.digitalhumanities.org/dhq/vol/5/1/000091/000091.html.

Flew, Terry. *New Media: An Introduction*, 3rd ed. Oxford, UK: Oxford University Press, 2008.

Galloway, Alexander R. *The Interface Effect*. New York, NY: Polity Press, 2012.

Gold, Matthew K. *Debates in the Digital Humanities*. Minneapolis, MN: University of Minnesota Press, 2012.

Jagoda, Patrick. "Critique and Critical Making." *PMLA* 132, no. 2 (2017): 356–363.

Jockers, Matthew. *Macroanalysis: Digital Methods and Literary History*. Urbana-Champaign, IL: University of Illinois Press, 2014.

McCarty, Willard. *Humanities Computing*. New York, NY: Palgrave Macmillan, 2005.

Ramsay, Stephen. *Reading Machines: Toward an Algorithmic Criticism*. Urbana-Champaign, IL: University of Illinois Press, 2011.

Staley, David. "On the 'Maker Turn' in the Humanities." In *Making Things and Drawing Boundaries: Experiments in the Digital Humanities*, edited by Jentery Sayers. Minneapolis, MN: University of Minnesota, 2017.

Vandendorpe, Christian. *From Papyrus to Hypertext: Toward the Universal Digital Library*. Urbana-Champaign, IL: University of Illinois Press, 2009.

CHAPTER 2

On Interdisciplinary Studies of Physical Information Infrastructure

lewis levenberg

Sometimes, in order to answer the questions that we ask as researchers, we need to combine more than one way of thinking about our questions. In situations when our objects of inquiry—the things in the world we question—are made up of some mixture of people, processes, and/or systems, we may find unusual juxtapositions of research methods particularly useful for discerning the important issues at stake. In these cases, our research benefits from the flexibility and breadth that we can bring to the ways that we ask, and answer, our research questions.

When we embrace this methodological diversity, we can decide how important it is for our approach to be **replicable**, our results **reproducible**, or our argument **intuitive**, and we can select a set of specific techniques and methods that fit these priorities. For example, to examine how **public policy** and **physical infrastructure** affect large-scale **digital communications**, we can use practices and techniques from any or all of computer science, policy analysis, literary studies, sociology, and history,

l. levenberg (✉)
Levenberg Services, Inc., Bloomingburg, NY, USA
e-mail: work@lewislevenberg.com

© The Author(s) 2018
l. levenberg et al. (eds.), *Research Methods for the Digital Humanities*,
https://doi.org/10.1007/978-3-319-96713-4_2

in varying proportions. In this chapter, I will demonstrate, through examples, how a beginning researcher of **information infrastructure**— the physical and technical elements of how we move information around—might use a similar combination of methodological approaches.

To illustrate the broad variety of specific research techniques that a Digital-Humanities perspective makes available, I will introduce examples from my own research on the **network infrastructure** across West Africa, where large-scale **telecommunications** network **architecture** remains unevenly distributed, both between and within the region's nation-states. Growth rates of **backbone** network infrastructure (the internet's 'highways', large-scale connections between cities, countries, or continents) outpace growth rates of access to those same networks for people in this region. The pattern contrasts with most of the rest of the world's demand-driven network development (in which larger backbone elements are only constructed once demanded by the scale of the networks trying to connect to each other). The internet—comprised of **physical network** infrastructure, technical **protocols, software**, and the movement of **data**—commonly enters public **discourse** in terms of a borderless, international, global phenomenon. On this basis, we might expect that telecommunications **policies** to influence how internet infrastructure is developed would tend to come from global political powerhouses. Yet we find that Ghana, Nigeria, and even Liberia, despite their apparent relative weakness in a **geopolitical** context, appear to pursue aggressive telecommunications policy with broader, regional effects. This anomaly raises the central **research question** that I wanted to answer: How and why would the telecommunications policy strategies of these ostensibly weak states lead to a backbone-first **architecture** for large-scale internetworking throughout West Africa?

Because a researcher might approach such a question from any of various perspectives, we have an opportunity to separate the project into its **epistemological** and **methodological** pieces. Epistemologically, the focus on its object of analysis—the effects of these case studies' telecommunications policies on large-scale physical network infrastructure over time—gives the study its place astride technological and humanities ways of thinking. Methodologically, the approach to each piece of this puzzle highlights its own set of research practices. For example, to understand the actual changes to the region's network infrastructure over time, we can use scanning and **topological** analysis techniques from computer science. To find out how we know what a particular telecommunications policy "means" or "intends", we can use both **computational** and **heuristic** reading practices. And to articulate whether there was actually a causal relationship between telecommunications policies and network infrastructure changes, we can use higher-order analyses from historical and public-policy perspectives. By combining the results of these methods, the study arrives at a unified argument to answer its question: the backbone-first telecommunications policies of these ostensibly weak states are rational initiatives in their historical context, and they have disproportionately effective results on large-scale network architecture across the region. This is because their policies rely on, favor, and reinforce the states' **"gatekeeper"** style **institutions** of **governance**—structures that work to concentrate political-economic **power** (and the perception of that power) at the state's physical and conceptual boundaries.

Procedure: Layering Methods

In holistic Digital Humanities studies of information infrastructure, we cannot rely solely on the selection of any given techniques from various disciplines. In addition to selecting our research methods pragmatically, for their relative efficacy at answering a part of a research question, we must also attend to the way in which those methods complement or contradict one another. In my study on West African network backbone infrastructure, I use the tools of different humanities, social-sciences, and computer science disciplines depending not only on the type of information that they help glean, but also on how they can build upon one another as I move through the phases of the study. Just as the architecture of information infrastructure includes discrete **"layers"** of machines, processes, human activity, and concepts, so too does the study of that architecture allow for multiple layers of **abstraction** and assumption, each a useful part of a unified, interdisciplinary approach.

To that end, I began my own study with background work, in the form of **historical** research. I reviewed the major developments in the cultural and political conditions of the region, and of each of the case studies, from 1965 to 2015. The challenge in this particular **historiography** was to connect the development of global internetworking, which mostly took place in North America and Europe at first, to the specific changes taking place in each of the West African case study countries during that period. In broad strokes, the social transformations in

Ghana, Nigeria, and Liberia in the late twentieth century were quite isolated from the technological work underway to create the internet. However, by concentrating on the **structural** forms of emerging **institutions**, we see in that period the first hints of gatekeeper-friendly governance, in both the case study states and for the internet.

Although that historical argument is superfluous to the present, methodologically focused chapter, I refer to it here in order to emphasize the importance of multi-disciplinary approaches to complex questions. Historical and regional-studies analysis of **macroscopic** narratives helped focus the next phases of my inquiry, by validating some **assumptions** about the time frame and relevance of my questions, and by providing necessary context to the examination of policy-making in the very recent past across those cases. In other words, it established the **historicity** of the material infrastructure under examination in the study. From there, I could undertake network data collection, and collection of the text **corpora**, with confidence that the period that I was studying was likely to prove itself significant for answering my question. These data-collection techniques would have worked just as well for studying any given period, but because I introduced them based on the historical layer, it helped validate some of my core **assumptions** before I delved too deeply into minutiae.

Next, based on the data I had collected, I moved into the **analytical** techniques, looking for the overarching patterns across the case studies. Without the data-collection stage for the network data, my network analysis would have been based on secondary sources. Likewise, without the text collection stage, I would have had to rely on the judgment of others to select which policies I would go on to read closely. And I was able to undertake my close reading of selected texts based on their prevalence in the **indexing** techniques I used across the whole collection. I could therefore lean on my own **interpretive** analysis of the texts in this phase, rather than on the biographical, historical, or other external context of the text or its creator.

I added other layers of abstraction as I collected more information from these disparate techniques, building towards the **theoretical** arguments that I would go on to make about the patterns that I perceived. Zooming out, as it were, to that theoretical level, I was able to test my assumption that nation-states do act, through their agents, to impact the shape of international networks under their purview, because I could review the evidence that I had already layered, through the earlier methods, of how these nation-states undertake their telecommunications policy agendas.

At this higher-order layer, I could draw the links between the changes I had identified in the network architecture of the region, distinctions between each state's political-economic structures. Theoretical literature helped frame how each of these weak states interacts with other (state and non-state) internet builders, how each uses the processes of internet-building and the products of internet connectivity to represent themselves to their citizens and to the international community, and how the logic that underpins their surprising impacts on large-scale internet architecture, from conception to implementation, is generated and reinforced.

From this vantage, I was able to articulate how and why backbone-first patterns of internetworking across the region occur, what they portend for the nation-states under study, and what I could **generalize** about this development strategy. The cases of Ghana, Nigeria, and Liberia demonstrate that the rationales of weak states, as they work to affect network-building, depend on the results of previous and ongoing network changes. They also depend on the particular **political economy** of weak states—but such network changes may themselves present significant political-economic potential for transitioning away from gatekeeper-state models in the region.

In the rest of this chapter, I will focus less on that specific set of data and arguments, and more on the specific methods that I used. First I will review the collection and analysis of network data, then the collection and analysis of unstructured texts, and finally the use of higher-order theoretical techniques for drawing inferences and conclusions based on the combination of those collections and analyses.

Collecting and Analyzing Network Infrastructure Data

To dissect how networks have changed over time, we use can use both active scans of existing computers in those networks, and passive collection of already-existing data in and about the same networks. To begin collecting my own data, I enumerated the **autonomous system** numbers (ASNs) and groups of **IP addresses** assigned by the internet **registries** for each case study state. To do this, I first copied the publicly available IP address and ASN assignment **database** from the public **FTP** server maintained by AFRINIC (the Africa region's registry).[1] Studies taking place in other regions of the world would use the appropriate regional registry for such databases. Next, using the publicly available 'ip2location' database of correspondences between geographical coordinates and IP addresses, I filtered this list of possible addresses by the geographical location of each case study.[2] These initial queries resulted in a list of groups of IP addresses, known as classless inter-domain **routing** (CIDR) blocks. The sizes of these blocks, limited by the registries, ranges from a single IP address, to as many as 16,777,216 addresses (thankfully, such addresses are listed in order). To run scans against each unique IP address in these sets, I wrote a small Python script, using the "netaddr" module,[3] to expand each CIDR block into a list of all the individual IP addresses contained therein. For ease of use, I built one list of addresses for each of my three case studies, and kept them in plain text format.

The resulting data was appropriately formatted for the actual active scanning of whether a given address had anything using it. To do this, I used 'nmap', which sends out and tracks the response of small **packets** of data on TCP, UDP, or ICMP ports to any number of addresses. With nmap, and a helper program similar to nmap called 'masscan', I tested whether, across any of the open **ports** on each of the IP addresses in each list, there existed a listening **service**. Here again, output from this step of the process became the input for the next step, in which I re-scanned those internet-facing hosts directly, using the 'curl', 'traceroute', 'bgpdump', and 'tcpdump' programs to get more information about each of those remote systems. Supplementary information in that database included the types of **servers** in use, common **response** data from the servers, and the most-reliable **paths** for data to travel to and from those endpoints. These tests resulted in my own 'snapshot' of current internet-facing infrastructure throughout the region. Repeating this process regularly for several months revealed clear growth patterns in that infrastructure over time.

To repeat this process, you need access to a computer with an internet connection. Each of the software programs and databases that I used are open-source and publicly available; I ended up needing to write very

---

[1] "Index of ftp://ftp.afrinic.net/pub/stats/afrinic/."

[2] "IP Address to Identify Geolocation Information," *IP2Location*, accessed October 15, 2016, https://www.ip2location.com/.

[3] https://github.com/drkjam/netaddr.

little of my own code for this project. While I used a GNU/Linux operating system on the local computer, and the correspondingly packaged versions of each software program listed above, as well as a plain text editor and the command line / terminal emulator installed on that machine, there are a vast number of resources—command-line and graphical alike—for replicating the same results using Windows, Mac OS, or any other modern operating system. The important parts of this method are not necessarily the specific software or tools that one uses, but the effort required to learn how to use one's tools effectively as well as the patience to perform the research.

In my own study, I supplemented those scan results with extensive information from existing public datasets, as well as from recent, similarly constructed studies. The latter served the additional function of validating the methods and results of those recent studies, although those had different research questions, and arrived at their approaches and conclusions separately. Secondary sources included data sets from universities and independent research institutions, dedicated research projects, and the regional internet registries.[4] Such programs collect quantifiable network data on a regular basis, using replicable methods that any beginning network researcher would be wise to try for themselves.

World Bank and IMF program data, such as the Africa Infrastructure Country Diagnostic (AICD) database, also provided some baseline, conservative estimates of telecommunications infrastructure projects in the region, though they tended to under-count both the contributions and the infrastructure of local programs and institutions.[5] Industry reports

[4] "Index of ftp://ftp.afrinic.net/pub/stats/afrinic/," accessed August 11, 2014, ftp://ftp.afrinic.net/pub/stats/afrinic/; "The CAIDA AS Relationships Dataset," accessed September 20, 2015, http://www.caida.org/data/as-relationships/; Y. Shavitt, E. Shir, and U. Weinsberg, "Near-Deterministic Inference of AS Relationships," in *10th International Conference on Telecommunications, 2009. Con_{TEL} 2009*, 2009, 191–198.

[5] "Homepage | Africa Infrastructure Knowledge Program," accessed June 3, 2016, http://infrastructureafrica.org/; "Projects : West Africa Regional Communications Infrastructure Project—APL-1B | The World Bank."; "World Development Report 2016: Digital Dividends"; "Projects : West Africa Regional Communications Infrastructure Project—APL-1B | The World Bank"; Kayisire and Wei, "ICT Adoption and Usage in Africa"; "Internet Users (per 100 People) | Data | Table"; "Connecting Africa: ICT Infrastructure Across the Continent"; World Bank, "Information & Communications Technologies"; The World Bank, Financing Information and Communication Infrastructure Needs in the Developing World. Public and Private Roles. World Bank Working Paper No. 65.

and other third-party sources, particularly those provided for marketing purposes, provided additional, but less-easily verifiable, estimates of existing infrastructure and internet usage. For example, the Internet World Statistics website, or the Miniwatts Marketing Group report, reliably over-estimate technological data in stronger consumer markets, and underestimate the same phenomena in areas with less per-capita purchasing power.[6]

Together, these primary and secondary data sets outlined the general patterns of networking growth across the region, and provided more insight into network infrastructure and ownership in Ghana, Liberia, and Nigeria than had previously existed. Despite rapid infrastructure development, the network topologies of Nigeria, Ghana, and Liberia remain thin within each state. They are each becoming denser at the backbone tier, and along network edges, while last-mile infrastructure, hosting services, and internal networking are still lacking in the region.

These results illustrated the validity of my research question, by showing that weak states are indeed developing strong backbone networks. More importantly, they provided a set of clear, verified network outcomes against which I could benchmark the perceived impact of weak states' telecommunications policies. However, to do so, we must turn to a different set of research methods—the collection and analysis of textual data.

COLLECTING AND ANALYZING UNSTRUCTURED TEXTS

To reliably collect and organize a large set of texts, we can use computational techniques from the branch of study known variously as **natural language processing, corpus linguistics, distant reading**, or **broad reading**.[7] This set of methods deals with the **aggregation** and analysis of large sets of **structured or unstructured texts**; different disciplinary approaches use distinct sets of algorithmic or programmatic approaches to understanding the contents of texts, depending on the purposes of their research.

---

[6] "Africa Internet Stats Users Telecoms and Population Statistics," accessed December 16, 2014, http://www.internetworldstats.com/africa.htm.

[7] For simplicity, I refer to the specific techniques that I outline here by the latter term, but you can find excellent resources on these techniques, and their histories, under any of those names.

In the approach that I describe here, the purpose of this stage of research was to collect and organize a great deal of writing in a consistent **format**, and then to identify the most promising documents out of that collection for closer analysis. In other projects, researchers might be looking to identify the occurrence of specific, predetermined terms, or particular uses of language, across a large body of writing (as an aside, this colloquialism of a "body" of work is why the terms "corpus" and "corpora" are used in these disciplines), or to create maps of relationships between distinct texts in a corpus based on their **metadata**. In those cases, various natural language processing techniques certainly suit the need, but the specific work to be done would differ from what I describe here.

For my own broad reading of the early twenty-first century telecommunications policies of Ghana, Liberia, and Nigeria, I first collected about two thousand documents, web pages, and transcripts, each of which was produced by the government or the officials of these states. I collected public record and news archive searches, conference proceedings, policy-making negotiations, technical documentation, and legal documentation, mostly through the web interfaces of governmental and agency websites, libraries, and databases maintained by third-party institutions such as the World Bank. These texts came in a huge variety of **formats**, so one major, early challenge in cleaning this "corpus" was to convert as many as possible of the files I had copied into a **machine-readable** format. I used the open PDF **standard** for this purpose, although certain documents were rendered as images rather than texts, which required some manual intervention to apply **optical character recognition** settings and/or quickly scan the documents into a different format. As with so many other projects that include the collection of **unstructured** data (textual or otherwise), a great deal of effort and time had to go into the cleaning and preparation of the data before it was feasible to process using automated tools.

Once that was done, though, I was able to proceed to the **indexing** of these texts. I used the open-source program Recoll, which is based on the Xapian search engine library, to create an index of all the documents in my collection.[8] There are a vast number of such programs and products available, so the specific program or software library that you might

---

[8] https://www.lesbonscomptes.com/recoll/.

use would certainly depend on your own project's requirements. At this stage, I used the index to search through all the texts at once, looking for higher-frequency occurrences of unusual words or phrases, such as proper nouns and technical terms.

Some of these patterns of language also helped classify the types of texts. For example, a frequent occurrence of terms related to the appa-ratuses, internal operations, and techniques of governance of the state, such as parliamentary names or legal references, tended to indicate texts produced by governmental bodies, such as legislative documents. Looser policy guidance documents tended to include more terminology distinct from the workings of the state itself, such as ideological or economic terms, or the use of terms like borders, security, identity, or control. Geographical or infrastructural terms were more likely than the baseline to appear in technical documentation, while historical or philosophical terms were likelier to pop up in speeches and arguments made by politi-cians and other public figures during policy negotiations or in transcripts.

The results of this process let me select a much smaller set of the col-lection of texts for my closer analysis, confident in the likelihood that each text would prove particularly technically, legally, academically, or politically significant. Next, I briefly reviewed each document in the selected set to ensure that I had eliminated duplicates, opinion articles and other similarly superficial pieces of writing, texts from countries or time periods outside the scope of my study, and other such false posi-tives. Finally, I used the same indexing program from earlier, Recoll, to search through the full text of each selected document for terms that I expected to indicate the concepts that I would be reading closely for, such as "network," "infrastructure", and so on. Your own such keyword searches, when you get to this stage, will depend on the specific object and question that you are studying, of course.

At this juncture, a researcher will have selected just a few of the many documents in their collections, but they will be able to reasona-bly argue that these texts are likely to have the most relevant information for answering their own research question. Combined with an analysis of network infrastructure, we can now cross-reference metadata such as comparing the dates at which selected texts were published and dissemi-nated with the dates when specific changes were measured in an observed network. However, we will not yet have understood the contents of these key documents. To proceed, we must do what humanities scholars have done for centuries—that is, we must read the texts for ourselves.

Any particular approach you take to reading a text closely will depend in large part on the specific research question you are trying to answer—and, by extension, the disciplinary tools at your disposal for answering it through reading. For example, in a literary study, you might read a text with special attention to its narrative structure, literary devices, or poetics. In a study of scientific discourse, you might instead read texts with a focus on the specialized terms, methods, results, or concepts that they cite, define, or change. And in a study of public policy outcomes, such as the one in this chapter's example study, close reading concentrates on identifying the ideological basis and implementation details of the policies described by the texts. As you can imagine, these different priorities can lead to very different observations and insights about the texts that you study.

In my own study's close reading, I hoped to understand how ostensibly weak states implemented large-scale technological policy, and effected very large-scale network changes. To that end, as I read through each text that I had selected, I noted the structural forms of the arguments that each policy set out as justification or incentive for its prescriptions, as well as the specific data that each policy cited. The overarching narratives and justifications for policy recommendations were not always explicitly named by the policies themselves. Still, enough of their underlying logic was expounded that when I would broaden my focus again to the overall theoretical and historical stakes of these policies' implementations, the close reading would serve as solid foundations for those arguments. I will not burden this chapter with examples of my close readings, but I mention the specific elements that I looked for because this was the part of the study that gathered my evidence for claims about how and why specific policies were enacted.

The basic techniques of close reading will be familiar to nearly all humanities researchers, but since they strike such a contrast to the computational research techniques that we have seen so far, we can spare a thought here for their mechanics. Effective close reading relies on your concentration on a specific text for a sustained period of time; speed-reading and skimming are useful techniques for gathering superficial information in greater volume from more texts, but they do not serve your ability to answer a research question through the observation of detail quite so well. Some useful tools in this context are quite ancient, but modern software for bibliographic management or for annotations of digital texts can support your readings. Whatever tools you prefer, the crucial undertaking is to read the texts with attention to the details that you need to find in order to answer your research question—in these cases, to move from the details of telecommunications policy back out towards an historical, political analysis of information infrastructure.

ARTICULATING THEORETICAL INSIGHTS

In this section, I connect the results of these disparate methods and disciplinary approaches to the larger project of 'doing Digital Humanities' in the study of information infrastructure. This is the point at which the evidence you have collected through each layered technique can be abstracted into an overarching argument, just as we rely on the underlying infrastructure of the internet to facilitate conversation with people around the world.

In my own study, I had found that, despite their noticeable political-economic and structural differences, Ghana, Liberia, and Nigeria each produced telecommunications network development policy specifically designed to target backbone network infrastructure development. Moreover, in each of these three cases, such policies have consistently preceded network infrastructure implementations which followed the architectures promoted by those policies. The network architectures of backbone-first or edge-first infrastructures are globally rare, and we would not expect to find many such architectural patterns in networks that are cobbled together ad hoc from existing smaller networks, or in the development of large centrally managed organizations. So, the fact that we find backbone-first architecture arising in the region where weak states have consistently produced technological policy calling for just such networks leads to the reasonable claim that these policies are working as intended.

Having examined how telecommunications policy affects ICT development beyond the expected capabilities of gatekeeper states in West Africa, I was then able to turn to the implications of that impact. Specifically, if network-building activity responds to aggressive telecommunications policy, then we can also observe long-term effects of network-building on the underlying political-economic conditions of the very states that produce telecommunications policies in the first place. Further, we might see here how weak, gatekeeping states can benefit from intensified investments of capital, labor, and policy attention on backbone infrastructure. Through the development of telecommunications infrastructure and social institutions that rely on it, Ghana, Nigeria, and Liberia engage in a "thickening" of both physical and figurative networks. By reinforcing their positions as gatekeeper states, they lay the foundations of a transition away from that precarious structure, and towards more administrative governmental institutions. This argument stems from observing the implementation of the disproportionately aggressive policies of the case study states, and noting that network backbone infrastructure development correspondingly increased.

Other factors beyond the policies themselves also mattered. Improved funding and, in some cases, easier access to domestic and international capital for large-scale infrastructure investors, including telecommunications providers, also proved consistent during this period. At the same time, few technical policy alternatives to the backbone-first approach to telecommunications development were offered by non-state actors such as corporations or international institutions, in the documented policy discussions from any of the three case studies. Under these conditions, supposedly weak states can wield outsize influence on international network architecture. This observation then forms our criteria for inferring some degree of causal relationship described by the correlation between the telecommunications policy of our case studies, and the subsequent appearance of networks described by those policies. However, confounding factors in these policies' implementations have ranged from funding sources for network ownership and construction that are located outside of the states in question, to economic demand for edge network providers (as opposed to local/end user/last mile demand). We can see that these confounding factors are accounted for by the weak states' policy initiatives, which in turn allows us to acknowledge the awareness of each state of their weak position in geopolitical context.

In other words, Ghana, Liberia, and Nigeria have pursued policies that reinforce their existing political-economic structures. Gatekeeper states pursue gate-keeping internet infrastructure—the backbone networks and connections described throughout this study—as opposed to last-mile service provisions, or dense data storage centers (or the non-ICT infrastructure that would support those other ICTs). This feedback loop reinforces the leverage held by gatekeeper states during negotiations with external interests such as other governments or international bodies, because it increases the degree of control that these states have over the "right of way" for global information flows. In this light, the back-bone-first telecommunications policies of these ostensibly weak states do make rational sense, and they have disproportionately effective results on large-scale network architecture across the region, because the policies rely on, favor, and reinforce the states' gate-keeping institutions of governance.

CONCLUSION

In this chapter, I have introduced the wide variety of techniques available to researchers who study information infrastructure. The appropriation of specific approaches for discrete parts of a larger research project has its drawbacks, of course. We must be cautious not to cherry-pick our data or methods, selecting only those approaches or pieces of information that support our biases or keep us in our comfort zones. To that end, it is worth remembering that other methods than those outlined in this chapter can also be useful for studying physical information infrastructure. For example, conducting interviews with those who create and maintain infrastructure, or with policymakers, or different demographic segments of the networks' users, would provide deeper insight into the perspectives of individual people on the issues at stake. Conversely, more targeted or sustained scans of specific hosts across the networks could provide further details of technological implementation of networking across the region, such as the distribution of routing or server software, or the relative usage of network address capabilities. The key to any particular combination of methods, however, remains its utility in the answering of a given research question from this peculiar position of digital humanist.

This chapter has also sought to highlight the benefits of the particular methods that I used in my own work, in order to illustrate their effectiveness for answering pieces of a complex research question. For example, the use of network scanning software in repeated passes helped identify the actual changes to network infrastructure across West Africa over a defined period of time. Broad reading practices applied to a large set of public documents helped to identify important texts, and close reading of those particular texts helped to illuminate what a particular telecommunications policy set out to accomplish. Then, moving up a level of abstraction, to higher-order theoretical analysis, articulated a direct relationship between the telecommunications policies and the network infrastructure changes that we mapped. Most importantly, I arrived at an overall answer to my initial research question precisely by layering all of these methods and ways of thinking. That ability to move between techniques and modes of inquiry, in order to ask original questions, and to answer them, is the great strength of the interdisciplinarity of Digital Humanities.

REFERENCES

"Africa Internet Stats Users Telecoms and Population Statistics." Accessed December 16, 2014. http://www.internetworldstats.com/africa.htm.

"Connecting Africa: ICT Infrastructure Across the Continent." World Bank, 2010.

"Homepage | Africa Infrastructure Knowledge Program." Accessed June 3, 2016. http://infrastructureafrica.org/.

"Index of ftp://ftp.afrinic.net/pub/stats/afrinic/." Accessed August 11, 2014.

"Internet Users (per 100 People) | Data | Table." Accessed March 16, 2014. http://data.worldbank.org/indicator/IT.NET.USER.P2.

"IP Address to Identify Geolocation Information." IP2Location. Accessed October 15, 2016. https://www.ip2location.com/.

Kayisire, David, and Jiuchang Wei. "ICT Adoption and Usage in Africa: Towards an Efficiency Assessment." *Information Technology for Development* (September 29, 2015): 1–24. https://doi.org/10.1080/02681102.2015.1081862.

lesbonscomptes. "Recoll Documentation." Accessed January 21, 2018. https://www.lesbonscomptes.com/recoll/doc.html.

"Projects : West Africa Regional Communications Infrastructure Project—APL-1B | The World Bank." Accessed January 24, 2016. http://www.worldbank.org/projects/P122402/west-africa-regional-communications-infrastructure-project-apl-1b?lang=en.

Shavitt, Y., E. Shir, and U. Weinsberg. "Near-Deterministic Inference of AS Relationships." In *10th International Conference on Telecommunications, 2009. Con$_{TEL}$ 2009*, 191–198, 2009.

"The CAIDA AS Relationships Dataset." Accessed September 20, 2015. http://www.caida.org/data/as-relationships/.

The World Bank. Financing Information and Communication Infrastructure Needs in the Developing World. Public and Private Roles. World Bank Working Paper No. 65. Washington, DC: The World Bank, 2005. http://wbln0037.worldbank.org/domdoc%5CPRD%5COther%5CPRDDContainer.nsf/All+Documents/85256D2400766CC78525709E005A5B33/$File/financingICTreport.pdf?OpenElement.

"West Africa Regional Communications Infrastructure Program—PID." Accessed January 23, 2016. http://www.icafrica.org/en/knowledge-publications/article/west-africa-regional-communications-infrastructure-program-pid-135/.

World Bank. "Information & Communications Technologies." Accessed December 14, 2012. http://web.worldbank.org/WBSITE/EXTERNAL/TOPICS/EXTINFORMATIONANDCOMMUNICATIONANDTECHNOLOGIES/0,,menuPK:282828~pagePK:149018~piPK:149093~theSitePK:282823,00.html.

"World Development Report 2016: Digital Dividends." Accessed February 9, 2016. http://www.worldbank.org/en/publication/wdr2016.

CHAPTER 3

Archives for the Dark Web:
A Field Guide for Study

Robert W. Gehl

This chapter is the result of several years of study of the Dark Web, which culminated in my book project *Weaving the Dark Web: Legitimacy on Freenet, Tor, and I2P*. *Weaving the Dark Web* provides a history of Freenet, Tor, and I2P, and it details the politics of Dark Web markets, search engines, and social networking sites. In the book, I draw on three main streams of data: **participant observation**, **digital archives**, and the experience of running the **routing** software required to access the Dark Web. This chapter draws on these same streams to provide a field guide for other digital humanists who want to study the Dark Web. I argue that, in order to study the cultures of Dark Web sites and users, the digital humanist must engage with these systems' technical infrastructures. I will provide specific reasons why understanding the technical details of Freenet, Tor, and I2P will benefit any researchers who study these systems, even if they focus on end users, aesthetics, or Dark Web cultures. To these ends, I offer a catalog of archives and resources that researchers could draw on, and a discussion of why researchers should build their own archives. I conclude with some remarks about the ethics of Dark Web research.

R. W. Gehl (✉)
The University of Utah, Salt Lake City, UT, USA
e-mail: robert.gehl@utah.edu

© The Author(s) 2018
l. levenberg et al. (eds.), *Research Methods for the Digital Humanities*,
https://doi.org/10.1007/978-3-319-96713-4_3

31

WHAT IS THE DARK WEB?

As I define the **Dark Web** in my book, the "Dark Web" should actually be called "Dark Webs," because there are multiple systems, each relatively independent of one another. I write about three in my book: Freenet, Tor, and I2P. With these systems installed on a computer, a user can access special Web sites through **network topologies** that anonymize the connection between the **client** and the **server**. The most famous of these systems is **Tor**, which enables Tor hidden services (sometimes called "onions" due to that system's Top Level Domain, .onion). But there is an older system, **Freenet**, which allows for hosting and browsing freesites. Freenet was quite influential on the Tor developers. Another system that drew inspiration from Freenet, the Invisible Internet Project (**I2P**), allows for the anonymous hosting and browsing of eepsites. Tor hidden services, freesites, and eepsites are all built using standard Web technologies, such as HTML, CSS, and in some cases server- and client-side scripting. Thus, these sites can be seen in any standard browser so long as that browser is routed through the accompanying special software. What makes them "dark" is their anonymizing capacities. A way to think of this is in terms of the connotation of "going dark" in terms of communications—of moving one's communications off of open networks and into more secure channels.[1]

Thus, I resist the definitions of "Dark Web" that play on the negative connotations of "dark," where the Dark Web is anything immoral or illegal that happens on the Internet. To be certain, there are illegal activities occurring on the Tor, Freenet, or I2P networks, including drug markets, sales of black hat hacking services or stolen personal information, or child exploitation images. However, there are also activities that belie the negative connotations of "dark," including political discourses, social networking sites, and news services. Even Facebook and the *New York Times* now host Tor hidden services. The Dark Web—much like the standard ("clear") World Wide Web—includes a rich range of human activity.

---

[1] The connotation of "dark" on which I draw to define the Dark Web is quite similar to that of former FBI Director James Comey. See James Comey, "Encryption, Public Safety, and 'Going Dark,'" Blog, *Lawfare*, July 6, 2015, http://www.lawfareblog.com/encryption-public-safety-and-going-dark.

Approaches Previously Taken to the Dark Web

Indeed, it is the presence of a wide range of activities on the Dark Web which leads me to my call: the Dark Web is in need of more humanistic inquiry. Currently, academic work on the Dark Web is dominated by **computer science**[2] and **automated content analysis**[3] approaches. The former is dedicated to developing new networking and **encryption algorithms**, as well as testing the security of the networks. The latter tends

[2] For examples, see Ian Clarke et al., "Freenet: A Distributed Anonymous Information Storage and Retrieval System," in *Designing Privacy Enhancing Technologies*, ed. Hannes Federrath (Springer, 2001), 46–66, http://link.springer.com/chapter/10.1007/3-540-44702-4_4; Ian Clarke et al., "Protecting Free Expression Online with Freenet," *Internet Computing, IEEE* 6, no. 1 (2002): 40–49; Jens Mache et al., "Request Algorithms in Freenet-Style Peer–Peer Systems," in *Peer-to-Peer Computing, 2002 (P2P 2002). Proceedings. Second International Conference on IEEE (2002)*, 90–95, http://ieeexplore.ieee.org/xpls/abs_all.jsp?arnumber=1046317; Hui Zhang, Ashish Goel, and Ramesh Govindan, "Using the Small-World Model to Improve Freenet Performance," in *INFOCOM 2002. Twenty-First Annual Joint Conference of the IEEE Computer and Communications Societies. Proceedings. IEEE*, vol. 3 (IEEE, 2002), 1228–1237, http://ieeexplore.ieee.org/xpls/abs_all.jsp?arnumber=1019373; Karl Aberer, Manfred Hauswirth, and Magdalena Punceva, "Self-Organized Construction of Distributed Access Structures: A Comparative Evaluation of P-Grid and FreeNet," in *The 5th Workshop on Distributed Data and Structures (WDAS 2003)*, 2003, http://infoscience.epfl.ch/record/54381; Jem E. Berkes, "Decentralized Peer-to-Peer Network Architecture: Gnutella and Freenet," University of Manitoba, Winnipeg, Manitoba, Canada, 2003, http://www.berkes.ca/archive/berkes_gnutella_freenet.pdf; Ian Clarke et al., "Private Communication Through a Network of Trusted Connections: The Dark Freenet," *Network*, 2010, http://www.researchgate.net/profile/Vilhelm_Verendel/publication/228552753_Private_Communication_Through_a_Network_of_Trusted_Connections_The_Dark_Freenet/links/02e7e525f9eb66ba13000000.pdf; Mathias Ehlert, "I2P Usability vs. Tor Usability a Bandwidth and Latency Comparison," in *Seminar*, Humboldt University of Berlin, Berlin, Germany, 2011, http://userpage.fu-berlin.de/semu/docs/2011_seminar_ehlert_i2p.pdf; Peipeng Liu et al., "Empirical Measurement and Analysis of I2P Routers," *Journal of Networks* 9, no. 9 (2014): 2269–2278; Gildas Nya Tchabe and Yinhua Xu, "Anonymous Communications: A Survey on I2P," *CDC Publication Theoretische Informatik–Kryptographie und Computeralgebra*, https://www.cdc.informatik.tu-darmstadt.de, 2014, https://www.cdc.informatik.tu-darmstadt.de/fileadmin/user_upload/Group_CDC/Documents/Lehre/SS13/Seminar/CPS/cps2014_submission_4.pdf; and Matthew Thomas and Aziz Mohaisen, "Measuring the Leakage of Onion at the Root," 2014, 11.

[3] Symon Aked, "An Investigation into Darknets and the Content Available Via Anonymous Peer-to-Peer File Sharing," 2011, http://ro.ecu.edu.au/ism/106/; Hsinchun Chen, *Dark Web—Exploring and Data Mining the Dark Side of the Web* (New York: Springer, 2012), http://www.springer.com/computer/database+management+%26+information+retrieval/book/978-1-4614-1556-5; Gabriel Weimann, "Going Dark: Terrorism

to use automated crawling software and large-scale content analysis to classify content on the various networks (predominantly on Tor). Very often, a goal of the latter is to demonstrate that Tor (or I2P or Freenet) is mostly comprised of "unethical" activity.[4]

More recently, given the explosion of interest in Dark Web drug markets, specifically the Silk Road during its run between 2011 and 2013, there is a growing body of research on Dark Web exchanges.[5] A significant part of this work is ethnographic, especially from Alexia Maddox and Monica Barratt, who not only have engaged in ethnographies of

---

on the Dark Web," *Studies in Conflict & Terrorism*, 2015, http://www.tandfonline.com/doi/abs/10.1080/1057610X.2015.1119546; Clement Guitton, "A Review of the Available Content on Tor Hidden Services: The Case Against Further Development," *Computers in Human Behavior* 29, no. 6 (November 2013): 2805–2815, https://doi.org/10.1016/j.chb.2013.07.031; and Jialun Qin et al., "The Dark Web Portal Project: Collecting and Analyzing the Presence of Terrorist Groups on the Web," in *Proceedings of the 2005 IEEE International Conference on Intelligence and Security Informatics* (Springer-Verlag, 2005), 623–624, http://dl.acm.org/citation.cfm?id=2154737.

[4] See especially Guitton, "A Review of the Available Content on Tor Hidden Services"; Weimann, "Going Dark."

[5] Nicolas Christin, "Traveling the Silk Road: A Measurement Analysis of a Large Anonymous Online Marketplace," in *Proceedings of the 22nd International Conference on World Wide Web, WWW'13* (New York, NY: ACM, 2013), 213–224, https://doi.org/10.1145/2488388.2488408; Marie Claire Van Hout and Tim Bingham, "'Silk Road', the Virtual Drug Marketplace: A Single Case Study of User Experiences," *International Journal of Drug Policy* 24, no. 5 (September 2013): 385–391, https://doi.org/10.1016/j.drugpo.2013.01.005; Marie Claire Van Hout and Tim Bingham, "'Surfing the Silk Road': A Study of Users' Experiences," *International Journal of Drug Policy* 24, no. 6 (November 2013): 524–529, https://doi.org/10.1016/j.drugpo.2013.08.011; James Martin, *Drugs on the Dark Net: How Cryptomarkets Are Transforming the Global Trade in Illicit Drugs*, 2014; James Martin, "Lost on the Silk Road: Online Drug Distribution and the 'Cryptomarket,'" *Criminology & Criminal Justice* 14, no. 3 (2014): 351–367, https://doi.org/10.1177/1748895813505234; Amy Phelps and Allan Watt, "I Shop Online—Recreationally! Internet Anonymity and Silk Road Enabling Drug Use in Australia," *Digital Investigation* 11, no. 4 (2014): 261–272, https://doi.org/10.1016/j.diin.2014.08.001; Alois Afilipoaie and Patrick Shortis, *From Dealer to Doorstep—How Drugs Are Sold on the Dark Net*, GDPO Situation Analysis (Swansea University: Global Drugs Policy Observatory, 2015), http://www.swansea.ac.uk/media/Dealer%20to%20Doorstep%20FINAL%20SA.pdf; Jakob Johan Demant and Esben Houborg, "Personal Use, Social Supply or Redistribution? Cryptomarket Demand on Silk Road 2 and Agora," *Trends in Organized Crime*, 2016, http://www.forskningsdatabasen.dk/en/catalog/2304479461; Rasmus Munksgaard and Jakob Demant, "Mixing Politics and Crime—The Prevalence and Decline of Political Discourse on the Cryptomarket,"

markets[6] but also have written about ethnographic methods in those environments.[7] This latter thread of Dark Web ethnography is, I would suggest, a key starting point for digital humanist work.

Thus, as should be clear, there are many underutilized approaches to the Dark Web, including political economy and semiotic and textual interpretation. The ethnographic work has mainly been directed at Dark Web markets, and not at other types of sites, including forums and social networking sites.[8] Moreover, most of the attention is paid to Tor Hidden Services; far less to I2P, Freenet, or newer systems such as **Zeronet**. Although the Dark Web is relatively small in comparison to the "Clear Web," there is much more work to be done, and critical humanists ought to be engaged in it.

WHY STUDY TECHNICAL INFRASTRUCTURES?

This leads me to a somewhat unusual point. To engage in critical humanist work on the Dark Web, I suggest that the potential researcher consider studying Dark Web infrastructures and technologies. I suggest this for a pragmatic reason: any qualitative research into the Dark Web will

International Journal of Drug Policy 35 (September 2016): 77–83, https://doi.org/10.1016/j.drugpo.2016.04.021; and Alice Hutchings and Thomas J. Holt, "The Online Stolen Data Market: Disruption and Intervention Approaches," *Global Crime* 18, no. 1 (January 2, 2017): 11–30, https://doi.org/10.1080/17440572.2016.1197123.

[6] Monica J. Barratt, Jason A. Ferris, and Adam R. Winstock, "Safer Scoring? Cryptomarkets, Social Supply and Drug Market Violence," *International Journal of Drug Policy* 35 (September 2016): 24–31, https://doi.org/10.1016/j.drugpo.2016.04.019; Monica J. Barratt et al., "'What If You Live on Top of a Bakery and You Like Cakes?'— Drug Use and Harm Trajectories Before, During and After the Emergence of Silk Road," *International Journal of Drug Policy* 35 (September 2016): 50–57, https://doi.org/10.1016/j.drugpo.2016.04.006; and Alexia Maddox et al., "Constructive Activism in the Dark Web: Cryptomarkets and Illicit Drugs in the Digital 'Demimonde,'" *Information, Communication & Society* (October 15, 2015): 1–16, https://doi.org/10.1080/13691 18x.2015.1093531.

[7] Monica J. Barratt and Alexia Maddox, "Active Engagement with Stigmatised Communities Through Digital Ethnography," *Qualitative Research* (May 22, 2016), https://doi.org/10.1177/1468794116648766.

[8] Robert W. Gehl, "Power/Freedom on the Dark Web: A Digital Ethnography of the Dark Web Social Network," *New Media and Society* (October 16, 2014): 1–17.

inevitably have to engage with the networks' technical capacities. As Barratt and Maddox argue, "Conducting digital ethnography in the dark net requires a strong working knowledge of the technical practices that are used to maintain anonymous communications."[9] Many of the discussions and interactions among Dark Web participants have to do with the technical details of these systems. Marshall McLuhan famously said "the medium is the message," and in the case of the cultures of the Dark Web, this is profoundly true. Those who administer and use Dark Web sites often engage in highly technical discussions about anonymizing networks, cryptography, operating systems, and Web hosting and browsing software. This also means that a researcher's literature review often ought to include much of the computer science work cited above. This is not to say that there are no other discourses on the Dark Web, but rather that the vast majority of interactions there involve these technical discourses in one way or another.

A **political economist**, for example, will have to understand **cryptocurrencies** (including Bitcoin, but also new systems such as Monero and Zcash), Web market software, and PGP encryption, in order to fully trace circuits of production, exchange, distribution, and consumption. Scholars of **visual culture** will see images and visual artifacts that are directly inspired by computer science, network engineering, and hacker cultures. Thus, such scholars require an understanding of how artists and participants are interpreting these technical elements of the network. **Textual analysts**, including those engaged in new Digital Humanities techniques of **distant reading** and **large corpus analysis**, will need to understand infrastructures and networking technologies in order to uncover the politics and cultures of Dark Web texts. And, just as in previous **ethnographies**, as the anthropologist Hugh Gusterson notes, the researcher's identity is a key aspect of the work.[10] Of course, the anonymizing properties of the Dark Web are predominantly used by

[9] Barratt and Maddox, "Active Engagement with Stigmatised Communities Through Digital Ethnography," 6.

[10] Hugh Gusterson, "Ethnographic Research," in *Qualitative Methods in International Relations*, ed. Audie Klotz and Deepa Prakash, Research Methods Series (Palgrave Macmillan, 2008), 96, https://doi.org/10.1007/978-0-230-58412-9_7.

people who hide many markers of identity, such as race, class, and gender.[11] Often, instead of those identity markers, Dark Web participants use technical knowledge of encryption, routing, network protocols, or Web hosting as substitutes for the markers that would be more prevalent in face-to-face settings. Ultimately, then, I recommend that humanist researchers familiarize themselves with technical details and language. This will aid in dealing with the inevitable "disorientation," which "is one of the strongest sensations of the researcher newly arrived in the field."[12]

For a humanist to study these networks and their participants on their own terms, then, it is necessary to have a solid grasp of the underlying technical infrastructures. This chapter is in large part a guide to resources to enable the study of those infrastructures. While I have selected these archives with this recommendation in mind, these archives also have the advantage of providing rich insights into many aspects of Dark Web cultures and practices.

ARCHIVES TO DRAW ON

Generally speaking, the materials that a researcher could draw on to study Dark Web infrastructures include:

- software (source code) repositories;
- mailing lists;
- forums; and
- hidden sites.

In terms of software repositories, as I have written about elsewhere, source code can offer a great deal of insight into how developers conceive of their software system's uses and users.[13] Many Dark Web

---

[11] This is definitely not to say that such markers don't emerge, or that racialized/gendered/classed discourses do not appear on the Dark Web. As I show in my book, such discourses do emerge, highlighting the overall arguments put forward by Lisa Nakamura that the Internet is not a perfectly "disembodied" medium. See Lisa Nakamura, *Cybertypes: Race, Ethnicity, and Identity on the Internet* (New York: Routledge, 2002).

[12] Gusterson, "Ethnographic Research," 97.

[13] Robert W. Gehl, "(Critical) Reverse Engineering and Genealogy," *Foucaultblog*, August 16, 2016, https://doi.org/10.13095/uzh.fsw.fb.153.

systems are open source, meaning their code is available for inspection in software repositories. Each and every contribution to the software is recorded, meaning software repositories provide an opportunity to study "software evolution," tracing production from initial lines of code to full-blown software packages. Most importantly for the digital humanist, this code is accompanied by comments, both within the code itself and added by developers as they upload new versions, so a researcher can trace the organizational discourses and structures that give rise to the software.[14]

Beyond code, however, the software developers engage in rich debates in mailing lists and forums. For example, since it dates back to 1999, Freenet has nearly two decades of mailing list debates that certainly engage in the technical details of routing algorithms and encryption **protocols**, but also discuss the role of spam in free speech,[15] the politics of post-9/11 surveillance states,[16] and network economics.[17] Tor also has highly active mailing lists.[18] I2P developers use Internet Relay Chat, archiving their meetings on their home page,[19] as well as a development forum hosted as an eepsite (at zzz.i2p*).[20] For my book, I focused on how these projects deployed the figure of "the dissident" as an ideal user to build for, as well as a political and economic justification for the projects' existences. Future researchers might draw on these archives to discover other such organizing concepts and discourses.

[14] Ahmed Hassan, "Mining Software Repositories to Assist Developers and Support Managers," 2004, 2, https://uwspace.uwaterloo.ca/handle/10012/1017.

[15] Glenn McGrath, "[Freenet-Chat] Deep Philosophical Question," January 2, 2002, https://emu.freenetproject.org/pipermail/chat/2002-January/000604.html.

[16] Colbyd, "[Freenet-Chat] Terrorism and Freenet," January 9, 2002, https://emu.freenetproject.org/pipermail/chat/2002-January/001353.html.

[17] Roger Dingledine, "[Freehaven-Dev] Re: [Freenet-Chat] MojoNation," August 9, 2000, http://archives.seul.org//freehaven/dev/Aug-2000/msg00006.html.

[18] See https://lists.torproject.org/cgi-bin/mailman/listinfo for a list of them.

[19] See https://geti2p.net/en/meetings/ for the archived chat logs.

[20] All URLs marked with an asterisk (*) require special routing software to access them. URLs ending in.i2p require I2P software; .onions require Tor, and Freesites require Freenet. For instructions on how to download, install, and run these routers, see each project's home page: https://geti2p.net/, https://torproject.org and https://freenetproject.org, respectively.

And of course, Dark Web sites themselves can provide rich streams of data, including archives that can help a researcher understand technical structures and the histories of these systems. For example, Freenet's Sone (SOcial NEtworking) **plugin** is an active, searchable microblog system, with posts dating back several years. I2P's wiki (i2pwiki.i2p) retains records of previous edits to wiki pages. Hidden Answers (on the Tor network and on I2P, at http://answerstedhctbek.onion and hiddenanswers. i2p, respectively), has tens of thousands of categorized questions and answers, dominated by questions on computer networking and hacking. These archives provide rich insight into the cultural practices of Dark Web network builders, administrators, and users. In what follows, I provide links to specific archives. This catalog is not exhaustive.

TOR HIDDEN SERVICES

Tor Project and Related Archives

The Tor Project home page (torproject.org) contains links to many specifications documents and public relations documents associated with Tor. Their blog (https://blog.torproject.org/) is now a decade old, with thousands of posts and tens of thousands of comments archived. Tor now uses Github as its software repository (https://github.com/ TheTorProject/gettorbrowser). This repository provides the sorts of data described above: bugs, comments, and of course lines of code.[21]

Prior to the Tor Project, key Tor people (including Roger Dingledine) worked on another, called Free Haven. Free Haven was to be an anonymous document storage system. It was never implemented, but the technical problems Dingledine and his colleagues encountered led them to onion routing and, from there, to what would become the Tor Project. The Free Haven site (freehaven.net) contains an archive of technical papers and the freehaven-dev mailing list. Similarly, onion routing creator Paul Syverson maintained a Web site dedicated to onion routing and the early years of Tor: https://www.onion-router.net/.

Research projects engaging with these archives might include historical analysis of the development of the Tor project as an organization,

---

[21] Achilleas Pipinellis, *GitHub Essentials* (Birmingham: Packt Publishing, 2015).

its peculiar relationship to state agencies, and how the culture of the Tor Project becomes embedded in the technical artifacts it produces.

Darknet Market Archives

Because of sites such as the Silk Road, a great deal of attention has been paid to Tor-based markets. Several researchers have used Web scraping software to download large portions of Dark Web market forums. These forums are important because they are where buyers, vendors, and market administrators discuss market policies and features, settle disputes, and engage in social and political discussion. A compressed, 50 GB archive of the results of this Web scraping, dating between 2011 and 2015, can be found at https://www.gwern.net/DNM%20archives. The page also includes suggested research topics, including analysis of online drug and security cultures.

Key Tor Hidden Services

Although a researcher can draw on the Gwern.org archives, those halt in 2015. To gather more recent data—as well as to engage in participant observation or to find interview subjects—one ought to spend time on market forums. For example, DreamMarket* is a long-running market, and its forum can be found at http://tmskhzavkycdupbr.onion/. For any researcher working on these forums, I highly recommend studying their guides to encryption and remaining anonymous. I also highly recommend Barratt and Maddox's guide to doing research in such environments, particularly because engaging in such research raises important ethical considerations (more on this below).[22]

As one of the longest-running Tor hidden service social networking sites, Galaxy2* (http://w363zoq3ylux5rf5.onion/) is an essential site of study. As I have written about elsewhere, such Dark Web social networking sites replicate many of the features of corporate sites such as Facebook, but within anonymizing networks.[23] Galaxy2 has over 17,000 registered accounts, which is of course very small compared to Facebook, but is quite large compared to many other Dark Web social networking

---

[22] Barratt and Maddox, "Active Engagement with Stigmatised Communities Through Digital Ethnography."

[23] Gehl, "Power/Freedom on the Dark Web: A Digital Ethnography of the Dark Web Social Network."

systems. It features blogs, social groups, and a microblogging system, dating back to early 2015.

By delving into market forums and Galaxy2, a researcher can begin to discover other key sites and services on the Tor network. Comparative work on the social dynamics of market forums versus social networking software would be a fruitful research project.

FREENET FREESITES

Freenet Project

Starting with Ian Clarke's Master's thesis in 1999, Freenet is the oldest of the Dark Web systems discussed in this chapter. The Freenet Project home page (freenetproject.org) is similar to the Tor Project's, in that it contains software specifications documents, guides on installation and use, and mailing lists. Mailing lists (https://freenetproject.org/pages/help.html#mailing-lists) date back to the year 2000. Unfortunately, the Freenet-chat mail list is no longer online (contact me for an archive). The Freenet Project also operates a user survey site at https://freenet.uservoice.com/forums/8861-general, where Freenet users suggest features and the developers discuss possible implementations of them.

One of the unique aspects of Freenet is its data storage structure. Freenet was designed to "forget" (i.e., delete) less-accessed data from its distributed data stores. This "forgetting" practice precedes contemporary discussions of "the right to be forgotten" or self-destructing media by over a decade. Thus, a researcher may draw insights from Freenet's unique place in a **genealogy** of forgetful media.

On Freenet

Freenet's home page currently lists directories as the first links. These directories—Enzo's Index,* Linkaggedon,* and Nerdaggedon*—are key ways into the network, but they are archives in their own right due to the structure of Freenet. Freenet's data storage system is distributed across every computer that participates in the network, leading much of the data on the network, including Freesites, to be stored for long periods of time. Thus, these directories, which offer links to Freesites, are a good way to get a sense of the content of the network. Enzo's Index is useful because it is categorized, with Freesites grouped by topic.

Unfortunately, it is not being updated. Nerdaggedon, however, is still active.

Two key resources, FMS* and Sone,* are additional plugins for Freenet. This means they do not come with the stock installation of Freenet, but have to be added to the base software. FMS—the Freenet Messaging System—is a bulletin board-style system with boards based on the topics. Sone, mentioned above, is a microblogging system, similar to Twitter in that it is structured in follower/followed relationships. However, unlike Tor and I2P, Freenet's file structure means that, in order to access older posts on either FMS or Sone, one has to run these systems for a long time, while they download older posts from the network. After doing so, a researcher has large archives of posts to examine.

I2P EEPSITES

Invisible Internet Project

As I discuss in my book, the Invisible Internet Project (I2P) is somewhat different from Tor and Freenet in that the latter two organizations decided to become registered nonprofits in the United States, which required them to disclose information about their founders and budgets. I2P, on the other hand, is what I call an "anonymous nonprofit," in that it did not formally file with the U.S. I.R.S. for nonprofit status, and it avoided revealing the real identities of its developers for most of its history. This organizational difference is reflected in how I2P developers do their work. Developer meetings are held predominantly over **IRC**. Their logs are archived at the I2P home page (https://geti2p. net/en/meetings/). In addition, I2P uses a forum hosted as an eepsite: zzz.i2p,* where developers consult about the project. While they have a public Github software repository (https://github.com/i2p), some development also occurs on another eepsite, http://git.repo. i2p/w?a=project_list;o=age;t=i2p.*

I2P did use a mailing list for several years, but Web-based access to it has been lost. Instead, researchers can access the mailing list archives via Network News Transfer Protocol (NNTP) from Gmane: news://news. gmane.org:119/gmane.network.i2p and news://news.gmane.org:119/ gmane.comp.security.invisiblenet.iip.devel. These have not been used since 2006, but both provide insights into the early years of I2P (including its predecessor, the Invisible IRC Project).

Key Eepsites

As described above, the I2P Wiki (i2piwiki.i2p*) is a collaboratively written guide to I2P, including eepsite directories and how to search the network. Moreover, it is built on MediaWiki (the same software as Wikipedia). Thus, a researcher can see edit histories and discussion pages.

Echelon.i2p* provides downloads of I2P software. Notable is the archive of older versions of I2P, stretching back to version 0.6.1.30. Because I2P (like Tor and Freenet) is open source, a researcher can trace changes to the software through these versions. Of particular interest are the readme files, hosts.txt (which includes lists of eepsites), and changelogs. Like Tor and Freenet, I2P has social networking sites. The oldest is Visibility.i2p*, which dates back to 2012. Visibility is a relatively low-traffic site, but its longevity allows a researcher to track trends in I2P culture over a period of years.

Finally, in addition to running the developer forum (zzz.i2p*), I2P developer zzz runs stats.i2p,* which includes data on I2P routers and network traffic (http://stats.i2p/cgi-bin/dashboard.cgi).* For a glimpse into zzz's early years as an I2P developer, visit http://zzz.i2p/oldsite/index.html.* Unfortunately, one of the largest archives on I2P, the user forum forum.i2p,* is no longer operational as of early 2017. There are discussions on the developer forum of bringing it back, archives intact. Any I2P researcher would want to watch—and hope—for the return of forum.i2p. If it does not, a major resource will be lost forever.

BUILDING YOUR OWN ARCHIVES

The disappearance of forum.i2p is not the only major Dark Web site to go offline and take its archives with it. For example, in my time on the Dark Web, I have seen dozens of social networking sites come and go.[24] The Darknet Market archives show that many markets have appeared and disappeared over the last five years, and the most recent victim is

---

[24]For an archive of screenshots of many of them, see https://socialmediaalternatives.org/archive/items/browse?tags=dark+web.

the largest market to date, Alphabay. Dark Web search engines and directories can also appear online for a few months, and then leave without a trace: there is no archive.org for the Dark Web. A site can be online one minute and gone the next. Therefore, my final recommendation for any Digital Humanities scholar studying the Dark Web would be to build your own archives.

The Firefox plugin Zotero is a good option here: it is a bibliographic management tool which includes a Web page archiver, and it is compatible with the Tor Browser. It must be used with caution, however: the Tor Project recommends avoiding the use of plugins with the Tor Browser, due to security considerations. Plugins are not audited by the Tor Project and they could leak a browser's identifying information. This includes other plugins, such as screenshot plugins. Such security considerations must be weighed against the researcher's need to document Dark Web sites.

As more Digital Humanities scholars engage with the Dark Web, they will develop their own archives on their local computers. I would also suggest that we researchers begin to discuss how such archives could be combined into a larger archival project, one that can help future researchers understand the cultures and practices of these anonymizing networks. This effort would be similar to what Gwern et al. achieve with the Darknet Markets archive (described above): the combination of ad hoc research archives into one larger, more systemic archive.

ETHICAL CONSIDERATIONS

Of course, given that many users of Dark Web sites do so to avoid revealing their personal information, any such combined archive—indeed, any Dark Web research—must be done only after deep consideration about research ethics. There are several guides to the ethics of Internet research, including the invaluable AOIR guidelines.[25] In addition, the Tor Project provides a research ethics guideline,[26] although it is geared

---

[25] Annette Markham and Elizabeth Buchanan, *Ethical Decision-Making and Internet Research: Recommendations from the Aoir Ethics Working Committee (Version 2.0)* (Association of Internet Researchers, 2012), https://pure.au.dk/ws/files/55543125/aoirethics2.pdf.

[26] "Ethical Tor Research: Guidelines," Blog, *The Tor Blog*, November 11, 2015, https://blog.torproject.org/blog/ethical-tor-research-guidelines.

toward large-scale analysis of the Tor network itself, does not say anything about research on Dark Web content, and is thus less valuable
to humanistic work. Current Dark Web researchers are tackling ethical
questions from a variety of disciplinary perspectives, including computer
science and ethnography. Two important guides to this subject are by
James Martin and Nicholas Christin[27] and by Monica Barratt and Alexia
Maddox,[28] both of which I draw on here.

The key takeaway of the AOIR ethics guide, the work of Martin and
Christin, and that of Barratt and Maddox is that the ethical quandaries
faced by a researcher exploring anonymizing networks will vary greatly
from site to site and from research project to research project. Thus,
rather than laying out hard-and-fast rules for ethical research practices,
Martin and Christin suggest that the researcher develop

> localised research practices that are cognizant of broader ethical norms and
> principles… while also remaining sufficiently flexible to adapt to the vari-
> ous contingencies associated with Internet research.[29]

They draw on Natasha Whiteman's *Undoing Ethics*, which suggests four
domains to draw upon for ethical insights: academic/professional bodies
and their norms, the researcher's own institution, the researcher's own
politics and beliefs, and the "ethics of the researched." I will focus next
on the last item in that list to suggest some ethical considerations arising
from social norms I have observed in my time on the Dark Web.

One of the social norms of many, if not all, Dark Web sites is a prohibition against **doxxing**, or publishing the personal details of, other
people. In terms of research ethics, this cultural prohibition means that
the researcher should not seek to connect online personae to their offline
counterparts. It may be tempting to use small pieces of information—say,
a subject's favorite food, ways of speaking, comments on the weather, or
political stances—to develop a detailed profile of that person. It may be
tempting to use these data to identify the person. But this would violate

[27] James Martin and Nicolas Christin, "Ethics in Cryptomarket Research," *International
Journal of Drug Policy* 35 (September 2016): 84–91, https://doi.org/10.1016/j.
drugpo.2016.05.006.

[28] Barratt and Maddox, "Active Engagement with Stigmatised Communities Through
Digital Ethnography."

[29] Martin and Christin, "Ethics in Cryptomarket Research," 86.

a fundamental aspect of the Dark Web: it is designed to anonymize both readers and producers of texts, and thus its users seek to dissociate their reading and writing from their real-world identities. For examples of such small bits of information, and how they could link pseudonymous people to real-world identities, as well as guidance about how to handle this information, see Barratt and Maddox.[30]

Another cultural norm is distrust, if not outright loathing, of the state. The Dark Web is largely comprised of persons with varying anarchist or libertarian political leanings, and along with these views comes a hatred of the state. Moreover, many of the activities that happen on Dark Web sites are illegal, and therefore participants in these sites fear law enforcement. In addition, Freenet, Tor, and I2P have all been developed by people who fear state censorship and repression. Thus, a research ethics developed in light of "the ethics of the researched" would call for the researcher to refuse active sponsorship from or collaboration with state agencies. To be certain, given the gutting of support for humanities research, it may be tempting to accept military/police/defense funding for Dark Web research, but such funding directly contradicts the ethical positions held by not only Dark Web participants, but many of the people who contribute to developing Dark Web technologies.

Finally, a very sticky issue: should researchers reveal their own identities to Dark Web site administrators and participants? This has a direct bearing on the ethical approaches of Institutional Review Boards (IRB), because IRBs often require the researcher to provide potential participants with contact information, which of course means the researcher cannot maintain pseudonymity/anonymity. The goal is to provide research participants with an avenue to hold the researcher responsible if the researcher violates their confidentiality or security. Following this standard, Barratt and Maddox revealed their identities to participants on the Silk Road drug market and other Tor hidden services, seeking to allay anxieties that they were, for example, undercover law enforcement agents. However, they note that this choice led to concerns for their own safety; Maddox received graphic death threats from a member of a forum.[31]

---

[30] Barratt and Maddox, "Active Engagement with Stigmatised Communities Through Digital Ethnography," 10.

[31] Ibid., 11.

Unfortunately, another cultural practice that emerges on some anonymous online spaces is harassment and trolling, and such harassment is far more effective if the victim's identity is known. Thus there is a conflict between standard IRB practice and contemporary online research. As Martin and Christin note, IRBs may not have the domain knowledge to help researchers navigate this issue.[32] In my research leading to my book project, I was fortunate to work with the University of Utah IRB, which recommended that I *offer* to provide my contact details to potential participants. This, in turn, allowed the participants to decide whether or not they wanted this information. The vast majority of participants I spoke to declined to know who I am.[33] This may have reduced the likelihood of incidents such as the one Maddox described.

CONCLUSION

As Ian Bogost and Nick Montfort argue, "people make negotiations with technologies as they develop cultural ideas and artifacts, and people themselves create technologies in response to myriad social, cultural, material, and historical issues."[34] This is decidedly the case with Freenet, Tor, and I2P, the Dark Web systems I've discussed here. Although my suggestion that Digital Humanities scholars must engage with Dark Web technical infrastructures may strike some as a form of techno-elitism— the privileging of technical knowledge over other knowledges—for better or worse, technical knowledge is the lingua franca of these systems. I hope this collection of resources will be valuable for future researchers as they explore the relationship between Dark Web technology and culture.

---

[32] Martin and Christin, "Ethics in Cryptomarket Research," 88.

[33] However, I should note that I was interviewing the builders of Dark Web search engines and the administrators and users of Dark Web social networking sites. These formats have different legal stakes than drug markets, the object Maddox and Barratt were studying. Thus, there may have been less anxiety among my participants that I was an undercover law enforcement agent. Again, this points to the difficulty of establishing hard-and-fast ethical rules for this line of research. I should also note that the Dark Web is a highly masculinized space. In the few cases where participants asked for my identity, they learned I identify as a cisgender male. In contrast, Maddox and Barratt discuss the specific harassment they received due to their female gender identities.

[34] I. Bogost and N. Montfort, "Platform Studies: Frequently Questioned Answers," in *Digital Arts and Culture 2009* (Irvine, CA: After Media, Embodiment and Context, UC Irvine, 2009), 3.

REFERENCES

Aberer, Karl, Manfred Hauswirth, and Magdalena Punceva. "Self-Organized Construction of Distributed Access Structures: A Comparative Evaluation of P-Grid and FreeNet." In *The 5th Workshop on Distributed Data and Structures (WDAS 2003)*. 2003. http://infoscience.epfl.ch/record/54381.

Afilipoaie, Alois, and Patrick Shortis. *From Dealer to Doorstep—How Drugs Are Sold on the Dark Net*. GDPO Situation Analysis. Swansea City: Global Drugs Policy Observatory, Swansea University, 2015. http://www.swansea.ac.uk/media/Dealer%20to%20Doorstep%20FINAL%20SA.pdf.

Aked, Symon. "An Investigation into Darknets and the Content Available Via Anonymous Peer-to-Peer File Sharing." 2011. http://ro.ecu.edu.au/ism/106/.

Barratt, Monica J., and Alexia Maddox. "Active Engagement with Stigmatised Communities Through Digital Ethnography." *Qualitative Research* (May 22, 2016). https://doi.org/10.1177/1468794116648766.

Barratt, Monica J., Jason A. Ferris, and Adam R. Winstock. "Safer Scoring? Cryptomarkets, Social Supply and Drug Market Violence." *International Journal of Drug Policy* 35 (September 2016): 24–31. https://doi.org/10.1016/j.drugpo.2016.04.019.

Barratt, Monica J., Simon Lenton, Alexia Maddox, and Matthew Allen. "'What If You Live on Top of a Bakery and You like Cakes?'—Drug Use and Harm Trajectories Before, During and After the Emergence of Silk Road." *International Journal of Drug Policy* 35 (September 2016): 50–57. https://doi.org/10.1016/j.drugpo.2016.04.006.

Berkes, Jem E. "Decentralized Peer-to-Peer Network Architecture: Gnutella and Freenet." University of Manitoba Winnipeg, Manitoba, Canada, 2003. http://www.berkes.ca/archive/berkes_gnutella_freenet.pdf.

Bogost, I., and N. Montfort. "Platform Studies: Frequently Questioned Answers." In *Digital Arts and Culture 2009*, 8. Irvine, CA: After Media, Embodiment and Context, UC Irvine, 2009.

Chen, Hsinchun. *Dark Web—Exploring and Data Mining the Dark Side of the Web*. New York: Springer, 2012. http://www.springer.com/computer/database+management+%26+information+retrieval/book/978-1-4614-1556-5.

Christin, Nicolas. "Traveling the Silk Road: A Measurement Analysis of a Large Anonymous Online Marketplace." In *Proceedings of the 22nd International Conference on World Wide Web, WWW'13*, 213–224. New York, NY: ACM, 2013. https://doi.org/10.1145/2488388.2488408.

Clarke, Ian, Oskar Sandberg, Brandon Wiley, and Theodore W. Hong. "Freenet: A Distributed Anonymous Information Storage and Retrieval System." In *Designing Privacy Enhancing Technologies*, edited by Hannes Federrath, 46–66. Springer, 2001. http://link.springer.com/chapter/10.1007/3-540-44702-4_4.

Clarke, Ian, Oskar Sandberg, Matthew Toseland, and Vilhelm Verendel. "Private Communication Through a Network of Trusted Connections: The Dark Freenet." *Network*. 2010. http://www.researchgate.net/profile/Vilhelm_Verendel/publication/228552753_Private_Communication_Through_a_Network_of_Trusted_Connections_The_Dark_Freenet/links/02e7e525f9eb66ba13000000.pdf.

Clarke, Ian, Scott G. Miller, Theodore W. Hong, Oskar Sandberg, and Brandon Wiley. "Protecting Free Expression Online with Freenet." *Internet Computing, IEEE* 6, no. 1 (2002): 40–49.

Colbyd. "[Freenet-Chat] Terrorism and Freenet." January 9, 2002. https://emu.freenetproject.org/pipermail/chat/2002-January/001353.html.

Comey, James. "Encryption, Public Safety, and 'Going Dark.'" Blog. *Lawfare*. July 6, 2015. http://www.lawfareblog.com/encryption-public-safety-and-going-dark.

Demant, Jakob Johan, and Esben Houborg. "Personal Use, Social Supply or Redistribution? Cryptomarket Demand on Silk Road 2 and Agora." *Trends in Organized Crime*. 2016. http://www.forskningsdatabasen.dk/en/catalog/2304479461.

Dingledine, Roger. "[Freehaven-Dev] Re: [Freenet-Chat] MojoNation." August 9, 2000. http://archives.seul.org//freehaven/dev/Aug-2000/msg00006.html.

Ehlert, Mathias. "I2P Usability vs. Tor Usability a Bandwidth and Latency Comparison." In *Seminar*. Humboldt University of Berlin, Berlin, Germany, 2011. http://userpage.fu-berlin.de/semu/docs/2011_seminar_ehlert_i2p.pdf.

"Ethical Tor Research: Guidelines." Blog. *The Tor Blog*. November 11, 2015. https://blog.torproject.org/blog/ethical-tor-research-guidelines.

Gehl, Robert W. "(Critical) Reverse Engineering and Genealogy." *Foucaultblog*. August 16, 2016. https://doi.org/10.13095/uzh.fsw.fb.153.

———. "Power/Freedom on the Dark Web: A Digital Ethnography of the Dark Web Social Network." *New Media and Society* (October 16, 2014): 1–17.

Guitton, Clement. "A Review of the Available Content on Tor Hidden Services: The Case Against Further Development." *Computers in Human Behavior* 29, no. 6 (November 2013): 2805–2815. https://doi.org/10.1016/j.chb.2013.07.031.

Gusterson, Hugh. "Ethnographic Research." In *Qualitative Methods in International Relations*, edited by Audie Klotz and Deepa Prakash, 93–113. Research Methods Series. Palgrave Macmillan, 2008. https://doi.org/10.1007/978-0-230-58412-9_7.

Hassan, Ahmed. "Mining Software Repositories to Assist Developers and Support Managers." 2004. https://uwspace.uwaterloo.ca/handle/10012/1017.

Hout, Marie Claire Van, and Tim Bingham. "'Silk Road', the Virtual Drug Marketplace: A Single Case Study of User Experiences." *International Journal of Drug Policy* 24, no. 5 (September 2013): 385–391. https://doi. org/10.1016/j.drugpo.2013.01.005.

———. "'Surfing the Silk Road': A Study of Users' Experiences." *International Journal of Drug Policy* 24, no. 6 (November 2013): 524–529. https://doi. org/10.1016/j.drugpo.2013.08.011.

Hutchings, Alice, and Thomas J. Holt. "The Online Stolen Data Market: Disruption and Intervention Approaches." *Global Crime* 18, no. 1 (January 2, 2017): 11–30. https://doi.org/10.1080/17440572.2016.1197123.

Liu, Peipeng, Lihong Wang, Qingfeng Tan, Quangang Li, Xuebin Wang, and Jinqiao Shi. "Empirical Measurement and Analysis of I2P Routers." *Journal of Networks* 9, no. 9 (2014): 2269–2278.

Mache, Jens, Melanie Gilbert, Jason Guchereau, Jeff Lesh, Felix Ramli, and Matthew Wilkinson. "Request Algorithms in Freenet-Style Peer-to-Peer Systems." In *Peer-to-Peer Computing, 2002. (P2P 2002). Proceedings. Second International Conference on IEEE (2002)*, 90–95, 2002. http://ieeexplore. ieee.org/xpls/abs_all.jsp?arnumber=1046317.

Maddox, Alexia, Monica J. Barratt, Matthew Allen, and Simon Lenton. "Constructive Activism in the Dark Web: Cryptomarkets and Illicit Drugs in the Digital 'Demimonde.'" *Information, Communication & Society* (October 15, 2015): 1–16. https://doi.org/10.1080/1369118x.2015.1093531.

Markham, Annette, and Elizabeth Buchanan. *Ethical Decision-Making and Internet Research: Recommendations from the Aoir Ethics Working Committee (Version 2.0)*. Association of Internet Researchers, 2012. https://pure.au.dk/ ws/files/55543125/aoirethics2.pdf.

Martin, James. *Drugs on the Dark Net: How Cryptomarkets Are Transforming the Global Trade in Illicit Drugs*. 2014.

———. "Lost on the Silk Road: Online Drug Distribution and the 'Cryptomarket.'" *Criminology & Criminal Justice* 14, no. 3 (2014): 351–367. https://doi.org/10.1177/1748895813505234.

Martin, James, and Nicolas Christin. "Ethics in Cryptomarket Research." *International Journal of Drug Policy* 35 (September 2016): 84–91. https:// doi.org/10.1016/j.drugpo.2016.05.006.

McGrath, Glenn. "[Freenet-Chat] Deep Philosophical Question." January 2, 2002. https://emu.freenetproject.org/pipermail/chat/2002-January/ 000604.html.

Munksgaard, Rasmus, and Jakob Demant. "Mixing Politics and Crime— The Prevalence and Decline of Political Discourse on the Cryptomarket." *International Journal of Drug Policy* 35 (September 2016): 77–83. https:// doi.org/10.1016/j.drugpo.2016.04.021.

Nakamura, Lisa. *Cybertypes: Race, Ethnicity, and Identity on the Internet.* New York: Routledge, 2002.

Phelps, Amy, and Allan Watt. "I Shop Online—Recreationally! Internet Anonymity and Silk Road Enabling Drug Use in Australia." *Digital Investigation* 11, no. 4 (2014): 261–272. https://doi.org/10.1016/j.diin.2014.08.001.

Pipinellis, Achilleas. *GitHub Essentials.* Birmingham: Packt Publishing, 2015.

Qin, Jialun, Yilu Zhou, Guanpi Lai, Edna Reid, Marc Sageman, and Hsinchun Chen. "The Dark Web Portal Project: Collecting and Analyzing the Presence of Terrorist Groups on the Web." In *Proceedings of the 2005 IEEE International Conference on Intelligence and Security Informatics,* 623–624. Springer-Verlag, 2005. http://dl.acm.org/citation.cfm?id=2154737.

Tchabe, Gildas Nya, and Yinhua Xu. "Anonymous Communications: A Survey on I2P." *CDC Publication Theoretische Informatik–Kryptographie und Computeralgebra.* 2014. https://www.informatik.tu-darmstadt.de/cdc. https://www.cdc.informatik.tu-darmstadt.de/fileadmin/user_upload/Group_CDC/Documents/Lehre/SS13/Seminar/CPS/cps2014_submission_4.pdf.

Thomas, Matthew, and Aziz Mohaisen. "Measuring the Leakage of Onion at the Root." 2014, 11.

Weimann, Gabriel. "Going Dark: Terrorism on the Dark Web." *Studies in Conflict & Terrorism,* 2015. http://www.tandfonline.com/doi/abs/10.1080/1057610X.2015.1119546.

Zhang, Hui, Ashish Goel, and Ramesh Govindan. "Using the Small-World Model to Improve Freenet Performance." In *INFOCOM 2002. Twenty-First Annual Joint Conference of the IEEE Computer and Communications Societies. Proceedings.* IEEE, 3: 1228–1237. 2002. http://ieeexplore.ieee.org/xpls/abs_all.jsp?arnumber=1019373.

CHAPTER 4

MusicDetour: Building a Digital Humanities Archive

David Arditi

When beginning a Digital Humanities project, it can be difficult to think through your goals and limitations. What follows will help the reader formulate a project that has academic relevance and addresses a real-world problem. In this chapter, I outline the purpose of a digital music archive, ways to create research questions, and the specific technological system that I used for MusicDetour: The Dallas–Fort Worth Local Music Archive. Finally, I address some of the problems that copyright creates for the Digital Humanities.

FINDING THE PROJECT'S PURPOSE

When I decided to create MusicDetour in December 2015, it was with an eye toward applying knowledge to everyday life. In my academic work, I recognized two problems inherent to the local production of music. First, local musicians often create music without recording it, or the recordings are not stored and disseminated effectively. In other words, a wealth of cultural creation is not accessible, because it is neither

D. Arditi (✉)
University of Texas at Arlington, Arlington, TX, USA
e-mail: darditi@uta.edu

© The Author(s) 2018
l. levenberg et al. (eds.), *Research Methods for the Digital Humanities*,
https://doi.org/10.1007/978-3-319-96713-4_4

archived nor widely distributed. Second, a number of scholars and musicians acknowledge the deep inequalities that exist in the music industry between record labels and musicians. Musicians, as labor, create all value in the recording industry, but record labels earn the bulk of all revenue and surplus value from the sale of music; few recording artists earn any revenue from recording, let alone the excess that we associate with pop stars. The **Internet,** and **Information Communication Technologies (ICTs),**[1] possess the potential both to create a permanent nonprofit record of music in a local scene, and to disrupt the exploitation of musicians within the music industry.

An archive of local music establishes a permanent record of a cultural process. **Culture** is the process through which people make meaning out of everyday things.[2] Therefore, cultural artifacts derive from previous cultural artifacts. However, copyright intervenes to construct artificial boundaries around cultural artifacts. **Copyright** is a set of regulatory privileges[3] that allow for the reproduction of intellectual work.[4] While copyright creates the potential to generate revenue from works, it also creates a mechanism to exploit labor and it eliminates the public aspect of culture.[5] As we demarcate boundaries around music through the copyrighting of culture, we foreclose the possible creation of future forms. Culture has always been public because it is shared meaning, but copyright makes culture private.[6] For example, musicians learn music by

[1] Christian Fuchs, *Internet and Society: Social Theory in the Information Age* (New York, NY: Routledge, 2008).

[2] Stuart Hall, Jessica Evans, and Sean Nixon, eds. *Representation*, 2nd ed. (London: Sage: The Open University, 2013), xix.

[3] William Patry, *Moral Panics and the Copyright Wars* (New York, NY: Oxford University Press, 2009), 110.

[4] Bethany Klein, Giles Moss, and Lee Edwards, *Understanding Copyright: Intellectual Property in the Digital Age* (Los Angeles, CA: Sage, 2015).

[5] David Arditi, "Downloading Is Killing Music: The Recording Industry's Piracy Panic Narrative," in *Civilisations, The State of the Music Industry*, ed. Victor Sarafian and Rosemary Findley 63, no. 1 (2014): 13–32.

[6] James Boyle. *The Public Domain: Enclosing the Commons of the Mind* (New Haven, CT: Yale University Press, 2008); Vaidhyanathan, *The Googlization of Everything* (Berkeley: University of California Press, 2011); and Siva Vaidhyanathan, *Copyrights and Copywrongs: The Rise of Intellectual Property and How It Threatens Creativity* (New York: New York University Press, 2003).

listening to other musicians perform—they learn from its publicness—but barriers exist to the wide dissemination of music.

Local music has an **oral history** because it is often unrecorded or unavailable to people beyond the space and time at which it was performed. However, that does not mean that local music lacks an impact on the creation of further music. H. Stith Bennett addresses the way that one rock group influences the formation of others within local music scenes. Bennett suggests:

> When someone has played with a first group and then that group has broken up, that musician has established an associative history. In the general case that history is the product of all the group formations and dissolutions the individual has participated in. To the extent that his previous groups performed to audiences, that history is a public history, and is a method of assessing the kind of musician he is ...[7]

For Bennett, this associative history is a means to boost one's performance resume, but the public aspect of performance is intrinsic to the associative history. Therefore, Bennett identifies two processes that influence the creation of further new music. First, the associative history is the social interaction that happens when performing with particular people; one learns to play a certain way by playing with specific musicians. Second, the publicness of performance means that people hear these performances, and that these performances can affect people. While one may never listen to musician A, musician A performed with musician B, and was heard by musician C. Musician D, who never played with or had even heard of musician A, would be influenced by musician A if she were to perform with musician B or listen to musician C. As a result, the cultural process of making music continues even without the original reference. According to Bennett, "A group's presentation to audiences is impossible to erase from the regional collective memory (although it naturally drifts away) and to the extent that a musician is known by associations with previous companions, public credentials are constructed."[8] The impact of a musician reverberates through the music scene long after they are no longer a part of it. The unwritten history is difficult

---

[7] Stith H. Bennett, *On Becoming a Rock Musician* (Amherst: University of Massachusetts Press, 1980), 35.

[8] Ibid.

to follow. MusicDetour aims to make a record of this cultural process available online. We hope to curtail the tendency for music to drift away from the regional collective memory by creating a permanent accessible record.

Accessibility is the other obstacle to maintaining the publicness of recorded music. When a musician performs in public, the audience experiences the music. The moment of performance is fleeting, and the audience is limited. In order to expand the audience, a musician must record their performance. However, recording and copyright limit the publicness of music. Even if a band records their music, that recording does not necessarily increase access to their music. In a commercial music regime, music exists as a commodity. Moreover, as a commodity, the driving logic behind music is to generate profit. The primary way to listen to recorded music is by paying for it. Many people have argued that ICTs create the opportunity for everyone to access all music made available on the Internet[9]; the only limitation is bands putting their music online. However, this is far from the truth,[10] and the real effect of ICTs has been the narrowing of commercially viable music (and by extension available music).[11] In order for an independent band or musician to have their music heard on Apple Music, for instance, they must upload their music through a third-party service such as CD Baby. These services cost money for the band/musician, and still do not include access to Apple Music's front page. In fact, so much music is on Apple Music that popular artists drown out independent musicians. Once they quit paying the fee to include their music on these services, these musicians lose access to their (potential) audience. Even when the access feels free on a service such as Bandcamp or SoundCloud, these services profit from artists' music by either selling data about them and/or through advertising. Furthermore, these services do not provide a permanent record of music, and their business models could change at any moment to exclude a band's music. There is a public need for a permanent open-access

[9] Lawrence Lessig, *Free Culture: The Nature and Future of Creativity* (New York: Penguin Press, 2004); Patrick Burkart, "Music in the Cloud and the Digital Sublime," *Popular Music and Society* 37, no. 4 (2013); and Chris Anderson, *The Long Tail: Why the Future of Business Is Selling Less of More*, 1st ed. (New York: Hyperion, 2006).

[10] David Arditi, *iTake-Over: The Recording Industry in the Digital Era* (Lanham, MD: Rowman & Littlefield Publishers, 2014).

[11] Boyle, *The Public Domain*; Vaidhyanathan, *The Googlization of Everything*.

repository of music, so people can always listen to music of the past and present. MusicDetour seeks to overcome the problem of distribution by giving everyone free access to music without exploiting a band/artist/musician in the process.

DEVELOPING A DIGITAL HUMANITIES RESEARCH PROJECT

Digital Humanities projects often address a problem from a theoretical position. For that reason, it is important to emphasize Digital Humanities as a means for **praxis**, in which theory is put to practice. Shifting from theory to practice allows scholars to address actual problems that appear unsolvable to a **capitalist** market-based system; at the same time, it gives students an opportunity to think about alternative solutions to real-world problems. Digital Humanities can address practical problems by raising the following two questions:

1. What theoretical problem is not being addressed in the real world that could be?
2. How can digital technology advance the gap between theory and practice?

MusicDetour aims to develop a digital nonprofit music distribution platform that provides an alternative to the major record label distribution model, while at the same time serving as an archive of local music.

I created MusicDetour with the following research question: how can ICTs be used to facilitate the cultural dissemination of music? This question is both limited and actionable. It is limited because it focuses specifically on music. If the question were about the dissemination of culture, more generally, then it would be difficult to build an apparatus that can smoothly take into account the characteristics of different aspects of culture. The question is actionable because it does not assume that one way of using ICTs will provide the means to create the archive. Since it frames the question about cultural dissemination, it focuses on the problems of access to culture as a public good. This means that the question is open enough to incorporate various technologies, while remaining limited enough to address a specific problem.

The question also remains open to different approaches and answers. While the question aims to think of ways to disseminate all music, the actual resolution has been to start on a small scale: local independent music in the Dallas-Fort Worth metropolitan area (DFW). There is room for future growth (Texas to the USA to Global reach), but initially, the scope remains limited. A criticism that I received about scope was that local independent music in DFW is still too broad. This criticism came in two forms: (1) limit the archive specifically to Arlington, TX, and (2) limit it to a specific genre. First, limiting the archive to Arlington, TX is difficult because city borders are arbitrary to the cultural realm. Would I limit the archive to the whole band living in/being from Arlington? Or at least one member from the city? What about people who perform in Arlington? What if they disavow that location? As a result, I err on the side of inclusivity, while at the same time acknowledging that the archive will never house everything. Second, the idea to limit MusicDetour to a **genre** seems reductive. The criticism claimed that the archive would be stronger if it became the go to place for a specific genre, because it would develop a certain gravity. I tend to agree with this sentiment, but at the same time, I see music genres as irrelevant, because they tend to be marketing categories in record stores, rather than descriptions that bands can easily articulate. It is better for the archive to have fewer visitors, and a weaker cultural position, than to reinforce marketing categories as cultural categories. MusicDetour aims to overcome limitations constructed by discourse about popular music genres.

These insights should help you conceive of the research side of creating a Digital Humanities project. When thinking about developing an archive, people must think about the need and scale of the archive. Next, I will explore the technical considerations pertinent to constructing a digital archive.

TECHNICAL CONSIDERATIONS

Since I possess limited computer programming skills, I reached out to the University of Texas at Arlington Library to see if they had any advice on creating digital archives. The library is a good place to start working on any digital archive. Librarians are very helpful not only for finding information, but also because they tend to be very knowledgeable about the tools that are available online. Most of the tools toward which librarians point faculty and students are **open-source** and **open-access**. As it turns out, the UTA library recently restructured, and they had added a new emphasis on coordinating digital projects with faculty. The library staff pointed me to Omeka, and they helped me to create the archive.

Omeka is a web-publishing software application that allows users to easily develop online archives, with little-to-no background in Information Technology (IT). Developed by George Mason University's Roy Rosenzweig Center for History and New Media (CHNM), Omeka is open-source, and allows everyone access to the free software. There are two versions of Omeka available to users. First, there is the full version designed for installation on a web server. This version is free and unlimited, but requires that the user have access (and the knowledge) to use a web server. Second, a web-based application is available via Omeka. net. CHNM hosts the Omeka.net version, but requires the user to sign-up for access. Free access on Omeka.net only provides 500 MB of server space and a limited numbers of plug-ins and sites. However, users can purchase larger space on the Omeka.net server through a variety of plans. While this costs money, it also adds a level of simplicity for people with no IT skills because they do not need to have access to server space, nor do they need to know how to install or manage the web software.

Part of the usefulness of Omeka comes from its **metadata**. Omeka uses Dublin Core, which is a metadata vocabulary used by many libraries. Specifically, it provides descriptive metadata in a standardized form recognized by other entities. While there are other descriptive metadata vocabularies, libraries frequently use Dublin Core. This allows music stored on MusicDetour to adhere to a widely used metadata standard, which will help with expansion in the future. If MusicDetour develops arrangements with other music and/or cultural archives, the common language will allow the databases to integrate with each other. Using the common language allows me to build MusicDetour upon an already-existing database instead of beginning from scratch. Omeka stores the music files and metadata, and MusicDetour has a user-interface for fans and musicians to access music and each other. By providing an abundance of descriptive metadata, MusicDetour will begin to highlight commonalities between different musicians. This will help listeners to identify new music that meets their taste.

THINKING ABOUT COPYRIGHT

As a project with the aim of providing music as a permanent record to everyone, all music in the archive is freely available to the public, online. However, this creates a set of issues, because musicians are granted copyright over the majority of their music in the United States. Because of the dominance of copyright across the **culture industry**, any Digital Humanities project dealing with music will have to consider the impact of copyright.

Whether the music is available free or access requires a fee, the Digital Humanities researcher must obtain copyright permission before uploading music. It is also important to note that if a project charges a fee for access, then that enters a different realm of copyright, because most copyright licenses guard against additional commercial interests. We decided that the best way to upload music to MusicDetour would be to require two assurances: (1) a nonexclusive copyright agreement; (2) confirmation that the musician(s) contributing the music own the copyrights to that music. The nonexclusive copyright agreement simply states that the contributor retains all rights to the music. At any time, they can request to have their music removed from the website, and MusicDetour claims no rights to the music. In other words, MusicDetour is only providing music to the public under limited terms, and the contributor preserves all their rights. The second assurance means that we cannot use cover songs, or songs written by anyone else, because in order to clear those copyrights it would strain our limited staff, and likely require MusicDetour to pay license fees to distribute or archive the music. We keep digital files of the nonexclusive copyright forms in digital storage in the cloud, to make sure that we maintain access to these forms. However, we put the responsibility of everything copyright-related on the copyright owner and archive contributor. As a Digital Humanities project at an institution of higher education, our business is not copyright, and we err on the side of caution.

Again, MusicDetour intends to provide an alternative to the recording industry and the commodification of music. Music is a cultural object that should be treated as a public good. Copyright is a hurdle that Digital Humanities projects must negotiate. Ideally, musicians would not have to worry about copyright issues. However, the copyright system is entrenched, and musicians think of music as their intellectual property. As such, MusicDetour tries to respect each musician's comfort level with free music. Some contributors to the archive request that we upload live recordings as advertisements for their shows and studio recordings. Other contributors only provide singles from an album, while others will only allow us to make older albums available. Still, some contributors make all of their music available. We leave this up to the musicians and their comfort levels, because copyright is entrenched in how musicians think about music.

CONCLUSION

Digital Humanities projects can help to expand culture by making more cultural objects available to the public. By using academic research to think about public needs, people can make Digital Humanities projects that emphasize praxis. A good Digital Humanities project starts from a research question that is both limited and actionable. Seek out support from librarians to find the types of resources available on your campus, and do not assume that a lack of technological knowledge is a barrier to producing a Digital Humanities project. The only way to transform the way that culture is produced and distributed is to begin to change the system.

REFERENCES

Anderson, Chris. *The Long Tail: Why the Future of Business Is Selling Less of More.* 1st ed. New York: Hyperion, 2006.

Arditi, David. "Downloading Is Killing Music: The Recording Industry's Piracy Panic Narrative." Edited by Victor Sarafian and Rosemary Findley. *Civilisations, The State of the Music Industry* 63, no. 1 (2014): 13–32.

———. *iTake-Over: The Recording Industry in the Digital Era.* Lanham, MD: Rowman & Littlefield Publishers, 2014.

Bennett, H. Stith. *On Becoming a Rock Musician.* Amherst: University of Massachusetts Press, 1980.

Boyle, James. *The Public Domain: Enclosing the Commons of the Mind.* New Haven, CT: Yale University Press, 2008.

Burkart, Patrick. "Music in the Cloud and the Digital Sublime." *Popular Music and Society* 37, no. 4 (2013): 393–407.

Fuchs, Christian. *Internet and Society: Social Theory in the Information Age.* New York, NY: Routledge, 2008.

Hall, Stuart, Jessica Evans, and Sean Nixon, eds. *Representation.* 2nd ed. London: Sage: The Open University, 2013.

Klein, Bethany, Giles Moss, and Lee Edwards. *Understanding Copyright: Intellectual Property in the Digital Age.* Los Angeles, CA: Sage, 2015.

Lessig, Lawrence. *Free Culture: The Nature and Future of Creativity.* New York: Penguin Press, 2004.

Patry, William. *Moral Panics and the Copyright Wars.* New York, NY: Oxford University Press, 2009.

Vaidhyanathan, Siva. *Copyrights and Copywrongs: The Rise of Intellectual Property and How It Threatens Creativity.* New York: New York University Press, 2003.

———. *The Googlization of Everything.* Berkeley: University of California Press, 2011.

CHAPTER 5

Creating an Influencer-Relationship Model to Locate Actors in Environmental Communications

David Rheams

INTRODUCTION

This chapter describes a method for locating actors in a corpus of disconnected texts by creating an archive of newspaper articles. The archive can be searched and modeled to find relationships between people who influence the production of public knowledge. My area of focus is an environmental communications project concerning groundwater debates in Texas. Groundwater is a valuable but hidden resource in Texas, often contested and yet little understood. An acute drought in 2011 intensified public interest in groundwater availability, usage, and regulations. News stories about drought, rainfall, and groundwater were a familiar sight in local newspapers, as public officials debated ways to mitigate the drought's effect. Though there was much discussion of groundwater during the drought, the agencies, politicians, and laws that manage groundwater resources remained opaque. I wanted to find out

D. Rheams (✉)
The University of Texas at Dallas, Richardson, TX, USA

© The Author(s) 2018
l. levenberg et al. (eds.), *Research Methods for the Digital Humanities*,
https://doi.org/10.1007/978-3-319-96713-4_5

how groundwater knowledge was produced and who influenced public knowledge about this essential environmental resource.

I started the project by reading newspaper articles and highlighting the names of relevant actors and places. After reading through a few dozen articles it quickly became evident that the study needed a more sophisticated approach. The relationship between the politicians, corporations, myriad state water agencies, and others was impossible to discern without creating a searchable archive of the relevant newspaper articles. The archive was intended to be a model of groundwater communications that allows a researcher to realize patterns within the texts. This chapter describes the method to create and model this archive. The humanities and social sciences are familiar sites of quantitative textual analysis. Franco Moretti's concept of "distant reading" describes a process of capturing a corpus of texts to find cultural trends through thousands of books.[1] Media Studies scholars use sentiment analysis and other techniques to discover patterns in public pronouncements. The method described in this chapter is similar in that it relies on quantitative analysis. However, the quantification of keywords or the model created from the archive is not the final outcome of the research; it is where one can begin to see the object of inquiry and begin to formulate a hypothesis. Questions are drawn from the model, rather than conclusions.

The method is applicable outside of environmental communications topics. Political, cultural, and social questions may benefit from this approach. I offer a detailed description of this method as a practice of methodically describing my research, but also in hopes that other researchers will continue to refine and improve the processes in this chapter. The chapter discusses each stage of the project in the sections. I conclude with a few thoughts for possible improvement to the method and ways to approach textual analysis critically.

The stages for creating an influencer-relationship model are best summarized by the C.A.G.E. method. The method requires the four following steps:

1. **C**onceptualize the model
2. **A**ssemble the model
3. **G**roup the actors
4. **E**valuate the results

[1] Franco Moretti, *Distant Reading* (London and New York: Verso, 2013).

Table 5.1 Software

Software/Technology	Description
Plot.ly	An online data visualization platform
Microsoft Excel	A spreadsheet program that can be substituted with Google sheets
MySQL Workbench	A free database management software suite
Import.io	An online web scraping application
MySQL database	A standard MySQL database hosted online or on a local machine
Text Parsing and Analytics tool	A small application written for this research project to parse and analyze text documents

The model is designed during the conceptualization phase as a manual prototype of the more extensive project. The next step, assembling the model, is the process of collecting and storing data in a searchable manner. The researcher can find patterns among different groups by coding the initial research results. For example, this project separated *politicians* from *aquifers* to assist in searching the database. The final stage, evaluating the results, renders the data into a usable format. Each of these steps required software to aid in data collection and management. While this list of applications in Table 5.1 is not meant as a recommendation or endorsement, they serve to illustrate the type of software available to a researcher. Software changes quickly, and there are always new methods and platforms to explore.

The concluding section of this chapter discusses alternatives to these applications. The technology used to perform the method is somewhat interchangeable. The platform required to assist with research is at the researcher's discretion, and should be chosen based on the requirements of the research design. The conceptual model determines the requirements for the research project.

The Conceptual Model

The conceptual model is the planning stage of creating an influencer-relationship model. During this phase, the constraints of the project are identified, along with potential sources of texts, and a method to analyze the texts. Essentially, the conceptual model is the prototype for the larger project. This phase also allows the researcher to validate the method by manually collecting a small amount of data and seeing if the study design accomplishes the desired results. I approach this stage by asking a series of questions:

1. **What texts are likely to contain influencers?** There is a range of texts where actors exert influence over public opinion: newspapers, blogs, government documents, speeches, or online videos. The medium of communication will, in part, determine the next two questions.

2. **How should the texts be collected?** When building the archive, texts need to be collected and stored in specific ways to ensure the researcher can ask questions of the data. This problem should help the researcher find the best method of collection either by using online repositories of information, manually collecting files stored online, or other locations. The key to this question rests on finding a way to save computer-readable text. A MySQL database is easy to use, but has limitations with large datasets. There are many types of databases, and I encourage the researcher to find the one that fits the research design criteria. There is no reason to invest thousands of dollars on a platform if the source material is only a few thousand words.

3. **How should the data be evaluated?** This question determines the way a researcher will interact with the data. Different data types and databases allow for different kinds of queries and visualizations, so it is essential to understand the strengths and limitations of the software platforms before creating the archive. The conceptual model is flexible enough to allow a researcher to make mistakes and start over before investing too much time (or money) into a particular technical approach.

My conceptual model consisted of arranging newspaper articles on a whiteboard. To begin this project, I read ten articles about groundwater and highlighted the names of all the actors quoted in the article. Journalists use a person's full name the first time they quote them in a story, so looking for two or more consecutive words with capital letters provided a list of the actors quoted in stories about drought and groundwater. The approach also captures geographic places and the names of state agencies, as most of these are multiple words. Next, I put these articles on a whiteboard and drew lines to the different news stories that quoted the same actors. These lines highlighted the relationship between actors. After I validated that the model was capable of producing the desired result, I focused on specific texts and a method of analysis. The process of viewing articles on a whiteboard helped to clarify the next steps of the research, which was to build an archive of newspaper articles.[2]

WHY NEWSPAPERS?

Newspapers are the basis for this study's communications model, because they play a significant role in shaping public opinion, disseminating information, and providing "knowledge claims" to the public.[3] Even with social media, citizens still turn to local newspapers for information about regional politics and other topics specific to the regional community.[4] Newspapers rank just above televised news programs regarding viewership within a local community in 2011.[5] However, the articles are not limited to print; the readership study includes digital versions of the news stories. Though the media landscape has changed from 2011 with digital distribution gaining prominence both in readership and newspaper revenue, both print and digital newspaper articles are a critical source of local information according to a 2017 Pew Research Center "Newspaper Fact Sheet."

Choosing the sources of the articles was one of the first steps in designing this study. Ideally, every item from every newspaper in Texas would be freely accessible, but this is not the case. I limited the archive by making a list of all newspapers in operation in Texas between 2010 and 2014, during the acutest drought years in the past few decades. I removed any paper catering to suburbs or small towns as they would likely be reproducing stories from larger papers and would be more

[2] I repeated the process of creating a conceptual model many times to arrive at a workable method and found it helpful to document each question and approach. First, research practices should be transparent, and it can be easy to forget to record critical choices. Second, the documentation can help to clarify the results later in the research process.

[3] Mats Ekström, "Epistemologies of TV Journalism," *Journalism: Theory, Practice & Criticism* 3, no. 3 (2002), 259–282.

[4] Tom Rosenstiel, Amy Mitchell, Kristen Purcell, and Lee Rainier, "How People Learn About Their Local Community," Pew Research Center, 2011; Maxwell T. Boykoff and Jules M. Boykoff, "Balance as Bias: Global Warming and the US Prestige Press," *Global Environmental Change* 14, no. 2 (2004), 125–136.

[5] Tom Rosenstiel, Amy Mitchell, Kristen Purcell, and Lee Rainier, "How People Learn About Their Local Community," Pew Research Center, 2011.

difficult to access. Therefore, my study limits the papers to only those printed in cities with a population over 50,000. I further reduced my list of sources to include only newspapers that allowed full-text access to articles either on their website or from Westlaw, LexisNexis, or ProQuest. I settled on nine newspapers and two monthly magazines that met these criteria. The research sample represented metro areas (e.g., the Dallas-Fort Worth metro area) and smaller cities (e.g., Midland and El Paso), coastal areas, and towns in both east and west Texas. The two nationally recognized state magazines, the *Texas Monthly* and the *Texas Observer*, concentrate on issues specific to Texas. I selected these sources to capture a cross section of the state: rural and urban articles, as well as articles written in the different ecosystems and economies across Texas.

QUALITATIVE CONTENT ANALYSIS

The mapping process is similar to creating a citation map. In a typical citation map, the researcher knows the actors they are searching for in advance. However, this technique is designed to uncover previously *unknown* actors and networks. Content analysis was a natural choice for a research method because it lends itself to projects that require examining large volumes of text and allowed a view of the conversations about hydraulic fracturing, agricultural groundwater, and domestic water conflicts. Additionally, this method is both predictable and repeatable.[6]

The output of this analysis provides a list of actors and articles to investigate further, and the results are quantifiable based on the number of articles that contain the actor. While there are well-documented issues with word frequency counts, this study mitigates the risk of connecting frequency to importance by combining quantitative identification methods with qualitative analysis.[7] Statistics is not the basis of observations found in this research project; instead, the quantitative results become a guide for further investigation. Krippendorff describes this method as

---

[6] Klaus Krippendorff, *Content Analysis: An Introduction to Its Methodology*, 2nd ed (Thousand Oaks, Calif: Sage, 2004); J. Macnamara, "Media Content Analysis: Its Uses, Benefits and Best Practice Methodology," *Asia Pacific Public Relations Journal* 6, no. 1 (2005), 1–34; Bernard Berelson and Paul Lazarsfeld, *Content Analysis in Communications Research* (New York: Free Press, 1946).

[7] Steve Stemler, "An Overview of Content Analysis," *Practical Assessment, Research & Evaluation* 7, no. 17 (2001).

qualitative content analysis, where "samples may not be drawn according to statistical guidelines, but the quotes and examples that the qualitative researcher present to their readers has the same function as the use of samples".[8] Content analysis separates the actors from the articles to render the texts abstract, but searchable.

The people who produced knowledge claims became clear once the articles became abstract. The process of grouping actors together revealed observations and insights into when, where, and to whom the public looks for information about groundwater. For example, this method identified each article where actors overlap, allowing a researcher to generate a list of *politician*s quoted in articles about the *Edwards Aquifer*. Another query located state senators' names in articles that contained the key-phrases *ExxonMobile, DuPont, TWDB*, or *Texas Railroad Commission*. Each of these queries was combined with the metadata.[9]

Assembling the Model

I collected 4474 articles from nine Texas news publications written between 2010 and 2014 using online newspaper repositories and collecting articles directly from newspapers' websites. Each method accompanied different technological challenges. The first data collection method was to search LexisNexis, ProQuest, and Westlaw for newspapers with the option to download full articles. Four newspapers met these criteria: *The Austin American-Statesman, The Dallas Morning News, The Texas Observer*, and the *El Paso Times*. The search queried the full text of articles published between 2010 and 2014 and returned results for all articles containing the words *drought* or *groundwater*. The search terms were kept deliberately broad, allowing the software to capture possibly irrelevant information. Irrelevant articles were filtered before downloading by using negative keywords to remove sports-related articles.[10]

---

[8] Klaus Krippendorff, *Content Analysis: An Introduction to Its Methodology*, 2nd ed (Thousand Oaks, Calif: Sage, 2004).

[9] The metadata for a text document contains the articles publication name, city, date, author, word count, and other identifying information.

[10] A negative keyword is any word that should not return results; it is used to narrow a search. For example, sports terms were made negative. One of the unintended and unofficial findings of this project is that "drought" is more common when describing a basketball team's win/loss record rather than a meteorological condition in local papers.

The repositories exported the news articles into a single text document containing **500** articles. While this format is acceptable for a human reader, the files must be converted from text into a table for purposes of digital content analysis. Each article needs to be separated into columns that allow for analysis; one column contains the author, another includes the publication date, another consists of the source, another contains the text of the article, and so on, to allow for content analysis. Otherwise, it is impossible to separate one result from another or to group articles that share common attributes together.

To overcome this challenge, I needed a data-parsing web application to convert the text file into rows within a table. The program had three requirements: first, the tool must upload the text file to a database; second, the application must run a *regular expression* to separate the text into rows based on pre-designated columns; and third, the application needs to write the results in a standard format (CSV).[11]

I was unable to find any software that performed this task, so I asked a colleague for help designing a small application to help separate the text files into a usable archive. I worked with that colleague, Austin Meyers, to design a lightweight PHP application, the Text Parsing and Analysis Tool, to build and analyze the archive.[12] The program converts output from LexisNexis, ProQuest, and Westlaw, from large text files into a MySQL table. The table columns contain the full text of a single article, links to images in the story, and other useful metadata. The second function of the Text Parsing and Analysis tool was to analyze the stories within the database. The next section discusses this feature in detail.

---

[11] A regular expression is a sequence of characters used to find patterns within strings of text. They are commonly used in online forms to ensure the fields are correctly filled out. For example, a programmer may use a regular expression to confirm a cell has the correct format for a phone number or address. If the user does not use the proper syntax, an error is returned. There are numerous online tutorials to help people write a regular expression. I used regex101.com and regexr.com to help write the expressions needed for this project.

[12] Austin Meyers, founder of AK5A.com, wrote the PHP scripts used in the application. Austin and I have collaborated over the past 15 years on numerous technical projects and applications. The process of web scraping is a method for extracting objects or text from HTML websites. There are many software companies producing applications to assist in mining website data. Researchers may also choose to build a web scraper for specialized research projects.

Table 5.2 Articles table

article_id	author	headline	publication	date	city	length	article_text	url

If newspapers were not available from the databases, I accessed them directly from the newspaper's website. However, I did not want to copy and paste each article into a database because manual processes are time-consuming and error-prone. Instead, I used a web scraping application[13] to collect the articles from newspaper websites. After experimenting with several scrapers, I decided on Import.io to automate text and image scraping from a group of websites.[14] Import.io had a simple user interface and did not require writing any complicated code. Import.io outputs the data in a comma separated value file (CSV) that is readable by any spreadsheet program. The table created by Import.io had the same column names as the tables created by Text Parsing and Analysis Tool, which avoided confusion and reduced the amount of time needed to match the sources.

GROUP THE ACTORS

Table 5.2 shows the organization of articles into a single table with columns for the publisher, the full text of the article, the publication date, and other identifying information. The table allows a user to search through all nine sources for specific phrases or patterns in the text and find relationships between the publications.

Text Parsing and Analysis Tool

Once the data existed in the table, another problem presented itself. Even though I had identified the textual patterns within the articles, there was not an efficient way to sort through each article using MySQL

[13] Web-scraping is a technique to transfer the content of a webpage to another format.

[14] Import.io is a free web scraping application that converts a webpage into a table. It can be automated to run against multiple websites or used to search within large sites. For example, the Brownsville Herald website has over 118,000 pages (as of December 19, 2017) and it would be impractical to search the entire site and copy and paste individual articles. The website accompanying this book has a video on how Import.io can be used to gather newspaper articles into a database.

```
1 ([A-Z][a-zA-Z0-9-])([\s][A-Z][a-zA-Z0-9-])+
```

Fig. 5.1   Regular expression for consecutive capitalized words

queries. The classification of two million words in the archive needed completion on both an individual level and within the context of other words.

The Text Parsing and Analysis Tool is designed to locate patterns within the syntax of the text, what Krippendorff calls syntactic distinctions, to identify unknown actors.[15] The syntactical distinction searched for in this scenario was any string of text where two or more consecutive, capitalized words were found. In effect, this method provided a list of proper nouns found in the dataset. For example, a search using this criterion will identify *Allan Ritter* (a Texas State Representative) or *Texas Railroad Commission* because there are two or more consecutive capitalized words in each phrase. The search could identify any phrase that contained two or more consecutive capitalized words, using the regular expression given in Fig. 5.1.

The process is similar to a Boolean phrase match[16] used in search engines; but rather than locating a distinct expression, the search determines proper nouns. A series of actions happen once the tool identifies a proper noun: the application records the phrase in a table, it applies a unique ID number to the words automatically, it records the article ID number, and the 60 characters preceding the text. An identification number was attached to each of the key phrases to assist in writing queries to find patterns between the articles.

The regular expression searched the articles and returned **244,000** instances of consecutive capitalized words (i.e., key-phrases). The majority of these phrases were not relevant or only appeared once or twice within the text. Any key-phrase found in less than **20** articles was removed from the list to reduce it to a manageable and meaningful size. While the frequency of a particular key phrase does not necessarily connote importance in groundwater conflict, it helps a researcher prioritize the list. I completed this process by sorting a frequency list in the

---

[15] Klaus Krippendorff, *Content Analysis: An Introduction to Its Methodology*, 2nd ed (Thousand Oaks, Calif: Sage, 2004).

[16] A Boolean phrase match allows a user to search for phrases using operators such as AND, OR, NOT to refine searches.

Table 5.3   Key phrase table structure

article_id	keyword	keyword_id	preceding_60_characters	following_60_characters

database and manually deleting the irrelevant results. The new table had the column defined in Table 5.3.

The Article ID column connects each key-phrase to the relevant article. The search located 362 relevant key-phrases. The table has considerably more rows than the Articles Table, because there are multiple key-phrases per article. The key-phrase table makes the data searchable, but the unwieldy size of the table makes it difficult to parse. The key phrases need to be grouped to help a researcher see the patterns of relationships between actors. The process of adding the group is another way to *code* the data.

CODING THE KEY PHRASES

The code for the key-phrases is descriptive words that follow five broad groups: people, places, agencies, industries, and activist groups. For example, the phrase *Allan Ritter*[17] appeared in 50 articles and was coded as a *politician*, thus grouping *Allan Ritter* with the other state politicians found throughout the articles. The Edwards Aquifer was coded as *aquifer*, and Ladybird Lake was coded as *lake*. The 27 codes were mutually exclusive and included:

- State Government Body
- Lake
- City Government Body
- River
- National Government Body
- Politician
- Aquifer Name
- Activist Group

[17] Allen Ritter is the Texas State Representative for District 21 and current chairman of the Texas House Committee on Natural Resources.

Though the codes for this project were relatively simple, this stage of research is critical. Different coding criteria changes the output and the way the researcher interacts with the data. There are risks in reliability problems that occur from "the ambiguity of word meanings, category definitions," and these risks are compounded when more than one person applies the codes.[18] The way to reduce reliability problems is to provide definitions of what each code means and ensure that the codes used are mutually exclusive. For this project, I wrote definitions of each code before assigning the codes. There are a number of textbooks on how to correctly code data for qualitative research methods, though I found Krippendorf's work to fit this project.[19]

I completed the task of coding by manually adding one of the 27 codes to each of the 362 key phrases (i.e., actors) on an Excel spreadsheet. Once the spreadsheet was complete, I uploaded the CSV as a new table in the MySQL database. This approach worked because I had relatively few key phrases and codes. Online security and performance were not issues because the database was not public[20] and relatively small. The upload added a column to the key phrases table, changing the structure to the following (Table 5.4).

Once coded this way, the actors are cross-indexed by time, location, mutual key phrases, or other variables. Every keyword phrase or keyword code was assigned a numerical identification number to assist with creating an accurate index and keep the MySQL queries short. The identification numbers also helped to verify the correctness of the query by not relying on text searches of the database. However, the techniques of creating the archive are less important than the questions a researcher

---

[18] Robert Philip Weber, *Basic Content Analysis*, 2nd ed. Sage University Papers Series, no. 07-049 (Newbury Park, CA: Sage, 1990).

[19] Klaus Krippendorff, *Content Analysis: An Introduction to Its Methodology*, 2nd ed (Thousand Oaks, Calif: Sage, 2004); Johnny Saldaña, *The Coding Manual for Qualitative Researchers*, 3rd ed (Los Angeles, CA and London, New Delhi, Singapore, Washington DC: Sage, 2016); Sharan B. Merriam and Elizabeth J. Tisdell, *Qualitative Research: A Guide to Design and Implementation*, 4th ed (San Francisco, CA: Jossey-Bass, 2016).

[20] A local server is a MySQL database hosted on the user's computer rather than hosted by a provider. Running the database on a local machine, as opposed to online, reduces risks allowing the user to experiment without worrying about security or performance issues. Instructions, best practices, and links to help get you started with a MySQL database on are on the website accompanying this book.

Table 5.4 Key phrase table structure with codes

article_id	keyword	keyword_id	preceding_60_characters	following_60_characters	keyword_code	keyword_code_id

asks of the archive. The technology enabled the ability to search, but did not dictate the search.

Once the phrases were identified and the tables existed in the database, I was able to query the database as needed to answer the question at hand. The answer to one question usually led to additional queries. For example, I wrote queries to elicit which politicians were most likely to be quoted in the same article that discussed aquifers. Another query created a matrix of each actor listed alongside all other key phrases and the article ID where the pair was located.

Use Case: Querying the Database

Each text analysis project will require some method of querying the database. One of the requirements for the influencer-relationship model is to locate places where two or more actors are quoted in the same article. The following query is an example of the method I used to create a table of news stories with both the phrase *Railroad Commission* and *Environmental Protection Agency* (shown as *keyword_id* 263 in the query). The following snippet of MySQL has been simplified (pseudo code) to show the method rather than the actual query.[21]

The query in Fig. 5.2 tells the database to combine two tables (the Articles table and the keywords table) and find all the articles with both keywords. There are also two comments in the query to remind the user where to input variables. I often include similar comments when using queries multiple times. These comments also help clarify the way the query functions. The query outputs a table with each of the objects under the SELECT statement (lines two through eight) as columns.

The query produces the table by using a *match against* expression to *match* the text in quotation marks *against* the article column and returns

---

[21] There are many ways to construct a MySQL query. I used a query similar to the one in Fig. 5.2 because it fit into my workflow; it was easy for me to find the keyword_id that associated with the keywords I was interested in. However, another researcher may have rewritten the query differently, but still arrive the same output.

```
1 SELECT
2       article_id,
3       keyword_id,
4       keyword_code_id,
5       keyword_code,
6       keyword,
7       author
8       publication
9 FROM
10            articles
11    JOIN
12            keywords ON articles.article_id = keywords.article_id
13
14 -- -------------------------------INSERT KEYWORD HERE -----------------
15 where
16    match(article)
17    against(' "KEYWORD" ' IN BOOLEAN MODE)
18 -- -------------------------------INSERT KEYWORD ID HERE -----------------

19 and keyword_id = 12345
20 group by article_id
```

Fig. 5.2 MySQL query example

Table 5.5 Results of the query

article_id	keyword_id	keyword_code_id	keyword_code	keyword	publication	author
1	287	22	Environmental Activist Group	Railroad Commission	*Austin-American Statesman*	Price
82	369	45	State Government Body	Environmental Protection Agency	*Brownsville Herald*	Smith

all of the articles with the phrase *Railroad Commission*. All rows are filtered using the *keyword_id* field within the search. I kept a table of each keyword ID as a reference when writing queries (Table 5.5).[22]

The result is displayed with both index numbers and their English language referents. Both are presented to assist with verification of the result. Querying a database is often a process of trial-and-error. I wrote many queries which did not work, or returned inaccurate results, while working through the data. Each new query was a refinement of a previous one and often lead to more questions. The output can be viewed in multiple ways. Either as tables or as charts, graphs, or other data visualizations.

[22] There are other ways to accomplish the same goal using MySQL, the only requirement for this type of project are that the results are accurate. Using identification numbers rather than the text searchers sped up the verification process.

EVALUATE THE RESULTS

Evaluating the results from the queries gives the data shape, and helps to render it into a usable format. I used data visualizations as a way to show the relationship between actors within newspaper articles by allowing a broad view of the database. All of the materials under review can be viewed at the same time, which is helpful when trying to determine the scope and impact of particular actors. There is a rich history of data visualization literature[23] and there are numerous methods of rendering data into a coherent image. One of the benefits of the Digital Humanities is that these practices are conducted in conjunction with considerations about visualizing complex datasets. Most critiques recognize that a visualization is not an exact representation of the object being studied, but a particular perspective of a specific database.[24] The visualization is not necessarily reality, but a guide to additional questions.

Johanna Drucker points to some of the limitations of humanities visualizations, warning that their uncritical use may serve as an intellectual "Trojan horse".[25] She argues that research in the humanities has long resisted the temptation to reduce all phenomena to data and that humanists need to recognize uncertainty and complexity. Lisa Otty and Tara Thomson explain how digital humanists alleviate some of the potential errors.[26] I stand in agreement with Otty and Thomson, that we must communicate the exact steps undertaken to make the design choices. The steps required to create the visualizations are "crucial components" of the visualization and the research project as a whole.[27] They cite Dörk

---

[23] Edward Tufte has written extensively on data visualization beginning in the 1970s (Tufte 2001, 2006). Ben Fry has not only written on the subject (Fry 2008) but has also developed a programing language around data visualization called Processing.

[24] Marian Dörk, Christopher Collins, Patrick Feng, and Sheelagh Carpendale, "Critical InfoVis: Exploring the Politics of Visualization," In *CHI'13 Extended Abstracts on Human Factors in Computing Systems*, edited by Wendy E. Mackay and Association for Computing Machinery (New York: ACM, 2013).

[25] Johanna Drucker, "Humanities Approaches to Graphical Display," *Digital Humanities Quarterly* 5, no. 1 (2011).

[26] Lisa Otty and Tara Thomson, "Data Visualization in the Humanities," In *Research Methods for Creating and Curating Data in the Digital Humanities*, edited by Matt Hayler and Gabriele Griffin. Research Methods for the Arts and Humanities (Edinburgh: Edinburgh University Press, 2016).

[27] Ibid.

et al.'s four principles of visualization defined in their article "Critical Info-Viz: Exploring the Politics of Visualization' as a way to visualize data in the Digital Humanities.[28] Dörk et al., Otty and Thomson, and Drucker each state the requirement to think critically about the potential ways visualizations shape knowledge. Visualizations should prevent preconceived ideas rather than entrench them. Models are representations of the data and should allow a researcher to explore the object of inquiry fully, without guiding the viewer to a specific conclusion.

Researchers can ensure models are open to interpretation by thinking through their methodology. Digital Humanities, like other disciplines, tend to reflect on their research to determine how the researcher impacts their results. For example, had I limited my model to show only the relationship between corporations and aquifers, my analysis would have been skewed towards corporations. The visualizations would not be open to exploration because that sort of approach limits the study to a single conclusion. To prevent this scenario, Dörk et al. recommend four principles to follow when creating visualizations: *disclosure, plurality, contingency*, and *empowerment*. I have found that these serve as a useful guide for most any project. A researcher must *disclose* the exact steps taken to create visualization to allow a viewer to understand the presentation of data. *Plurality* asks that a visualization be holistic, answering multiple different questions so as not to present only one side of the data. The contingency principle "acknowledges the situation of the viewer in relation to the phenomenon being represented" by allowing a viewer to explore the visualization, on their terms. For a map-based visualization this can mean orienting the map towards their location. The final principal, *empowerment*, acknowledges the way a viewer can interact with the visualization by leaving comments or making updates available for all viewers. This research project followed these principles as closely as possible, and in doing so, proved an early hypothesis regarding the influence of corporations on groundwater knowledge claims wrong.

During the research project, I created numerous tables to help sort the data in different ways. The visualization helped to provide a different perspective of the entire dataset. The first visualization I produced is

---

[28] Marian Dörk, Christopher Collins, Patrick Feng, and Sheelagh Carpendale, "Critical InfoVis: Exploring the Politics of Visualization," In *CHI'13 Extended Abstracts on Human Factors in Computing Systems*, edited by Wendy E. Mackay and Association for Computing Machinery (New York: ACM, 2013).

Frequency of Actors

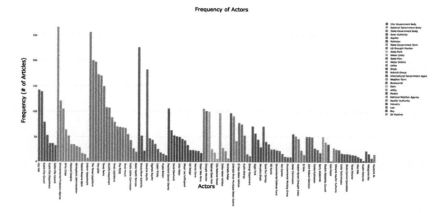

Fig. 5.3 Frequency of actors

Actor Relationship Matrix

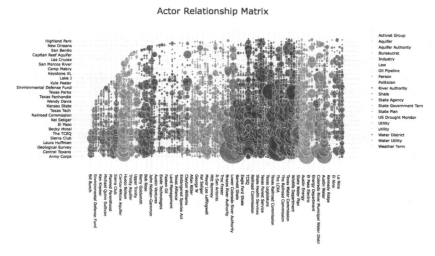

Fig. 5.4 Actor relationship matrix

a bar chart of the frequency of each actor as they appear in the dataset. The bars are grouped by color to denote the category of the actor; these categories were based on the codes I applied to the keyword phrases. I used data visualization software, Plot.ly, to create Figs. 5.3 and 5.4.

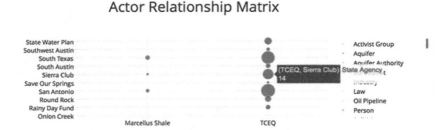

Fig. 5.5 Magnified view of the actor relationship matrix

Figure 5.3 does not prove anything on its own; however, in context, it is a useful way to visualize the collection of articles and allows the viewer to explore the data on their own terms. The blue, orange, and green bars represent the city, federal, and state agencies. A quick look at the chart shows the frequency of quotes and stories from official sources, which shows where journalists are getting much of their information. To validate this finding, I sent emails to Texas journalists writing about environmental and water issues.

To address the relationship between actors, I created the Actor Relationship Matrix chart shown in Fig. 5.4. Thinking back to Dörk et al.'s, principles, this chart helps to answer questions about *plurality* and *contingency*. The size of the sphere represents the frequency of stories that contain both actors. The colors represent the groups of key phrases to make the chart easier to parse. When viewed in its entirety, as it is in Fig. 5.4, the chart is similar to the visualization in Fig. 5.3. However, once the chart is magnified, the viewer can explore the data via the relationship between actors within the articles. Figure 5.5 is a magnified view of the Actor Relationship Matrix that allows a user to examine the database and the relationship between actors.

The magnified view shows that 14 articles listed both the Texas Commissions on Environmental Quality and the Sierra Club. The journalistic practice of creating balanced stories by quoting opposing viewpoints within the same story is evident when looking at this chart.[29]

---

[29] Maxwell T. Boykoff and Jules M. Boykoff, "Balance as Bias: Global Warming and the US Prestige press," *Global Environmental Change* 14, no. 2 (2004), 125–136.

The practice of indexing that Lance Bennett described is also evident in this dataset, along with other takeaways.[30] The data in this matrix is designed for a user to explore and help to see the articles in a productive way. While I used environmental topics for this paper, any relevant topic or dataset could be presented in a similar matrix.

I used the free version of Plot.ly to create these visualizations.[31] While Plot.ly allows a user to connect the visualization program directly with a MySQL database, it was easier for me to export the results of a query as a CSV and upload the CSV to Plot.ly. I chose Plot.ly as the visualization platform because it was accurate, has an accessible user interface, and is free for basic users. There was no need here to invest in expensive software options. Especially for scholars who are new to this type of software, it is often easiest to start simple and explore. I created quite a few visualizations before I found ones that were useful. Again, the process is trial and error, with each iteration being a refinement of the one before.

OUTCOMES AND NEXT STEPS

Another way to think of the output of this project is to think of it as a small-scale search engine, for a particular group of articles that would have been unavailable in any other context. For this project, the quantitative analysis leads to more rigorous qualitative research. I used the analysis from the visualizations to locate actors to interview, articles to examine, agency websites to explore and environmental laws to review. In other words, the broad view of the data enabled and clarified further research. I used the model as a reference while conducting interviews with state hydrologists, water district managers, and environmentalists. For example, the influencer-relationship model showed that journalists relied heavily on state agencies, especially the Texas Water Development Board, for information about groundwater, but that they did not cite spokespeople from industries which use groundwater. This result led to an interview with a prominent Texas environmental journalist and became the genesis of a conversation about how journalists located sources for groundwater stories.

---

[30] See Lance Bennett's (2016) *The Politics of Illusion* (10th edition) by the University of Chicago Press.

[31] The specific steps required to create these charts are available on the website accompanying this book.

All the choices made during this project had an impact on its results. It is helpful to be aware of each of one's design decisions, and the impact that these decisions have on the outcome when thinking critically about Digital Humanities projects. If I had chosen to use a different database schema, or a slightly different regular expression, or if I had visualized the output differently, it may have altered the results. The technology used to create the influencer-relationship model is not static, however, and should be expanded to include new platforms.

If I were to rebuild the Text Parsing and Analysis Tool, I would consider using Python, rather than PHP with regular expressions. Python's Natural Language Toolkit is designed to assist with language analysis.[32] However, I had to choose whether to take time off to learn a new language or to work with the tools readily available. I chose the latter because it was enough to arrive at the model I needed, and the improvements were not evident until we had completed the first version of the application. Alternatively, if the project required modeling millions of texts, one could use a NoSQL database such as MongoDB, and/or employ Dgraph to query the archive. However, the technologies used are less important than the methodology. This process can be used with any technique or technological tool. The key aspect of the method presented here is the ability to locate influential actors across multiple sources of texts. The specific patterns and techniques are decided by the research question. I considered this project a success because I was able to ask questions of the data, and it helped shape the next phase of research, which included interviews with actors, close reading of the articles, and examinations of new documents that were alluded to within the news stories. Like software, research is an iterative process that gets more accurate with each new phase. Each new look at the object offers new opportunities to refine methods in the Digital Humanities.

References

Berelson, Bernard, and Paul Lazarsfeld. *Content Analysis in Communications Research*. New York: Free Press, 1946.

---

[32] Python is a general-purpose high-level programming language and is ideal for small-scale applications. Python's Natural Language Toolkit (NLTK) is a platform that allows Python application to work with English language data. The NLTK is a free, open-source project used by researchers across disciplines.

Boykoff, Maxwell T., and Jules M. Boykoff. "Balance as Bias: Global Warming and the US Prestige Press." *Global Environmental Change* 14, no. 2 (2004): 125–136. https://doi.org/10.1016/j.gloenvcha.2003.10.001.

Dörk, Marian, Christopher Collins, Patrick Feng, and Sheelagh Carpendale. "Critical InfoVis: Exploring the Politics of Visualization." In *CHI'13 Extended Abstracts on Human Factors in Computing Systems*, edited by Wendy E. Mackay and Association for Computing Machinery. New York: ACM, 2013. http://mariandoerk.de/criticalinfovis/altchi2013.pdf.

Drucker, Johanna. "Humanities Approaches to Graphical Display." *Digital Humanities Quarterly* 5, no. 1 (2011). http://www.digitalhumanities.org/dhq/vol/5/1/000091/000091.html#p4.

Ekström, Mats. Epistemologies of TV Journalism. *Journalism: Theory, Practice & Criticism* 3, no. 3 (2002): 259–282.

Fry, Ben. *Visualizing Data*. Sebastopol, CA: O'Reilly Media, Inc., 2008.

Krippendorff, Klaus. *Content Analysis: An Introduction to Its Methodology*. 2nd ed. Thousand Oaks, Calif: Sage, 2004.

Macnamara, J. "Media Content Analysis: Its Uses, Benefits and Best Practice Methodology." *Asia Pacific Public Relations Journal* 6, no. 1 (2005): 1–34.

Merriam, Sharan B., and Elizabeth J. Tisdell. *Qualitative Research: A Guide to Design and Implementation*. 4th ed. San Francisco, CA: Jossey-Bass, 2016.

Moretti, Franco. *Distant Reading*. London, New York: Verso, 2013.

Otty, Lisa, and Tara Thomson. "Data Visualization in the Humanities." In *Research Methods for Creating and Curating Data in the Digital Humanities*, edited by Matt Hayler and Gabriele Griffin. Research Methods for the Arts and Humanities. Edinburgh: Edinburgh University Press, 2016.

Rosenstiel, Tom, Amy Mitchell, Kristen Purcell, and Lee Rainier. "How People Learn About Their Local Community." Pew Research Center, 2011. http://www.journalism.org/2011/09/26/local-news/.

Saldaña, Johnny. *The Coding Manual for Qualitative Researchers*. 3rd ed. Los Angeles, CA and London, New Delhi, Singapore, Washington DC: Sage, 2016.

Stemler, Steve. "An Overview of Content Analysis." *Practical Assessment, Research & Evaluation* 7, no. 17 (2001). http://PAREonline.net/getvn.asp?v=7&n=17.

Tufte, Edward R. *The Visual Display of Quantitative Information*. 2nd ed. Cheshire, CT: Graphics Press, 2001.

———. *Beautiful Evidence*. Cheshire, CT: Graphics Press, 2006.

———. *Envisioning Information*. Fourteenth printing. Cheshire, CT: Graphics Press, 2013.

Weber, Robert Philip. *Basic Content Analysis*. 2nd ed. Sage University Papers Series, no. 07-049. Newbury Park, CA: Sage, 1990.

CHAPTER 6

Digital Humanities for History of Philosophy: A Case Study on Nietzsche

Mark Alfano

INTRODUCTION

Nietzsche scholars have developed an interest in his conceptions of moral psychological phenomena, such as drives and instincts[1], as well as virtue(s)[2]. However, the quality and systematicity of engagement in

[1] M. Alfano, "The Tenacity of the Intentional Prior to the *Genealogy*," *Journal of Nietzsche Studies* 40 (2010): 123–140; M. Alfano, "Nietzsche, Naturalism, and the Tenacity of the Intentional," *Journal of Nietzsche Studies* 44, no. 3 (2013b): 457–464; P. Katsafanas, "Nietzsche's Philosophical Psychology," in *Oxford Handbook of Nietzsche*, ed. J. Richardson and K. Gemes (Oxford: Oxford University Press, 2013a), 727–755; P. Katsafanas, *Agency and the Foundations of Ethics: Nietzschean Constitutivism* (Oxford: Oxford University Press, 2013b); P. Katsafanas, "Value, Affect, and Drive," in *Nietzsche on Mind and Nature*, ed. P. Kail and M. Dries (Oxford: Oxford University Press, 2015).

[2] M. Alfano, "The Most Agreeable of All Vices: Nietzsche as Virtue Epistemologist," *British Journal for the History of Philosophy* 21, no. 4 (2013a): 767–790; M. Alfano, "An Enchanting Abundance of Types: Nietzsche's Modest Unity of Virtue Thesis," *Journal*

M. Alfano (✉)
Delft University of Technology, Delft, The Netherlands
e-mail: m.r.alfano@tudelft.nl; mark.alfano@acu.edu.au

M. Alfano
Australian Catholic University, Melbourne, VIC, Australia

© The Author(s) 2018
l. levenberg et al. (eds.), *Research Methods for the Digital Humanities*,
https://doi.org/10.1007/978-3-319-96713-4_6

this area leave much to be desired. In this chapter, I explain a synoptic Digital Humanities approach to Nietzsche interpretation and demonstrate its explanatory value.

This methodology integrates and extends both **close reading** and **distant reading** techniques developed by philosophers and other humanists.[3] The latter has been available for years, but despite promising to lead to new insights and complement existing approaches, they have made almost no inroads in philosophy. Of the two million articles, chapters, and books housed at www.philpapers.org, only twenty-one unique publications (approximately 0.001%) are returned when one searches for 'Digital Humanities', and I am an author or co-author of three of them.[4]

Here is the plan for this chapter: first, I explain my methodology. Next, I present the results of applying the methodology to the study of Nietzsche's discussion of drives, instincts, and virtues. In the interpretive section of the paper, I marshal the resources developed in the previous section to argue that, for Nietzsche, instincts and virtues are (partially overlapping) subsets of drives. Instincts are innate drives, whereas virtues

---

of Value Inquiry 49, no. 3 (2015a): 417–435; M. Alfano, "How One Becomes What One Is Called: On the Relation Between Traits and Trait-Terms in Nietzsche," *Journal of Nietzsche Studies* 46, no. 1 (2015b): 261–269; M. Alfano, "Review of Christine Swanton's *The Virtue Ethics of Hume and Nietzsche*," *Ethics* 126, no. 4 (2016): 1120–1124; J. Annas, "Which Variety of Virtue Ethics," in *Varieties of Virtue Ethics*, ed. D. Carr, J. Arthur, and K. Kristjánsson (London: Palgrave, 2017); C. Daigle, "Nietzsche: Virtue Ethics... Virtue Politics?" *The Journal of Nietzsche Studies* 32 (2006): 1–21; T. Hurka, "Nietzsche: Perfectionist," in *Nietzsche and Morality*, ed. B. Leiter and N. Sinhababu (Oxford: Oxford University Press, 2007), 9–31; S. May, *Nietzsche's Ethics and His War on 'Morality'* (Oxford: Oxford University Press, 1999); P. Railton, "Nietzsche's Normative Theory? The Art and Skill of Living Well," in *Nietzsche, Naturalism, & Normativity*, ed. C. Janaway and S. Robertson (Oxford: Oxford University Press, 2012), 20–51; B. Reginster, *The Affirmation of Life* (Cambridge: Cambridge University Press, 2006); S. Robertson, "The Scope Problem—Nietzsche, the Moral, Ethical, and Quasi-Aesthetic," in *Nietzsche, Naturalism, & Normativity*, ed. C. Janaway and S. Robertson (Oxford: Oxford University Press, 2012), 81–110; A. Thomas, "Nietzsche and Moral Fictionalism," in *Nietzsche, Naturalism, & Normativity*, ed. C. Janaway and S. Robertson (Oxford: Oxford University Press, 2012), 133–159; A. White, "The Youngest Virtue," in *Nietzsche's Post-Moralism*, ed. R. Schacht (Cambridge: Cambridge University Press, 2001), 63–78.

[3] F. Moretti, *Distant Reading* (London: Verso, 2013).

[4] Search conducted 23 January 2017. Gemes (2001, 2008) makes brief forays into the sort of word-counting that grounds the analysis in this paper, but he does not monitor overlaps. In addition, his papers were written before the Nietzsche Source was available as a resource.

are well-calibrated drives. A well-calibrated instinct is therefore also a virtue. What it takes for a drive to be calibrated involves both internal synergy and social harmony (or at least non-interference). In the final section, I make a few observations and recommendations for future research in Nietzsche scholarship and history of philosophy more generally.

METHODOLOGY

Philosophers—especially those who favor a hermeneutic approach to "great figures"—may be prejudiced against Digital Humanities and distant reading, but they should rest assured that this approach complements and contextualizes the methods with which they are familiar. Since there is no single method associated with Digital Humanities, in this section I explain my approach. There are six steps:

1. select core **concepts**;
2. **operationalize** concepts to search your source (in this case study, Nietzsche Source);
3. conduct **searches**;
4. clean **data**;
5. **analyze** and **visualize** data; and
6. **close read** relevant passages.

The first and most important step is to select the core **concepts** for the study. For this study, I selected the concepts of *virtue, drive,* and *instinct.* As Katsafanas[5] remarks, Nietzsche sometimes seems to use the latter two equivalently. In addition, some interpretations in the secondary literature[6] claim based on passages such as D 30, GS 21, BGE 10, and GM III.8 that virtues are a subset of drives.[7] For these reasons, it is worthwhile to ask whether Nietzsche does in fact refer to drives and

---

[5] P. Katsafanas, "Nietzsche's Philosophical Psychology," in *Oxford Handbook of Nietzsche*, ed. J. Richardson and K. Gemes (Oxford: Oxford University Press, 2013a), 727–755.

[6] M. Alfano, "The Most Agreeable of All Vices: Nietzsche as Virtue Epistemologist," *British Journal for the History of Philosophy* 21, no. 4 (2013a): 767–790. M. Alfano, "How One Becomes What One Is Called: On the Relation Between Traits and Trait-Terms in Nietzsche," *Journal of Nietzsche Studies* 46, no. 1 (2015b): 261–269.

[7] I use the standard abbreviations for the titles of Nietzsche's texts (http://www.hunter.cuny.edu/jns/style-guide). All translations are Cambridge University Press critical editions, with a few minor emendations for clarity.

instincts interchangeably, and to which sorts of drives or instincts he grants the honorific 'virtue'.

Once these questions have been formulated, a methodological challenge immediately arises. There is no reliable, valid catalogue of which concepts Nietzsche deploys (and whether he does so ironically) in which passages. The closest thing we have is the Nietzsche Source (www. nietzschesource.org), a digital repository of all of his writings that includes published works (e.g., HH, D, GS, BGE), private publications (e.g., NCW), authorized manuscripts (e.g., A, EH), posthumous writings (e.g., PTAG), posthumous fragments, and letters.[8] This brings us to step 2: we need to **operationalize** the concepts under study by developing a list of words that Nietzsche characteristically uses to express them. This list will be neither comprehensive (there will be some false negatives) nor complete (there will be some false positives). Nevertheless, if the researcher is sufficiently familiar with Nietzsche's corpus, it should have high validity and reliability.

Such searching is aided by the **query** functionality of the Nietzsche Source: it is possible to return all passages containing words that begin with a given text string if one appends a wildcard (denoted by an asterisk) to the end of the string (e.g., '*tugend**'). Of course, it is possible to discuss virtue in German without using one of these words, and it is also possible for one of these words to turn up without the author discussing virtue in a serious way. Despite these drawbacks, operationalizing in this way is the best, most reproducible method we currently have for systematically studying Nietzsche's texts, and the texts are the best evidence we have for what he thought. In addition, because it makes explicit what the inclusion and exclusion criteria are, this method is transparent in a way that most other interpretive methods are not.

For the present study, I operationalized *drive* by searching for '*trieb**'. Likewise, I operationalized *instinct* with both '*instinkt**' and '*instinct**' (Nietzsche uses both until 1882, at which point he stops using the spelling with 'c'). I operationalized *virtue* with '*tugend**' and '*keusch**'. These are both typically translated as some variant of 'virtue' in English, though the latter is more gendered and often refers specifically to

---

[8]For a full introduction, see D'Iorio (2010). To my knowledge, the only papers to use the Nietzsche Source to comprehensively study Nietzsche's use of particular words are Alfano (2013a, 2017). The complete data-sets for these study as well as the present study are freely available at http://www.alfanophilosophy.com/dh-nietzsche/.

chastity. The same ambiguity exists in English of the nineteenth century, as we see in Austen's *Pride and Prejudice*.[9]

The next methodological hurdle is to determine which of Nietzsche's writings to include in the search. In keeping with standard interpretive practices, I refrain from using Nietzsche's unpublished works, or poems. That leaves me with the published works, private publications, and authorized manuscripts. Future work can easily supplement this chapter by including the letters, the poetry, and the kitchen sink.

Given these constraints, the next choice is to determine what researchers in the field of natural language processing call the '**window**'. The basic idea is that if an author tends to use word W near word V, then the author probably associates the concepts expressed by W and V (whether positively or negatively). However, there is no hard-and-fast rule for determining what counts as **nearness**. One appealing window is co-sententiality: if W and V are used in the same sentence, they are probably associated. Another is co-paragraphicality: if W and V are used in the same paragraph, they are probably associated. Alternatively, one can determine a window of length *n*, where *n* is the number of words between W and V. For instance, a window of 3 around W would include all words up to three before or after W (including words that occur across sentence and paragraph breaks). As you might imagine, choosing a window size is a dark art. Fortunately for Nietzsche scholars, he wrote in sections that—at least after the *Untimely Meditations*—tend to be of roughly the same brief length. These are standardly used in Nietzsche scholarship, making it straightforward to link this methodology to the existing secondary literature. In addition, the Nietzsche Source returns separate results for each such section, which makes it a simple task to reproduce results. For these reasons, I set the window at the level of the section for this study. As before, this may not be ideal, but it is documentable, and therefore both criticizable and corrigible.

I now describe my method for preparing or "**cleaning**" the data. In order to clean the data for optimal use in the visual analytics platform Tableau Public, one must arrange them in a tabular format. The rows in this table represent individual query results from the Nietzsche Source. The columns represent every datum of interest about the query result in

---

[9]J. Austen, "*Pride and Prejudice*," (Penguin Classics. Harmondsworth: Penguin, 1813/2002).

question. When querying this database, one chooses a subset of writings to search and inputs a search term.

This query returned 148 passages: 15 from *The Birth of Tragedy*, 5 from *David Strauss, the Confessor and the Writer*, 3 from *The Uses and Disadvantages of History for Life*, and so on. The results include 'Trieb' (drive), 'Triebe' (drives), 'Triebfedern' (driving forces), and 'trieblos' (impotent). Some of the surrounding text for the first two passages is also returned. For each passage, I recorded five items in separate columns: the book in which it occurs, the passage within that book in which it occurs, the year of publication of the book, which search term I used, and which concept the term operationalizes.

Once the data have been cleaned, they can be **analyzed and visualized**. Perhaps the simplest analytic technique is to count the number of passages per concept in each book. For instance, in BT, virtue is referred to in five passages, chastity in none, drive in fifteen, and instinct in nine. We can also look for overlaps: passages in which more than one relevant concept is referred to. More sophisticated analyses involve various descriptive and inferential statistics. In this chapter, I focus primarily on visualization as a defeasible guide to close-reading. The idea is to achieve a synoptic view of both the books and the sections within each book in order to identify the most important passages and steer a systematic reading of those passages. To accomplish this, I fed the cleaned data into Tableau Public.[10]

After reading the data into Tableau Public, I created three interactive visualizations:

1. a timeline indexed to books and concepts,
2. a treemap of all concepts of interest indexed to books, and
3. a section-by-section map of each book, indexed to concepts of interest.

To create the **timeline**, I placed the year of publication and the book title in the Columns shelf (in that order), Number of Records in the Rows shelf, and Concept in both the Filters card and the Color card. To create the **treemap**, I placed Number of Records in the Size card, Book in the Label card, and Concept in both the Color card and the Filters

---

[10] Available at https://public.tableau.com/en-us/s/download. Tableau Public is a highly intuitive interface that automatically employs best practices in visual analytics.

card. Finally, to create the **section-by-section map**, I placed Passage in the Columns shelf, Number of Records in the Rows shelf, Concept in the Color card, and Book in the Filters card.

RESULTS

In this section I present the results of the analytics exercise described above. On the website associated with this chapter (alfanophilosophy. com), all of these visualizations are dynamic and interactive. Using the filter functionality to select one concept at a time, Tableau Public automatically visualizes the data from the timeline described above, as a histogram with two horizontal axes (year and book) and one vertical axis (number of passages per book in which the concept of interest occurs at least once). We can quickly see from such a visualization that *Daybreak* is the only book in which there are over 30 passages that refer to drives.

Likewise, Tableau Public automatically visualizes the treemap data described above as a chart, in which the books with the most passages that contain one of the concepts of interest are represented by larger rectangles. The books with the least such passages are represented by smaller rectangles.

As Nietzsche moved beyond the *Untimely Meditations* (DS, HL, SE, and RWB), he began to speak more and more frequently of drives. However, after *Beyond Good and Evil*, his engagement with drive-talk dropped off precipitously. Thus, scholars interested in Nietzsche's conception of drives would benefit from looking to the works associated with his so-called "free spirit" period (D, GS, and HH).

Nietzsche barely used the language of instinct until the 1880s. Indeed, the passages from GS in which Nietzsche uses instinct-talk are mostly from sections in the re-release that included book 5. Thus, unlike drives, instincts receive little attention from Nietzsche until his mature works (which I count as everything from BGE onwards). And, with the exception of the anti-Wagner works (CW and NCW), his use of instinct never drops off. Scholars interested in Nietzsche's conception of instincts would benefit from looking less to the free spirit works and more to the mature works (TI, BGE, A, EH, and GM).

Nietzsche started talking of virtue in the free spirit works and continued to do so until 1886 (plus TI in 1889). The discussions of virtue occur during the transition from an emphasis on drives to an emphasis on instincts. Thus, scholars interested in Nietzsche's conception of virtue should look to both the free spirit works and the mature works.

Nietzsche talks of chastity less frequently than the other concepts. Several books have no passages in which it crops up. *The Antichrist* has the most relevant passages, and there are only four of them. By contrast, virtue proper is referenced at least five times in almost every book, and in many books there are over thirty-five relevant passages (HH, D, GS, Z, and BGE). Moreover, whereas virtue is barely discussed in the anti-Wagner books, chastity comes up in them multiple times. Scholars interested in Nietzsche's differentiation between virtue proper and chastity should therefore look to the anti-Wagner books as well as to A, Z, and GS.

Here, I present visualizations of all concepts together in both timeline (Fig. 6.1) and treemap (Fig. 6.2) visualizations. These visualizations allow us to see everything at once. In addition, they make it possible to see what proportion of the relevant passages in a given text refer to a particular concept. This is important because the number of sections in

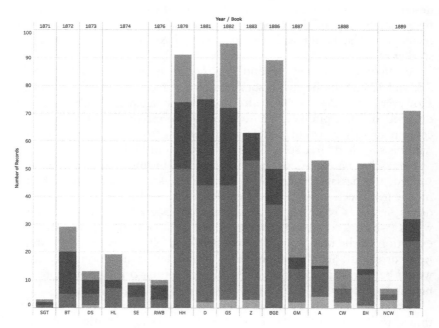

Fig. 6.1 All concepts timeline

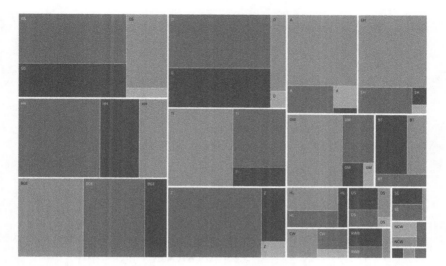

Fig. 6.2 All concepts treemap

a given book is highly variable. For example, HL is arranged in ten long sections, whereas A has sixty-two numbered sections plus a preface and a concluding "Law against Christianity." In addition, not every passage in each book—regardless of the total number of passages—contains a section that refers to drive, instinct, virtue, or chastity. Some books demonstrate relatively little engagement with the concepts under study, others much more. Graphing everything together enables us to see this.

As Fig. 6.2 shows, Nietzsche's engagement with concepts of interests begins in earnest with HH and continues—with the exception of the anti-Wagner books—to the end of his writing career. The replacement of drives with instincts is even clearer in this figure, which shows that the sum total of passages that refer *either* to drives or to instincts remains relatively stable while the proportion shifts decisively from drives to instincts. The treemap in Fig. 6.2 also makes it easy to see the relevant proportions of engagement on a book-by-book basis. For example, BGE engages most with instincts, virtues, and drives (in that order) without once mentioning chastity. By contrast, GS engages most with virtues, followed by drives, instincts, and chastity. The only books in which drives receive the most engagement are BT, DS, and RWB (SE is a tie), and the only book in which references to chastity predominate is NCW.

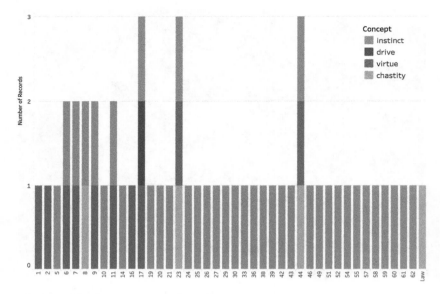

Fig. 6.3   All relevant passages from A

Next, I present an example of a section-by-section visualization (Fig. 6.3) of relevant concepts within a single book (A).[11]

In the interactive version of this visualization online, it is possible to see a similar graph for each book under study. This figure shows that, in A, Nietzsche engages with instinct throughout, whereas he addresses virtue primarily in the first seventeen sections. Drives are mentioned only once (section 17), and chastity crops up three times in the same passage as instinct (sections 8, 23, and 44), two of which also refer to virtue (23 and 44). This sort of analysis allows us to see both the order in which various concepts appear within a book and what Nietzsche also talks about when he talks about one of the concepts under study.

Finally, consider Fig. 6.4, which maps the overlaps among the concepts under study.

[11] All data, methods, and visualizations (including section-by-section visualizations for the other books) are freely available for perusal and download at https://public.tableau. com/profile/mark.alfano#!/vizhome/Virtuedriveinstinct/Story1.

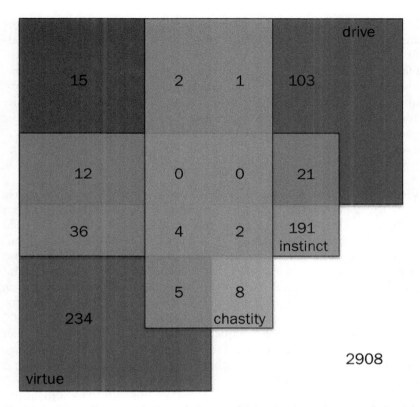

Fig. 6.4 Venn diagram of Nietzsche's use of drive, instinct, virtue, and chastity. Numbers represent the number of passages in which a combination of concepts is discussed

Tableau Public does not support Venn diagrams, so I constructed Fig. 6.4 manually. In addition, this Venn diagram represents four sets, which makes it tricky to read. I'll therefore walk through it starting with the cells with the least overlap and moving to those with the greatest overlap. There are **2908** passages in which none of the concepts under study occur. There are **234** passages in which virtue but none of the other concepts is referenced. Along the same lines, there are **8** chastity-only passages, **191** instinct-only passages, and **103** drive-only passages. Next, consider the "doubles"—passages in which exactly two concepts are referenced. Virtue and chastity occur together in 5 passages, virtue and instinct in 36, virtue and drive in 15, chastity and instinct in 2, chastity and drive in 1, and instinct and drive in 21. Finally, consider the "triples" (there are no quadruples): virtue, chastity, and instinct in 4; virtue, instinct, and drive in 12; virtue, chastity, and drive in 2; and chastity, instinct, and drive in 0. In the next section, I will focus on the doubles and triples, since these are the passages most likely to indicate how the concepts under study are related in Nietzsche's thinking.

INTERPRETATION

Visualizations are food for thought. They do not do the interpretive work themselves. Nevertheless, by providing a synoptic view of the texts to be interpreted, they can guide our reading. For example, I should emphasize a point that is already clear from Fig. 6.4: Nietzsche is significantly more likely to refer to one of the concepts under study if he also refers to at least one of the other three. Consider virtue by way of example. There are 3542 total passages in the works under consideration, of which 308 refer to virtue. The probability that a randomly selected passage will refer to virtue is therefore $308/3542 = 8.696\%$. There are 400 passages that refer to drives, instincts, or chastity, of which 74 also refer to virtue. The conditional probability that a randomly selected passage that refers to at least one of the other concepts will also refer to virtue is therefore $74/400 = 18.500\%$.

The discrepancies are similar for the other concepts. The prior probability of a passage referring to chastity is $22/3542 = 0.621\%$, while the conditional probability of a passage referring to chastity given that it refers to at least one of the other three concepts is 2.234%. The prior probability of drive is 4.348%, while the conditional probability is 9.605%. And the prior probability of instinct is 7.510%, while the conditional probability is 16.930%. Generalizing, the probability of one of these terms occurring in a passage is more than doubled if that passage contains at least one of the other terms. Not to put too fine a point on it: these concepts are strongly correlated in Nietzsche's thinking.

Determining more precisely how they are related, however, demands close-reading that is attentive to the possibility of changes in Nietzsche's view from the free spirit works to the mature works, alertness to his use of irony and sarcasm, and an eye to the linguistic context in which a term crops up. Because this chapter must be brief, I here offer the conclusions of my close-readings along with the main passages on which they are based. In other work,[12] I walk through the passages in more detail and connect my interpretation to the secondary literature.

My first claim is that, in Nietzsche's framework, *both instincts and virtues are subsets of drives: instincts are innate, whereas drives can be either innate or acquired; virtues are well-calibrated, whereas drives can be either well- or poorly calibrated*. This claim is based primarily on HH I.99, D 26, D 30, GS 1, GS 8, GS 21, GS 116, GS 123, BGE 199, A 2, EH Clever 1, A 9, and TI Skirmishes 37. My second main interpretive claim is that *drives are standing motivational dispositions to token actions of a particular type*. When they are also instincts, such drives are biologically given (because innate); when they are not instincts, they are part of what Nietzsche sometimes calls "second nature" (*zweite Natur*, cf. HL 3, HL 4, D 38, D 455). This claim is based primarily on D 38, GS 21, GS 296, BGE 189, BGE 201, GM II.2, GM II.16, and TI Socrates. My third main interpretive claim is that, while drives can be modified and modulated both by the agent who possesses them and by others, *drives are resistant to change and cannot be modified without limit*. As early as HL, Nietzsche insists that people have types,[13] and that a person's type constrains the psychology that she can develop.

To make sense of this idea, I here borrow and modify the capabilities approach.[14] Sen develops this approach by starting with the notion of a *functioning*, which is a way of doing or being, such as reading. He then defines a *functioning vector* as the set of functionings a person actually achieves (e.g., not just reading but also eating, walking, not being sick, etc.) and a *capability* as the power to exercise a functioning (e.g., literacy). A person's *capability set* is then the set of functioning vectors within that person's reach. Sen emphasizes that a person's capability set is constrained both by their current psychology and by their material and social environment. We can build a Nietzschean version of this framework starting from the notion of an *action-type*. As I argued above, a *drive* is a standing motivational disposition to token actions of a given

---

[12] M. Alfano, "Virtue in Nietzsche's Drive Psychology," in *The New Cambridge Companion to Nietzsche*, ed. T. Stern (Cambridge University Press, Forthcoming).

[13] A. Jensen, *An Interpretation of Nietzsche's* On the Uses and Disadvantages of History for Life (New York: Routledge, 2016).

[14] A. Sen, "Well-Being, Agency and Freedom," *The Journal of Philosophy* 82, no. 4 (1985): 169–221.

type; for example, all tokens of aggression are associated with the aggressive drive, and all tokens of inflicting suffering are associated with the cruel drive. We can then define a *drive vector* as the set of drives a person actually embodies. Finally, define a *drive set* as the set of drive vectors within a person's reach. This, I claim, is what Nietzsche means by a *type*: a type is just a drive set. And, just like a capability set, a person's drive set is constrained both by their current psychology and by their material and social environment.

This brings us to what I have elsewhere[15] called Nietzsche's *person-type-relative unity of virtue* thesis, according to which a person's flourishing is a matter of developing and acting upon particular drives that fit both the type she embodies, and the material and social environment in which she finds herself. This is what I mean above by a drive's being "well-calibrated." If someone attempts to embody drives that result in catastrophe, are outside her drive set (incompatible with her type), or meet with intense social and moral disapproval, she will not turn out well. Different people have different types, which means that some people will find it easier to embody virtue in one social context while others will find it easier to do so in another context. Thus, both internal (type-dependent) and external (social) factors conspire to determine whether someone's drives are, or count as, virtues. I suggest that, for Nietzsche, a drive merely counts as a virtue if it meets with approbation from the agent's community, whereas a drive is a virtue if it not only is approved but also fits the agent's type. This view is supported by many passages, including D 202, D 204, Z Tree, Z Chastity, BGE 206, BGE 224, GM III.8, A 11, TI Socrates 11, TI Skirmishes 45, and TI Errors 2.

CONCLUSION

In this brief section, I articulate some of the limitations of the Digital Humanities method employed in this chapter. Next, I point to future directions in Nietzsche scholarship that could benefit from this method. I conclude with a few broader remarks about the use of Digital Humanities methods in history of philosophy.

As I mentioned in the methodology section, my approach is liable to miss some relevant passages, and to tag as relevant some passages that are

---

[15] M. Alfano, "An Enchanting Abundance of Types: Nietzsche's Modest Unity of Virtue Thesis," *Journal of Value Inquiry* 49, no. 3 (2015a): 417–435.

actually irrelevant. For example, while I captured all passages that contain a word starting with 'trieb', I missed passages that contain a word starting with 'antrieb'. Prefixes are trickier than suffixes. More generally, I ended up ignoring many passages that contain words that express concepts that arguably should have been included in the analysis, such as affect (*Affekt*), will (*Wille*), power (*Macht*), vice (*Laster*), and character (*Charakter*). This is why I pointed out from the start that the first and perhaps most important step is to select the core concepts to study, and to do so explicitly so that the results are criticizable and corrigible. Future research can and should expand on the work in this chapter to include these and probably other concepts. What it should not do is engage in reckless and overblown readings of Nietzsche's entire corpus that depend on a single, idiosyncratically-chosen passage (e.g., HH 95 for Swanton 2015, BGE Preface for Clark and Dudrick 2012). There are 3542 passages in Nietzsche's entire published and authorized corpus. If Nietzsche scholarship is to advance, we need to read and relate these passages systematically.

Because he wrote in short, numbered sections, Nietzsche's works are especially amendable to the kind of visual analytics employed in this chapter. That said, similar methods could be adapted to the textual structures used by other philosophers. For instance, Plato and Aristotle could easily be visualized in this way based on Stephanus pagination and Bekker numbering, and Aquinas helpfully organized the *Summa Theologiae* into parts, questions, and articles. When such standardized numbering is unavailable, it is of course possible just to divide the text in question into paragraphs or sentences – or to use a "window" of *n* words as explained above. For Digital Humanities of the history of philosophy to avoid a crisis of replication, they must use rigorous, criticizable, corrigible, and reproducible methods.

REFERENCES

Alfano, M. The Tenacity of the Intentional Prior to the *Genealogy*. *Journal of Nietzsche Studies* 40 (2010): 123–140.

Alfano, M. The Most Agreeable of All Vices: Nietzsche as Virtue Epistemologist. *British Journal for the History of Philosophy* 21 (4) (2013a): 767–790.

Alfano, M. Nietzsche, Naturalism, and the Tenacity of the Intentional. *Journal of Nietzsche Studies* 44 (3) (2013b): 457–464.

Alfano, M. An Enchanting Abundance of Types: Nietzsche's Modest Unity of Virtue Thesis. *Journal of Value Inquiry* 49 (3) (2015a): 417–435.

Alfano, M. How One Becomes What One Is Called: On the Relation Between Traits and Trait-Terms in Nietzsche. *Journal of Nietzsche Studies* 46 (1) (2015b): 261–269.

Alfano, M. Review of Christine Swanton's *The Virtue Ethics of Hume and Nietzsche. Ethics* 126, no. 4 (2016): 1120–1124.

Alfano, M. A Schooling in Contempt: Emotions and the *Pathos of Distance.* In *Routledge Philosophy Minds: Nietzsche,* edited by P. Katsfanas. London: Routledge, 2017.

Alfano, M. Virtue in Nietzsche's Drive Psychology. In *The New Cambridge Companion to Nietzsche,* edited by T. Stern. Cambridge University Press, Forthcoming.

Annas, J. Which Variety of Virtue Ethics. In *Varieties of Virtue Ethics,* edited by D. Carr, J. Arthur, and K. Kristjánsson. London: Palgrave, 2017.

Austen, J. *Pride and Prejudice.* Penguin Classics. Harmondsworth: Penguin, 1813/2002.

Clark, M., and D. Dudrick. *The Soul of Nietzsche's* Beyond Good and Evil. Cambridge: Cambridge University Press, 2012.

Daigle, C. Nietzsche: Virtue Ethics... Virtue Politics? *The Journal of Nietzsche Studies* 32 (2006): 1–21.

D'Iorio, P. The Digital Critical Edition of the Works and Letters of Nietzsche. *Journal of Nietzsche Studies* 40 (2010): 70–80.

Gemes, K. Postmodernism's Use and Abuse of Nietzsche. *Philosophy and Phenomenological Research* 62, no. 2 (2001): 337–360.

Gemes, K. Nihilism and the Affirmation of Life: A Review of and Dialogue with Bernard Reginster. *European Journal of Philosophy* 16, no. 3 (2008): 459–466.

Hurka, T. Nietzsche: Perfectionist. In *Nietzsche and Morality,* edited by B. Leiter and N. Sinhababu, 9–31. Oxford: Oxford University Press, 2007.

Jensen, A. *An Interpretation of Nietzsche's* On the Uses and Disadvantages of History for Life. New York: Routledge, 2016.

Katsafanas, P. Nietzsche's Philosophical Psychology. In *Oxford Handbook of Nietzsche,* edited by J. Richardson and K. Gemes, 727–755. Oxford: Oxford University Press, 2013a.

Katsafanas, P. *Agency and the Foundations of Ethics: Nietzschean Constitutivism.* Oxford: Oxford University Press, 2013b.

Katsafanas, P. Value, Affect, and Drive. In *Nietzsche on Mind and Nature,* edited by P. Kail and M. Dries. Oxford: Oxford University Press, 2015.

May, S. *Nietzsche's Ethics and His War on 'Morality'.* Oxford: Oxford University Press, 1999.

Moretti, F. *Distant Reading.* London: Verso, 2013.

Railton, P. Nietzsche's Normative Theory? The Art and Skill of Living Well. In *Nietzsche, Naturalism, & Normativity,* edited by C. Janaway and S. Robertson, 20–51. Oxford: Oxford University Press, 2012.

Reginster, B. *The Affirmation of Life*. Cambridge: Cambridge University Press, 2006.

Robertson, S. The Scope Problem—Nietzsche, the Moral, Ethical, and Quasi-Aesthetic. In *Nietzsche, Naturalism, & Normativity*, edited by C. Janaway and S. Robertson, 81–110. Oxford: Oxford University Press, 2012.

Sen, A. Well-Being, Agency and Freedom. *The Journal of Philosophy* 82, no. 4 (1985): 169–221.

Swanton, C. *The Virtue Ethics of Hume and Nietzsche*. Hoboken: Wiley-Blackwell, 2015.

Thomas, A. Nietzsche and Moral Fictionalism. In *Nietzsche, Naturalism, & Normativity*, edited by C. Janaway and S. Robertson, 133–159. Oxford: Oxford University Press, 2012.

White, A. The Youngest Virtue. In *Nietzsche's Post-Moralism*, edited by R. Schacht, 63–78. Cambridge: Cambridge University Press, 2001.

CHAPTER 7

Researching Online Museums: Digital Methods to Study Virtual Visitors

Natalia Grincheva

In the twenty-first century, digital technologies, social media, and mobile devices add a new interactive dimension to cultural experiences. Online environments provide spaces for a more advanced level of engagement for contemporary audiences, which increasingly intersect with influential and interactive marketing.[1] Marketing with social media is not just about delivering a message to consumers, but about building two-way relationships with key audiences. Effective audience engagement involves the online public in a number of cultural and social activities that include online conversations and social media forums, public contests and viral campaigns with mega-popular YouTube videos or even "advergames" consisting of interactive virals with subtle branding.[2]

---

[1] Glen Drury, "Social Media: Should Marketers Engage and How Can It Be Done Effectively?" *Journal of Direct, Data and Digital Marketing Practice* 9, no. 3 (2008): 274–277.

[2] Ibid.

N. Grincheva (✉)
The University of Melbourne, Melbourne, VIC, Australia
e-mail: natalia.grincheva@unimelb.edu.au

© The Author(s) 2018   103
l. levenberg et al. (eds.), *Research Methods for the Digital Humanities*,
https://doi.org/10.1007/978-3-319-96713-4_7

All of these online activities leave online "traces," which are constantly recorded in the digital realm as a visitor comments, posts, likes, visits, or shares. This online data on virtual audience behavior provides opportunities for a more nuanced and comprehensive audience research that aims to enhance relationships between institutions and the public. **Visitor or audience research** refers to the interdisciplinary study of human experiences based on a systematic collection and analysis of data to inform institutional decisions about their programs and offerings.[3] This chapter builds a framework of digital methods to study virtual visitors through a presentation of three key methodologies applied in online audience research, including quantitative, behavioral, and qualitative approaches.

Quantitative methods[4] in this field are concerned with audience statistics, including quantity, demographics, and geographic distribution of online visitors. This quantitative approach is especially valuable for building an audience social-demographic profile to answer such questions as who the virtual visitors are, where they come from, and what segments of population they represent. **Behavioral analysis**[5] complements statistical methods by offering insights into what people do online and how they interact with online content. This method's concern with the online behavior of virtual visitors explores audiences' pathways, and communication with each other and online content.

Qualitative methodologies[6] aim to explain online visitors' activities by revealing their motivations, interests, and preferences. These methods require not only a complex observation of virtual visitors but more nuanced research of online communities. This research is usually based on surveying and interviewing key audiences to get more comprehensive and realistic explanations of what drive visitors' interests and motivations, what define their preferences and how exactly they perceive content and messages delivered to them online. All three methods complement each other by offering insights from different, but interrelated perspectives.

---

[3] "Glossary of Visitor Studies Terms," Visitor Studies Association, accessed May 10, 2017, http://www.visitorstudies.org/glossary-of-terms.

[4] Alan Bryman, "The End of the Paradigm Wars?" In *The SAGE Handbook of Social Research*, eds. Pertti Alasuutari, Leonard Bickman, and Julia Brannen (Thousand Oaks, CA: Sage, 2008).

[5] Abbas Tashakkori and Charles Teddlie. *Handbook of Mixed Methods in Social & Behavioral Research* (Thousand Oaks, CA: Sage, 2003).

[6] Bryman, "The End of the Paradigm Wars?"

Together, they help us to understand: (1) *who* online audiences are; (2) *what* they do online; as well as, (3) *how* and *why* they do what they do.

This chapter focuses on the application of visitor studies methodologies to museums as cultural institutions that incorporate digital media into their cultural programming and social activities. Museums have traditionally been defined as major repositories of cultural heritage, the main keepers and exhibitors of historical, scientific, artistic, or cultural artifacts.[7] While in a physical museum, public access to collections can be quite limited, new media technologies provide unique opportunities to "visit" museums 24 hours a day. More importantly, contemporary museum visitors can participate in online discussions, share their opinions, curate their own exhibitions, rate museum objects in online galleries, collaborate with other visitors, and even contribute to museum online collections with their own creations.

Museums do not solely engage their audiences in new, digital interactive experiences for marketing purposes. However, as examples of this chapter highlight, they are based on similar social media marketing principles, such as "participatory" activities and public contests. These online "interactives" involve clicking through links, browsing pages, manipulating views of digital objects, as well as adding various textual, visual, or audio information to the online content of museums. Recorded through online applications, this data provides an advanced database of evidence illustrating museum visitor behavior online. **Museum audience (visitor) research** is a very important part of museum work, which is based on research activities and evaluation of actual, potential, and virtual visitors.[8]

Since the emergence of museum studies, a variety of methodologies have been successfully employed both by museum professionals and academic scholars. Counting heads, gathering demographics, mapping visitor paths in the museum, surveying audiences, and evaluating visitors' understanding of exhibitions have shaped the majority of museum visitor research in the past decades.[9] Through time, audience research has

---

[7] "Museum Definition," ICOM (International Council of Museums), accessed May 10, 2017. ICOM, http://icom.museum/the-vision/museum-definition/.

[8] Eilean Hooper-Greenhill, *"Studying Visitors,"* in *A Companion to Museum Studies*, ed. Stuart McDonald (Oxford: Blackwell, 2006).

[9] Steve Bitgood, "Introduction: Visitor Studies—1988." *Visitor Studies* 1, no. 1 (1989): 5–8; George Hein, *Learning in the Museum.* (London: Routledge, 1999); and Boris Schiele, Ruth Rentschler, and Eve Reussner, *Museum Marketing Research: From Denial to Discovery* (Melbourne: Deakin University Press, 1992).

significantly advanced from a simple quantification of visitors and their characteristics to complex observations, interviews, and focus groups that aim to analyze and interpret visitors' behaviors in their interactions with objects in a museum setting.

With the development of the Internet and new media, museum visitor studies have been supplied with a plethora of new digital tools to study virtual museum "goers." If in a museum physical space video or audio recording is required to collect data demonstrating how people interact with museum objects, an online environment is a perfect recording tool in itself. It instantly traces all user activities and displays the visible records. From a marketing perspective, online audience research is a significantly faster, easier, and less expensive means of data collection than traditional interviews or focus groups, because it is based on the collection of data that people freely share online.[10] However, both in social media marketing[11] and in a museum world[12] there are important ethical issues that require further discussion. This chapter starts with a section "Studying Virtual Human Subjects," which specifically focuses on ethical considerations that define audience research in a museum setting.

The following sections provide a comprehensive guide to three types of research methods employed by contemporary museums to study online visitors. Illuminating how traditional museum visitor research tools informed emerging digital methods, the chapter describes important procedures of online museum audience studies. Step by step, three sections introduce more sophisticated online methods, which add new dimensions to the understanding of virtual visitors. The chapter commences its methodological framework with a section "Who Comes to Online Museums" that presents quantitative research, including statistics and demographics on online audiences. Then, it proceeds with details about behavioral research in the section "What Virtual Visitors Do in Online Museums." This section describes methods based on tracking online visitor pathways and observing their activities. Finally, the section

---

[10] Robert Kozinets, *Netnography: Doing Ethnographic Research Online* (London: Sage, 2010).

[11] Ibid.

[12] Natalia Grincheva, "Museum Ethnography in the Digital Age: Ethical Considerations," in *Internet Research Ethics for the Social Age: New Cases and Challenges*, eds. Michael Zimmer and Kataharina Kinder-Kurlandan (New York: Peter Lang, 2017).

"How and Why Virtual Visitors Communicate with Museums" presents qualitative methodologies that are based on complex observations and interpretations of online museum communities.

STUDYING VIRTUAL HUMAN SUBJECTS: ETHICAL RESEARCH

Traditional museum visitor research activities should comply with the internationally accepted Code of Ethics for Museums, established by the International Council of Museums.[13] This Code of Ethics undergoes continuing updates, as new media technologies facilitate new research methods for visitor studies. Despite the fact that the majority of online museum spaces are public and easily accessible for anyone who wishes to join and contribute, observation in such "open" online communities can be quite controversial.

"Lurking" presupposes an invisible presence on a site, based on a one-way process in which a researcher acquires a powerful position to gaze on others, "appropriating their actions for the purposes of research."[14] Nonetheless, non-obtrusive "lurking" has established itself as a major strand of social science research on the internet,[15] because of the convenience of the data collection procedure, which does not affect participants' behavior.[16] Being non-disruptive, this method allows digital researchers to investigate large numbers of online participants and to achieve a high degree of accuracy in data analysis.

However, if engaged in passive methods of data collection, museums need to inform the online public that all user contributions in the form of comments, posts, or visual materials are widely and freely accessible in the public domain and can be used for the purposes of research. Many online museum spaces require participants to read and agree with

[13] "Code of Ethics for Museums," ICOM (International Council of Museums), accessed May 10, 2017, http://icom.museum/fileadmin/user_upload/pdf/Codes/code_eth-ics2013_eng.pdf.

[14] Debora Heath, Erin Koch, Barbara Ley, and Michael Montoya, "Nodes and Queries: Linking Locations in Networked Fields on Inquiry," *American Behavioral Scientist* 43, no. 3 (1999): 450–463.

[15] Christine Hine. *Virtual Ethnography* (London: Sage, 2000).

[16] Nigel Fielding, Raymond Lee, and Grant Blank. *Sage Book of Online Research Methods* (London: Sage, 2008).

their terms and conditions as a part of registration procedures. In these agreements, it is usually specified that participants' contributions automatically become part of a larger internet community and in certain cases are being employed by third parties for educational and research purposes.

In cases when museum online communities emerge on third-party social networks, like Facebook or YouTube, museums and researchers need to clarify their terms and conditions for nonreactive data collection. Even though social media audiences are usually informed by the networks' Terms of Use that data on visitor activities is potentially collected and reused, some special measures to protect the confidentiality and anonymity of online audience data is crucial for ethical research. These measures include avoiding using the personal information provided by online participants, such as their online names, age, nationality, profession, etc. Furthermore, confidentiality may require the omission of visual/textual user-generated content if it contains personal information on sensitive issues or if it could result in threats to participants' material or psychological well-being.

Although "passive" methods can appear to be quite convenient ways to collect reliable data based on simple unobtrusive observations, more active engagement with online communities can be very beneficial.[17] By crossing the line of online observation and initiating a dialogue with potential respondents through online interviews and focus-groups, museum managers can develop a more nuanced and detailed understanding of their audiences. In online dialogues, museum researchers are obligated to explain the purpose of their research, how data will be used and the protection of users confidentiality to participants. This helps a museum to establish a trustworthy reputation among their online public and, in many cases, it leads to a more candid and loyal relationship with online museum fans, supporters and active contributors.

Making sure that online visitors feel "safe" in online museum communities is a crucial component of any digital research that provides an important basis for making museums truly public spaces for enjoyment and interaction. While this section provides foundations for setting up a "safe" museum research environment, the next part illuminates initial methods for building productive virtual visitor research.

---

[17] Hine, *Virtual Ethnography*, 257.

WHO COMES TO ONLINE MUSEUMS: COUNTING VIRTUAL VISITORS

The earliest visitor studies were mostly based on gathering *quantitative data* on museum audiences. These methods consisted of collecting information about museum visits on site and counting specific social and demographic characteristics of visitors such as their gender, age, social and family status, occupation, and place of residence. The huge popularity of statistical approaches that aim to understand the social composition of museum public can be explained by the growing importance for museums to become more socially inclusive spaces that can engage audiences from different social classes.[18]

In London, the major British museums began gathering audience statistics as early as the 1830s. They concentrated on gross visitor numbers in different seasons as well as on days of the week.[19] More advanced research about the demographic profiles of museum visitors started to demonstrate various patterns of museums use in 1884[20] and remains one of the most important methods to understand museum audiences. For example, interviews with the directors of major museums in London, New York, and Washington, DC, confirmed that the simplest quantitative methods are still the most popular methodology for measuring museum performance.[21] Museum professionals and academics consider individual characteristics of visitors to be important factors, which have a profound effect on how different social groups interact and engage with museum spaces, objects, and activities.[22]

With the development of the Internet, online visitor studies immediately employed the quantitative approach. In many museums, evaluating online audiences has largely been based on gathering and analyzing statistics that demonstrate unique site visits over a period of time, as well as web demographic data about online visitors. Furthermore, assessing success in social media spaces is heavily dependent on quantitative data that demonstrates the number of connections created in social networks

---

[18] Tony Bennett, *The Birth of the Museum: History, Theory, Politics* (London: Routledge: 1995), 8.

[19] Ibid.

[20] Bitgood, "Introduction: Visitor Studies," 5–8.

[21] Ibid.

[22] Hooper-Greenhill, "Studying Visitors," 368.

online.[23] Contemporary museums constantly track online visitors and compile results in reports over regular intervals (daily, monthly, weekly, annually) in order to evaluate their performance online.[24] That is why, in the professional museum world, the audience engagement factor is very often understood in terms of quantitative data, such as the number of visits, number of visitors, and the length of time a user spends on a museum site.[25]

For example, Facebook data collection tools provide an excellent opportunity to explore online museum fans and their social demographics. Facebook Insights records the number of people who connected to the museum page by subscribing to its newsfeed or by "liking" its page. It provides invaluable details,[26] which allow museum managers to see who these people are, in terms of their gender, age, country of origin or location, as well as what languages they speak. The Facebook Insights page of the Hermitage Museum Foundation UK (see Fig. 7.1) demonstrates that there are slightly more female audience members than male. It also shows that people from the age groups 25–34 and 35–44 are the most engaged in the Facebook community. Finally, it reveals that people from 45 countries speaking 17 different languages follow the Museum Foundation page. This information is very valuable for museum managers as it helps to identify which potential audience segments need more careful targeting, and which age or gender groups could be more engaged with the museum activities and collections in social media spaces.

[23] Charles Van den Heuvel, Sandor Spruit, Leen Breure, and Hans Voorbij, "Annotators and Agents in a Web-Based Collaboratory Around Cartographical Collections in Cultural Heritage Institutions." Museums and the Web 2010, accessed May 10, 2017, http://www.archimuse.com/mw2010/papers/heuvel/heuvel.html; Georgia Angelaki, Rossella Caffo, Monika Hagedorn-Saupe, and Susan Hazan, "ATHENA: A Mechanism for Harvesting Europe's Museum Holdings into Europeana," *Museums and the Web* 2010, accessed May 10, 2017, http://www.museumsandtheweb.com/mw2010/papers/angelaki/angelaki.html; Wayne LaBar, "Can Social Media Transform the Exhibition Development Process: Cooking the Exhibition—An Ongoing Case Study." *Museums and the Web* 2010, accessed May 10, 2017, http://www.archimuse.com/mw2010/papers/labar/labar.html.

[24] Barbara Soren and Nathalie Lemelin, "'Cyberpals!/Les Cybercopains!': A Look at Online Museum Visitor Experiences." *Curator: The Museum Journal* 47, no. 1 (2004): 55–83.

[25] Ibid.

[26] Facebook Insights shows the demographics and geographic distribution of audiences in total absolute numbers, not normalized to the Facebook demographics.

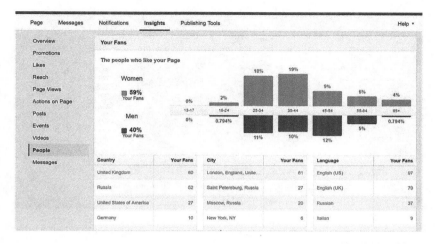

Fig. 7.1 Facebook insights: Hermitage Museum Foundation UK

Another good example is the quantitative research conducted by the Van Gogh Museum in 2010 about their online audiences across various social media platforms. Highly visible and active on social media, the Van Gogh Museum engages its online visitors by providing participatory opportunities on its blog and various social media sites, such as Facebook, Twitter, and YouTube. The 2010 research revealed that people from different countries have particular social media preferences regarding their interaction with the museum. With foreign visitors constituting more than 80% of their total audience, the Van Gogh Museum has outstanding international appeal and recognition.[27] In 2010, the museum reached online audiences from around 135 countries, with the majority of audiences coming from Europe and North America. Social media significantly helps the Van Gogh Museum to engage wider international communities; 63% of visits to the museum website were from international users, compared to 90% of Facebook fans and Twitter followers[28] (see Fig. 7.2). The Van Gogh Museum's online audience

[27]"Annual Report 2010–2015," Van Gogh Museum, accessed May 10, 2017, https://www.vangoghmuseum.nl/en/organisation/annual-report.

[28]Natalia Grincheva, "How Far Can We Reach? International Audiences in Online Museum Communities." *The International Journal of Technology, Knowledge and Society 7*, no. 4 (2012): 29–42.

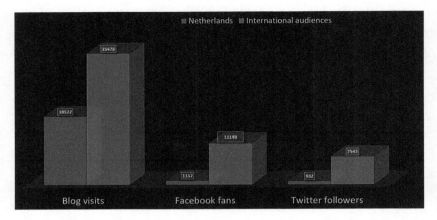

Fig. 7.2   Van Gogh Museum blog, Facebook and Twitter: domestic and international audiences

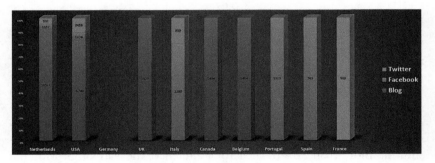

Fig. 7.3   Van Gogh Museum blog, Facebook, Twitter: top countries audiences

research drew on quantitative data collection through the museum blog and social networks, including the collection of statistical data on the geographical distribution of virtual museum audiences.[29]

The analysis of social network use among the top represented countries indicated different preferences in the social media tools they employed to connect to the museum. Figure 7.3 illustrates that only Dutch and American audiences actively used all social media spaces (blog, Facebook, and Twitter) to follow the museum online. People

[29] Grincheva, "How far can we reach?"

from other countries mainly connected to the museum through a preferred social media channel. For example, Twitter attracted more of a French population, Facebook appealed more to Spanish and Portuguese online users. Virtual visitors from the UK, Belgium, and Canada enjoyed following the museum blog the most. Interestingly, while Germany was among the top five in the geographic distribution of the museum site visits, it was an underrepresented country on the social web (see Fig. 7.3).

Even though this quantitative research clearly demonstrated significant cross-cultural differences in the use of the museum social media, it left many questions unanswered. For instance, researchers could explore the motivations behind the usage of specific social networks by people from different countries in their engagement with the museum activities. However, this is difficult to investigate, relying only on the quantitative methods. Indeed, quantitative data points to a social strength and power of museums as social institutions that are capable of attracting local and international audiences. Nevertheless, this data fails to evaluate the qualities of online visitors experiences as well as their motivations, interests, and values. To address these limitations in demographic and statistical methods, one has to employ a behavioral approach in audience research.

What Virtual Visitors Do in Online Museums: Exploring Audience Behavior

Behavioral studies are based on observing visitor actions within a museum area in order to comprehend what visitors do and how they interact with each other and with museum objects while they explore a museum. Behavior research is usually linked to the educational agenda of museums, striving to provide an effective learning environment for its visitors.[30] Data that helps to analyze visitor behavior inside a museum includes the total time of museum visits, choice of exhibition areas, and focus of attention on certain objects or displays. As visitors proceed through the exhibition halls of a museum, personal tastes, cultural preferences and other psychological and social factors make certain exhibitions, objects or museum spaces popular while others remain unnoticed or purposefully ignored.

Tracking visitor movement through exhibit and gallery spaces is one of the oldest methods of studying visitor behavior, dating to the early 1900s. One of the earliest forms of visitor behavioral research is "mapping." Mapping involves tracking the differences between visitor behaviors in

[30] "Museum Definition," ICOM.

particular exhibition spaces. As a result, maps can indicate the most and least interesting places in exhibitions according to the time spent at these sites, as well as the number of people who followed similar tracks.[31]

The use of surveillance technology is very important for mapping and other behavior studies methodologies. Museums rely on the use of monitoring and recording devices that can help observe people's behavior and collect evidence on visitor activities. One of the methods for studying visitors that is frequently used in museums now is audio recording people's conversations or video recording their behavior.[32] Through observation of body movements and analysis of verbal behavior, museums analyze visitor responses to installation designs to assess exhibitions' learning outcomes.

Online, the behavior-focused approach is quite popular among museum scholars and managers. Online mapping is frequently used to track visitor paths on websites and gather statistics: for example, the number of unique visits to a particular page, the time spent on the page, and the particular browsing path to the page. The data indicates the interest of the visitors in the museum content and the most and least popular web pages, galleries, or blog postings. Evaluating the effectiveness of online communication through an analysis of website statistics can highlight most requested or popular pages, the average time spent on site, as well as the main sequence of pages browsed.[33] These patterns of use indicate which parts of websites are most visited and which are seldom selected by different online audiences. This information tells museum managers and curators how the content that they display online is relevant to visitors' interests and needs and how quickly and easily online visitors can find it.

More importantly, the online environment provides a plethora of evidence, which not only demonstrates various patterns of online content consumption, but also illuminates the degree of audience engagement

[31] Arthur Melton, *Problems of Installation in Museums of Art* (Washington, DC: American Association of Museums, 1935), 114.

[32] Arthur Lucast, Paulette McManus, and Gillian Thomas, "Investigating Learning from Informal Sources: Listening to Conversations and Observing Play in Science Museums." *International Journal of Science Education* 8, no. 4 (1986): 341–352; Kevin Crowley and Maureen Callanan, "Describing and Supporting Collaborative Scientific Thinking in Parent-Child Interactions," *Journal of Museum Education* 23, no. 1 (1998): 12–17; and Dirk vom Lehn, Charles Heath and John Hindmarsh, "Video-Based Field Studies in Museums and Galleries," *Visitor Studies Today* 5, no. 3 (2002): 15–23.

[33] Patricia Gillard and Anne Cranne-Francis, "Evaluation for Effective Web Communication: An Australian Example," *Curator: The Museum Journal* 45, no. 1 (2002): 35–49, 38.

with museum spaces through different types of activities. There are four important types of online behavior, among which *involvement*, is an initial stage of audience engagement based on visits to the museum site or social media spaces. Other, more advanced levels of involvement include *participation*, defined as taking an active part in online museum activities by commenting, "liking," sharing, or submitting content. A higher degree of engagement is *interaction*, meaning establishing relationships with other online participants and creating a sort of online community around a museum. Finally, the highest level of audience engagement is *influence* which refers to promotional activities that online visitors voluntarily involve themselves in on behalf of a museum by sharing and circulating museum content within their own social media spaces[34] (see Fig. 7.4).

Behavioral analysis of audiences' levels of engagement usually employs a mixture of computation tools applied by researchers to identify various stages of virtual visitors' engagement and to measure this engagement on each of the levels. This methodological framework was developed by combining two engagement measurement systems: the metric of engagement, proposed by Brian Haven, a Forrester researcher in social computing, and the hierarchy of social participation developed by Nina Simon, a famous museum consultant and author of the book *The Participatory Museum*.[35] This framework is based on **audience segmentation**, a process of dividing audiences into categories based upon their online communication preferences and behaviors within social media spaces.[36]

While various social media platforms, for example Facebook, offer their own benchmarks and metrics for categorizing users' online activities, in a museum setting it is usually done by a researcher through behavioral observation. In certain cases purposefully created online museum "participatory" portals provide research platforms, which allow museums to measure different levels of online audience engagement. A really good example of such a platform is World Beach Project (WBP) map, created by the Victoria and Albert Museum in 2007.[37] This social media

[34] Grincheva, "How Far Can We Reach?"; Natalia Grincheva, "'The World Beach Project' Going Viral: Measuring Online Influence (Case Study of the Victoria & Albert Online Museum Project)," *Journal of Creative Communications* 10, no. 1 (2015): 39–55.

[35] Grincheva, "How far can we reach?"

[36] Graham Black, *The Engaging Museum: Developing Museums for Visitor Involvement* (Abingdon: Routledge, 2005).

[37] "The World Beach Project," Victoria and Albert Museum, accessed May 10, 2017, http://www.vam.ac.uk/content/articles/w/world-beach-project/.

Degree of engagement	Type of behavior	Characteristics	Quantitative Indicators	Qualitative Indicators
Low	Involvement	The initial level of engagement that audiences have with an online museum. It refers to the general level of interest the audiences express in the content, activities, and collections of online museums.	Site visits Time spent per page Number of pages viewed Frequency of site visits Social media connections	N/A
Medium	Participation	Online actions the audiences take to establish a relationship or a connection with the project. This participation metric is based on measuring events in which people contribute their own creative content, make comments and participate in surveys, rate and tag museums' content online, and request additional information about exhibitions or projects.	Number of posts Number of comments Number of online submissions (text, video, audio, image) Number of ratings	Quality and content of submissions, posts and comments
Upper Medium	Interaction	It illustrates how individuals within the online project are connected to each other and if these connections are strong enough to sustain a live online community. The interaction component is usually measured through qualitative and quantitative data that indicate whether individuals exchange information, content and opinions in collaborative or interactive activities around the project.	Number of partnerships established among the participants Number of collaborative contributions and submissions Number of messages exchanged between each other Number of comments left to each other's posts.	Quality and content of messages and collaborative contributions
High	Influence	It is the potential of online participants to promote the museum and the online project to wider audiences. The influence metric is based on identifying the 'influencers' among the audiences and measuring the scope of their influence in terms of how big and diverse their personal networks are and what actions they take in order to promote the museum.	Number of active 'influencers' Frequency of their promotional actions on behalf of the museum Number of their followers and fans	Quality and content of their promotional messages

Fig. 7.4 Levels of online audience engagement

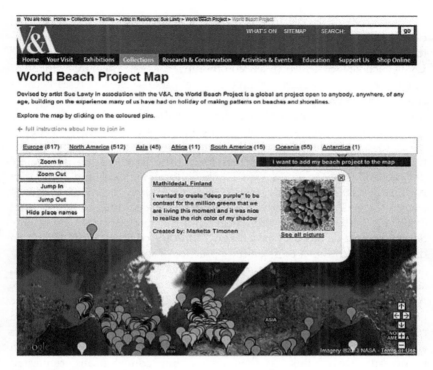

Fig. 7.5 World Beach Project map, Victoria & Albert Museum

platform collected stories and photographs of individual art pieces based on stone patterns, created by people on a beach, and displayed them on the digital global map (see Fig. 7.5). The database of the platform provided a great data resource to measure *participation* and *interaction* levels of participants' engagement with the project.

In terms of *participation*, the online portal-map featured photographs and stories of user art creations and allowed monitoring and data collection of online submissions, as well as tracking the geographical origins of contributions on the map. The portal instantly calculated total participants' submissions and displayed exact geo-locations where participants created their submissions. Furthermore, the platform collected participants' stories which provided a database to indicate and assess the level of online audience *interaction* through **data mining** techniques.

Data mining is a digital research method, based on sorting through a large amount of data to identify patterns and establish relationships between different types of data.[38] In this project, a keyword search was conducted on the project database, which aimed to identify participants' stories submitted to the portal-map and illustrate social engagement with the project.[39] Using such key search words as "community," "group," "family," "friends," "together," and "joint activity" on the portal database allowed researchers to collect and analyze examples to demonstrate that the WBP provided interactive social experiences not only in a virtual but also in a physical reality.

Stories shared by participants in the project's online platform illuminated that many families, schools, communities, and artists actively participated in joint outdoor activities for artistic practices, environmental projects and many other relevant events on local, national, and even international levels. For example, the John Muir Award, organized by the St Mary's Cathedral community from Glasgow was dedicated to discovering, exploring and conserving wild nature, and the International Community School project at Bawdsey beach (UK) in 2009 connected children from different countries in a cross-cultural practice of stone art creation.[40]

More advanced levels of audience engagement with the project, such as *influence*, were identified and explored beyond the WBP map. A focused behavioral analysis of social media spaces through which the project was promoted, such as Facebook, Twitter and YouTube allowed researchers to identify online posts circulated by the project participants among their broader circles of family and friends. Online posts in which participants shared links to their own online contributions, requested additional information about the WBP initiative, or forwarded the project information to their friends, constituted data for the *influence* metrics and indicated a high level of audience engagement with this project.

The highest expression of *influence* in the project manifested in the launching of an independent, dedicated fan page on Facebook where fans shared their online creations and celebrated their experiences with the project. The group was created by Becky Rendell, a Welsh artist, who shared that the group was created as a quick favor to help promote the project... "I felt it was important to have something on Facebook as a point of contact for WBP, it's such a vital communication tool that I felt we could attract more participants by making a group."[41]

[38] Jiawei Han, Jian Pei, and Micheline Kamber, *Data Mining: Concepts and Techniques* (New York: Elsevier, 2011).

[39] Grincheva, "'The World Beach Project' Going Viral."

[40] "The World Beach Project," Victoria and Albert Museum.

[41] Becky Rendell, E-mail Message to Author, November 15, 2010.

The group had members from the USA, UK Australia, Canada, Italy, Germany, Czech Republic, Switzerland, France, and other countries which indicates the international nature of the self-generated online community.

It is important to clarify that the online interview with Rendell to explore her motivations behind creating the fan community constitutes a different type of audience research that goes beyond the limits of behavioral observations. Observing online audiences is certainly a more advanced method in comparison to merely counting. However, even though it provides more insights into online user activities, it is still very limited as it cannot explain why certain online museum spaces attract traffic while others fail to grab visitors' attention. In addressing these limitations, digital ethnography stands out as a comprehensive method for a more nuanced and detailed audience analysis.

How and Why Virtual Visitors Communicate with Museums: Understanding Online Audiences

If behaviorist analyses are concerned with how various factors and designs stimulate visitor response, ethnographic methods in museum studies aim to understand how and why online environments and artifacts become relevant and important to the public. **Ethnography** is a method of studying culture and society that originated in the late nineteenth century and was first employed to study aboriginal communities in colonized territories.[42] It entails observations of people and their way of life in their own local context. This methodology tells stories about a group of people based on detailed descriptions and interviews with community members. **Museum ethnographic research** is based on the visitors' observations, listening to their conversations, and conducting in-depth interviews with museum audiences that explore specific questions of interest. These methods help to expose and explore nuances of interactions between a visitor's social sphere and the world of museum objects.

Ethnographic methods employed to research computer-mediated communication derive their power from the open exploratory settings of the Internet that are equipped with the tools for observational research on virtual communities.[43] **Digital ethnography** is a branch of

---

[42] David Fetterman, *Ethnography: Step-by-Step* (London: Sage, 2010).

[43] David McConnell, *Implementing Computer Supported Cooperative Learning* (London: Psychology Press, 2000), 72.

ethnographic studies that aims to explore the culture of online communities. It is immersive, descriptive and as multilateral as the traditional ethnographic approach. Digital ethnography requires a researcher to become immersed in virtual culture and the life of online participants in order to observe their interactions and communications.[44]

Though the online community is, in itself, a device of data recording and an archive of evidence of visitor behavior, the ethnographer retains a dedicated role within this system. An online ethnographer serves as an interpreter who makes sense of the signals and signs of an online community. The method of digital ethnography requires the researcher to analyze a large amount of qualitative data, such as audience online expressions through text messages, comments, or through audio and visual material that they share within museum spaces. Usually, such an analysis of audiences' digital "traces" presupposes a content analysis.

Content analysis is a qualitative research technique based on interpreting and coding textual, visual, or audio material through a systematic evaluation.[45] It aims to interpret raw qualitative data to produce meaningful knowledge about a specific social or cultural phenomenon. In the digital realm, content analysis is very frequently employed to explore online audience perceptions, preferences, concerns, and motivations. In cases when researchers need to deal with a large amount and scope of online data, for example, thousands or millions of user comments on social media spaces, scholars can employ automated software for a more systematic content analysis. Examples of this software include NVivo and HyperResearch. These digital automated tools are designed to help qualitative research by storing, coding, categorizing, and searching large amounts of qualitative raw data that allows researchers to quickly sort coded data and draw correlations, patterns, and links among various materials.

A good example of an ethnographic research project, which applied content analysis to a large amount of qualitative data investigated the 2010 YouTube Play project created by the Guggenheim Museum in cooperation with Google.[46] The main goal of YouTube Play was to

[44] Steven Jones. *Cybersociety 2.0: Revisiting Computer-Mediated Communication and Community* (London: Sage, 1998).

[45] Kimberly A. Neuendorf, *The Content Analysis Guidebook* (Thousand Oaks, CA: Sage, 2016).

[46] Natalia Grincheva, "Cultural Diplomacy of a Different Kind: A Case Study of the Global Guggenheim" (PhD dissertation, Concordia University, 2015).

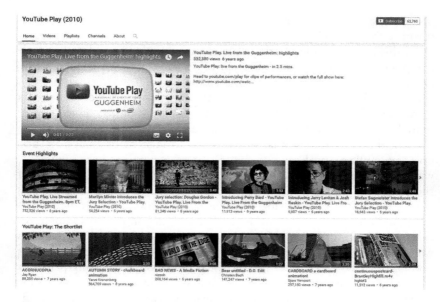

Fig. 7.6 YouTube play platform, Guggenheim Museum

showcase the best creative video from around the world. Posted on YouTube, 14 invitations in different languages invited creative video artists to participate in the contest and to compete for a prestigious award to be presented in the Guggenheim Museum in New York. Less than two months after the official call for contribution was announced, the museum received **23,358** online videos from **91** countries, **125** of which were shortlisted and featured in the YouTube Play channel[47] (see Fig. 7.6).

The channel garnered more than 10 million online viewers the day of the live event in the Guggenheim museum celebrating 25 winners of the contest. This amount of views exceeded the total number of online visits the Guggenheim website usually receives annually. Over a year after completion of the project, the YouTube Play site attracted over 23 million viewers and to date it remains a popular YouTube channel with around

[47] Nora Semel and Francesca Merlino, "YouTube: Play at Guggenheim Museum," *Museum Next* 2011, accessed May 10, 2017, https://www.museumnext.com/insight/youtube-play-at-guggenheim-museum/.

65,000 subscribers and constantly updated feedback on the videos constituting the channel archive.[48]

In this project digital ethnographic research helped to identify which components of the project design, in terms of its *content, form* and *targeted audiences*, made it so appealing to the global YouTube community. The research was based on the content analysis of audience comments from the 176 video clips on the YouTube Play channel, which represented 21,215 posts. First, the posts were collected through a YouTube CommentThread toolkit that enabled the storage of original YouTube posts and collection of key information on who submitted the comment, when, and to what specific stream or to what exact video. The sample of the audiences' comments was selected by collecting not more than 500 comments for each of the videos. In cases where a single video generated less than 500 comments, all of them were included in the final sample. In cases where the total number of comments exceeded 500, the comments were selected by collecting 500 available comments posted by audiences around or closer to October 2010 (when the contest was taking place).

Next, content analysis was employed to code collected comments, using a single comment as a unit of analysis. First, it included identification of the language in which each of the comments was posted. The linguistic analysis of the YouTube Play comments helped to answer a question regarding the *targeted audiences*. First, it exposed that online followers of the project communicated in 26 different languages, including non-European languages, such as Hebrew or Arabic, for example, as well as Japanese, Malay or Russian, pointing to a strong global appeal of the project.

Furthermore, a more focused analysis of comments collected from 14 video invites posted by the museum on YouTube in 14 languages confirmed that such as strategic multilingual promotion ensured a high visibility of the project among various online linguistic communities, eliminating language barriers in the digital realm. Specifically, the linguistic analysis revealed that 14 languages chosen for the project promotion were the most frequently used by online audiences among other non-English languages. The linguistic analysis of comments also attested to a high level of diversity of the YouTube Play audiences indicating the YouTube Play campaign's successful targeting of a global public, including non-English speakers.

---

[48] Ibid.

The content analysis of the project also included a thematic analysis of messages with the most favorable feedback or sentiment. Sentiment analysis or **opinion mining** is a method that aims to extract audience opinions from natural language text using computational tools. It helps to identify positive and negative opinions expressed through social media messages in relation to targets of these sentiments.[49] Messages with positive sentiment about the project were coded and distributed in broad categories according to important questions about the *content* and *form* design components of the project. In terms of the *content*, the analysis focused on positive messages and comments discussing the channel clips as representatives of various video genres. A comparative analysis of the amount of positive feedback (exact number of messages with a favorable view) submitted to clips representing different video genres revealed audience favorites. The largest amount of positive comments posted on video clips representing so-called "remix" or "mash-up" videos confirmed that the Guggenheim made a strategically correct choice by prioritizing this genre among contest submissions.

"Mash-up" is based on taking samples from pre-existing video or audio materials to combine them into new forms according to personal taste practices of "cut/copy and paste."[50] The massive audience for remix YouTube clips, which can go viral on the Internet, enthusiastically praised the museum's idea of making this type of video as a part of contemporary museum collection. Hundreds of users' positive comments, some of which called the "mash-up" video a "YouTube Orchestra," "YouTube Art," "Future of art" or "The Bible of Sampling!", explained why the *content* of the Guggenheim museum online project was so enjoyable to the global public.[51]

As for the *form*, the analysis focused on messages with favorable feedback about the design and organizational component of the project. Specifically, this analysis illuminated that the interactive or "participatory" nature of the project predetermined its success among online audiences. One of the most prevalent arguments in favor of this project was

[49] Liu, Bing. *Sentiment Analysis: Mining Opinions, Sentiments, and Emotions* (Cambridge: Cambridge University Press, 2015).

[50] Betsy Rymes, "Recontextualizing YouTube: From Macro–Micro to Mass-Mediated Communicative Repertoires," *Anthropology & Education Quarterly* 43, no. 2 (2012): 214–227.

[51] Grincheva, "Cultural Diplomacy of a Different Kind."

the contest's objective to invite ordinary people to share their artistic talents: "What I like about the YouTube Play," a passionate fan of the project shared, "is the images of ordinary people, youtubers, not highly paid professional actors and actresses. Regular people, real life. It feels much realer than movies or tv." Many similar comments demonstrated that YouTube audiences strongly supported the museum in giving a chance to ordinary people and amateur creators: "I reckon, it should extend... There are a ton of talented artists on the internet that don't get the recognition they deserve." The contest gave the opportunity to YouTube audiences to share their talent and celebrate a living "culture of today."[52]

In this project, digital ethnographic research, which included sentiment mining, and linguistic and content analyses combined with quantitative methods, helped to identify important components of the project design which made YouTube Play a global and viral phenomenon. Such deep ethnographic research usually not only documents specific outcomes of museum online programs but, more importantly, informs strategic institutional choices about developing new activities for online audiences. A rich world of social media comments provides a diverse spectrum of the online visitors' thoughts and points of view, which expose museum staff to what they can improve, what they can take on board for future initiatives, what they have to leave in the past in order to create a more meaningful engagement with online audiences.

Conclusion

This chapter explored three important dimensions of visitor studies methods in online museum communities, including *quantitative, behavioral* and *qualitative* methodologies. It demonstrated that each of these methods is important for understanding virtual visitors and provides vital details answering such questions as *who* interact with online museums as well as *how* and *why*. Quantitative research, with its statistical approaches, constitutes the foundational methodological basis for drawing a social-demographic profile of audiences and highlighting how many people are engaged and what segments of the population they come from. It provides invaluable information for museums who employ this data to diversify their audiences and enhance their social inclusion strategies.

---

[52] Ibid.

These quantitative methods in many cases inform behavioral research which intends to bring audience studies to the next level by offering observations on what virtual museum "goers" actually do online and how they involve themselves in museum online activities. This method helps to track visitor paths in online museum environments and measure levels of social engagement in specific campaigns. By looking at how people interact with each other and with the museum in social media communities, behavioral research complements quantitative analysis and offers a new criteria of audience segmentation based on types of user behavior rather than mere social-demographic factors.

Finally, qualitative research, such as digital ethnography, provides important methodological tools to understand museum audiences and collect feedback on museum programming. This method is the most time-consuming, however, it offers a high degree of accuracy in explaining virtual visitor behavior, preferences, and motivations behind their online actions. All these methods work the best when they are integrated or combined with one another. In some cases, it is not possible to apply them separately, as this chapter demonstrated through numerous examples. Quantitative and behavioral data provide details about online audiences and aid decision making processes.

Museum visitor research is a rapidly developing field, which employs digital and mobile media to provide new avenues for cultural and museum experiences. For example, innovative developments in the museum world include museum virtual reality (VR) tours, museum augmented realities, and activities that are predominantly designed for human-object interactions in between on site and online spaces and communities. These new museum activities across physical and virtual worlds urge a development of new methods that need to combine path mapping and public tracking through sensors and security cameras installed in gallery spaces with data collected through Internet, media platforms, and mobile devices. New research will need to look at how "big data" and **cultural analytics** can be applied to advance museum audience research[53] through the integration of new data sources. Researchers can explore information streams and the circulation of people, objects, and ideas across digital and physical realities.

[53] Lev Manovich, "Cultural Data," In *Museum and Archive on the Move: Changing Cultural Institutions in the Digital Era*, ed. Oliver Grau (Berlin: De Gruyter, 2017).

REFERENCES

Angelaki, Georgia, Rossella Caffo, Monika Hagedorn-Saupe, and Susan Hazan. "ATHENA: A Mechanism for Harvesting Europe's Museum Holdings into Europeana." *Museums and the Web* 2010. Accessed May 10, 2017. http://www.museumsandtheweb.com/mw2010/papers/angelaki/angelaki.html.

"Annual Report 2010." Van Gogh Museum. Accessed May 10, 2017. https://www.vangoghmuseum.nl/en/organisation/annual-report.

Bennett, Tony. *The Birth of the Museum: History, Theory, Politics.* London: Routledge, 1995.

Bitgood, Steve. "Introduction: Visitor Studies—1988." *Visitor Studies* 1 (1989): 5–8.

Black, Graham. *The Engaging Museum: Developing Museums for Visitor Involvement.* Abingdon: Routledge, 2005.

Bryman, Alan. "The End of the Paradigm Wars?" In *The SAGE Handbook of Social Research*, edited by Pertti Alasuutari, Leonard Bickman, and Julia Brannen. Thousand Oaks, CA: Sage, 2008.

"Code of Ethics for Museums." ICOM (International Council of Museums). Accessed May 10, 2017. http://icom.museum/fileadmin/user_upload/pdf/Codes/code_ethics2013_eng.pdf.

Crowley, Kevin, and Maureen Callanan. "Describing and Supporting Collaborative Scientific Thinking in Parent-Child Interactions." *Journal of Museum Education* 23, no. 1 (1998): 12–17.

Fetterman, David. *Ethnography: Step-by-Step.* London: Sage, 2010.

Fielding, Nigel, Raymond Lee, and Grant Blank. *Sage Book of Online Research Methods.* London: Sage, 2008.

Gillard, Patricia, and Anne Cranne-Francis. "Evaluation for Effective Web Communication: An Australian Example." *Curator: The Museum Journal* 45, no. 1 (2002): 35–49.

Glen Drury, "Social Media: Should Marketers Engage and How Can It Be Done Effectively?" *Journal of Direct, Data and Digital Marketing Practice* 9, no. 3 (2008):274–277.

"Glossary of Visitor Studies Terms." Visitor Studies Association. Accessed May 10, 2017. http://www.visitorstudies.org/glossary-of-terms.

Grincheva, Natalia. "How Far Can We Reach? International Audiences in Online Museum Communities." *The International Journal of Technology, Knowledge and Society* 7 (2012): 29–42.

Grincheva, Natalia. "Cultural Diplomacy of a Different Kind: A Case Study of the Global Guggenheim." PhD dissertation, Concordia University, 2015a.

Grincheva, Natalia. "'The World Beach Project' Going Viral: Measuring Online Influence (Case Study of the Victoria & Albert Online Museum Project)." *Journal of Creative Communications* 10 (2015b): 39–55.

Grincheva, Natalia. "Museum Ethnography in the Digital Age: Ethical Considerations." In *Internet Research Ethics for the Social Age: New Cases and Challenges*, edited by Michael Zimmer and Kataharina Kinder-Kurlandan. New York: Peter Lang, 2017.

Han, Jiawei, Jian Pei, and Micheline Kamber. *Data Mining: Concepts and Techniques*. New York: Elsevier, 2011.

Heath, Debora, Erin Koch, Barbara Ley, and Michael Montoya. "Nodes and Queries: Linking Locations in Networked Fields on Inquiry." *American Behavioral Scientist* 43 (1999): 450–463.

Hein, George. *Learning in the Museum*. London: Routledge, 1999.

Hine, Christine. *Virtual Ethnography*. London: Sage, 2000.

Hooper-Greenhill, Eilean. *"Studying Visitors."* In *A Companion to Museum Studies*, edited by Stuart McDonald. Oxford: Oxford, Blackwell, 2006.

Jones, Steven. *Cybersociety 2.0: Revisiting Computer-mediated Communication and Community*. London: Sage, 1998.

Kozinets, Robert. *Netnography: Doing Ethnographic Research Online*. London: Sage, 2010.

LaBar, Wayne. "Can Social Media Transform the Exhibition Development Process: Cooking the Exhibition—An Ongoing Case Study." *Museums and the Web* 2010. Accessed May 10, 2017. http://www.archimuse.com/mw2010/papers/labar/labar.html.

Liu, Bing. *Sentiment Analysis: Mining Opinions, Sentiments, and Emotions*. Cambridge: Cambridge University Press, 2015.

Lucast, Arthur, Paulette McManus, and Gillian Thomas. "Investigating Learning from Informal Sources: Listening to Conversations and Observing Play in Science Museums." *International Journal of Science Education* 8, no. 4 (1986): 341–352.

Manovich, Lev. "Cultural Data." In *Museum and Archive on the Move: Changing Cultural Institutions in the Digital Era*, edited by Oliver Grau. Berlin: De Gruyter, 2017.

McConnell, David. *Implementing Computer Supported Cooperative Learning*, 72. London: Psychology Press, 2000.

Melton, Arthur. *Problems of Installation in Museums of Art*. Washington, DC: American Association of Museums, 1935.

"Museum Definition." ICOM (International Council of Museums). Accessed May 10, 2017. ICOM. http://icom.museum/the-vision/museum-definition/.

Neuendorf, Kimberly A. *The Content Analysis Guidebook*. Thousand Oaks, CA: Sage, 2016.

Rendell, Becky. E-mail Message to Author, November 15, 2010.

Rymes, Betsy. "Recontextualizing YouTube: From Macro–Micro to Mass-Mediated Communicative Repertoires." *Anthropology & Education Quarterly* 43, no. 2 (2012): 214–227.

Schiele, Boris, Ruth Rentschler, and Eve Reussner. *Museum Marketing Research: from Denial to Discovery*. Melbourn: Deakin University Press, 1992.

Semel, Nora, and Francesca Merlino. "YouTube: Play at Guggenheim Museum." *Museum Next* 2011. Accessed May 10, 2017. https://www.museumnext.com/insight/youtube-play-at-guggenheim-museum/.

Soren, Barbara, and Nathalie Lemelin. "'Cyberpals!/Les Cybercopains!': A Look at Online Museum Visitor Experiences." *Curator: The Museum Journal* 47, no. 1 (2004): 55–83.

Tashakkori, Abbas, and Charles Teddlie. *Handbook of Mixed Methods in Social & Behavioral Research*. Thousand Oaks, CA: Sage, 2003.

Van den Heuvel, Charles, Sandor Spruit, Leen Breure, and Hans Voorbij. "Annotators and Agents in a Web-Based Collaboratory Around Cartographical Collections in Cultural Heritage Institutions." *Museums and the Web*, 2010. Accessed May 10, 2017. http://www.archimuse.com/mw2010/papers/heuvel/heuvel.html.

vom Lehn, Dirk Charles Heath, and John Hindmarsh. "Video-based Field Studies in Museums and Galleries." *Visitor Studies Today* 5, no. 3 (2002): 15–23.

CHAPTER 8

Smart Phones and Photovoice: Exploring Participant Lives with Photos of the Everyday

Erin Brock Carlson and Trinity Overmyer

Even when we have significant access to our research participants, it is difficult to study other people's personal, in-the-moment thoughts and experiences, which often hold important insights. During interviews and focus groups, participants might not remember how they felt at a particular moment in the past. They may even dismiss those insights as unimportant and, therefore, fail to bring them up. If our research techniques depend primarily on participants' abilities to discuss insights from memory—as many qualitative methods do—we risk losing valuable information in our research studies.

Photovoice methods help researchers capture this covert data by asking participants to take photographs over a span of time—ranging from a couple of weeks to several months—in order to document experiences and catalog their perceptions. With this method, photographs are used,

E. B. Carlson (✉) · T. Overmyer
Purdue University, West Lafayette, IN, USA
e-mail: brock7@purdue.edu

T. Overmyer
e-mail: tcovermy@purdue.edu

© The Author(s) 2018
l. levenberg et al. (eds.), *Research Methods for the Digital Humanities*,
https://doi.org/10.1007/978-3-319-96713-4_8

129

both as data for the study, and as memory aids that help participants articulate their viewpoints. Together with interviews and focus groups, the photos provide rich, narrative data for qualitative inquiry.

As researchers, we often think about our work as the search for and collection of evidence, and then the use of that evidence, alongside our own expertise, to construct new knowledge. But photovoice is a participatory method, which positions both researchers *and participants* as the collectors of data and the makers of meaning. Photovoice is flexible enough to help us pursue a variety of research questions in the Digital Humanities.

This chapter outlines how the photovoice method operates, and we offer practical advice for implementing this technique in your own research projects. With this in mind, we outline our study on the value and pitfalls of community engagement, which investigates the various ways that students, partner organizations, and instructors navigate collaborative projects between the community and the university. We asked people from each of these groups to take pictures while their work together unfolded, in order to explore the relationships between these different stakeholders throughout their collaboration. Our goal was to understand the impacts and obstacles of engagement work. The photos ultimately helped us recognize that each participant group had very different goals and expectations for the project, which were sometimes in tension with other stakeholders' goals. This gives us valuable insight into building more productive relationships in engagement work. Throughout this chapter, we lay out the strengths and weaknesses of this method, and offer a step-by-step guide to using photovoice in an informed and innovative way.

An Interdisciplinary and Participatory Method

In 1997, Caroline Wang and Mary Ann Burris published an article outlining photovoice as a method used in participatory research. Wang and Burris note that photovoice is powerful because it gives participants the opportunity to "identify, represent, and enhance their community" using their own pictures.[1] Photovoice is grounded in

---

[1] Caroline Wang and Mary Ann Burris, "Photovoice: Concept, Methodology, and Use for Participatory Needs Assessment," *Health Education & Behavior* 24, no. 3 (1997): 369–387.

Paulo Freire's theories of social transformation and community activism, aimed at raising critical consciousness and using methods that interrogate power dynamics. With Freire as a starting point, Wang, Burris, and Ping first developed photovoice methods to help women document the Women's Reproductive Health and Development program in Yunnan, China. They framed the process as a combination of empowerment education, feminist practice, and documentary photography. Since the 1997 article, Wang has published a string of articles expanding upon this method.[2] Caricia Catalini and Meredith Minkler also offer an excellent overview of the method and its many applications.[3] Photovoice's versatility has inspired researchers in many fields to apply it, including public health,[4] community action scholarship,[5] environmental studies,[6] and technical writing.[7]

In addition to its applications across disciplines, photovoice also aids reflection and collaboration within the communities it seeks to study. In Joyce Yi-Frazier et al.'s study on public health and diabetes noted above, participants uploaded their photos to Instagram and tagged them with

[2] See "Photovoice as a Participatory Health Promotion Strategy," *Health Promotion International* 13, no. 1 (1998): 75–86; "Photovoice: A Participatory Action Research Strategy Applied to Women's Health," *Journal of Women's Health* 8, no. 2 (1999): 185–192; "Who Knows the Streets as Well as the Homeless? Promoting Personal and Community Action Through Photovoice," *Health Promotion Practice* 1, no. 1 (2000): 81–89; "Youth Participation in Photovoice as a Strategy for Community Change," *Journal of Community Practice* 14, no. 1–2 (2006): 147–161; and many others.

[3] Caricia Catalani and Meredith Minkler, "Photovoice: A Review of the Literature in Health and Public Health," *Health Education & Behavior* 37, no. 3 (2010): 424–451.

[4] Joyce P. Yi-Frazier, Katherine Cochrane, Connor Mitrovich, Michael Pascual, Emil Buscaino, Lauren Eaton, Neil Panlasigui, Bailey Clopp, and Faisal Malik, "Using Instagram as a Modified Application of Photovoice for Storytelling and Sharing in Adolescents with Type 1 Diabetes," *Qualitative Health Research* 25, no. 10 (2015): 1372–1382.

[5] Alix Holtby, Kate Klein, Katie Cook, and Robb Travers, "To Be Seen or Not to Be Seen: Photovoice, Queer and Trans Youth, and the Dilemma of Representation," *Action Research* 13, no. 4 (2015): 317–335.

[6] Caroline Fusco, Fiona Moola, Guy Faulkner, Ron Buliung, and Vanessa Richichi, "Toward an Understanding of Children's Perceptions of Their Transport Geographies: (Non)active School Travel and Visual Representations of the Built Environment," *Journal of Transport Geography* 20, no. 1 (2012): 62–70.

[7] Patricia Sullivan, "Participating with Pictures: Promises and Challenges of Using Images as a Technique in Technical Communication Research," *Journal of Technical Writing and Communication* 47, no. 1 (2017): 86–108.

specific hashtags linked to the project.[8] As a result, researchers could easily access photo data and participants were able to interact with each other through Instagram. During focus groups, Yi-Frazier et al. found that social networks were an important tool for dealing with chronic diseases like diabetes. While in many photovoice studies participants upload their photographs to private folders and share them with others for the first time during focus groups, this study reveals a different model, which emphasizes community-building.[9]

As a result, photovoice has two major benefits. First, the method can be used to study a wide variety of topics that are often subjective in nature, including processes, practices, habits, and perceptions. Photos, when paired with other methods, provide more robust participant reflection when compared with traditional focus groups or interviews. Second, photovoice allows participants to collect data quickly and easily throughout their day using just their phones. Therefore, participation does not require major investments in time, money, or training, which is especially important when working with community organizations.

Photovoice has three main goals:

1. to enable individuals to record and reflect their community's strengths and concerns;
2. to promote critical dialogue and knowledge about important issues through large and small group discussion of photographs;
3. and to reach policymakers and spur change with these insights.[10]

While more traditional qualitative methods, like interviews, require participants to respond to questions that researchers develop, photovoice allows participants more freedom to interpret photo prompts as they see fit. As a result, participants produce unique photos and then have a chance to analyze their photos during interviews and focus groups *alongside* researchers. The collaboration between researchers and participants

---

[8]Yi-Frazier et al., "Using Instagram as a Modified Application of Photovoice for Storytelling and Sharing in Adolescents with Type 1 Diabetes."

[9]Using social media as the means through which participants store and share their photos would require careful consideration and cooperation with your university's Institutional Review Board, the governing body at your university that oversees research on human beings.

[10]Caroline C. Wang, "Photovoice: A Participatory Action Research Strategy Applied to Women's Health," *Journal of Women's Health* 8, no. 2 (1999): 185–192.

throughout the study allows us to see clearly how both groups are involved in interpreting the data.

Photovoice creates a space for people to represent themselves, as opposed to having their voices mediated only through a researcher's analysis. It operates like an autoethnography, which allows a researcher to explore their own experiences through self-narration. Participants make rhetorical choices about the timing, content, and framing of photos, meaning, they decide how and what to communicate through these images. In order to provide some guidance, however, researchers usually craft specific prompts to help participants take photos that are relevant to the study's research questions. This is yet another way that both researchers and participants construct meaning together using this method.

This kind of collaborative knowledge work became important in our study, particularly because we were exploring how students, instructors, and community partners (the organizations that agree to partner with college classes) navigated their relationships with each other inside the university engagement framework. In the next section, we discuss our study in depth. This case illustrates how photovoice operated in our own research, while also providing a detailed discussion of the inner workings of the method. This section and the subsequent discussion takes you from our initial pilot test, through the intricacies of research design and revision, and finally to other considerations you might make before you implement a study like this. Even for more exploratory research, it is important to consider how our method impacts the kinds of data we are able to gather and, therefore, how it affects the insights that are drawn from a study such as this one.

Using Photos in Community Engagement Research: An Illustrative Case

The bulk of research on course-driven community engagement focuses on teacher perceptions or student reflections, but there are few studies that examine the experience of community partners or the relationships between these different groups. This case examines a range of projects typical of engagement work in upper-level business writing and technical writing courses at Purdue University. Because most engagement scholarship focuses on student experiences and learning, instead of on the

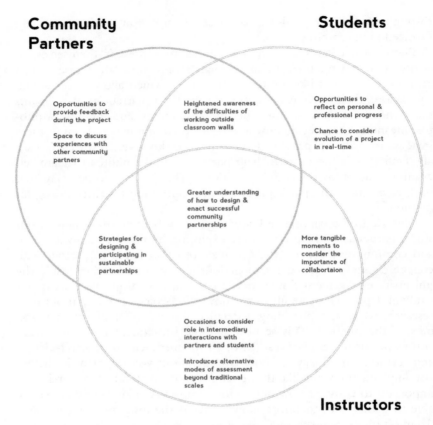

Community Partners

Students

Opportunities to provide feedback during the project

Space to discuss experiences with other community partners

Heightened awareness of the difficulties of working outside classroom walls

Opportunities to reflect on personal & professional progress

Chance to consider evolution of a project in real-time

Greater understanding of how to design & enact successful community partnerships

Strategies for designing & participating in sustainable partnerships

More tangible moments to consider the importance of collabortaion

Occasions to consider role in intermediary interactions with partners and students

Introduces alternative modes of assessment beyond traditional scales

Instructors

Fig. 8.1 Intended outcomes for stakeholders involved in the photovoice engagement study

complex ecology of goals, concerns, and standpoints of community partners, instructors, and students together, we started to wonder how these other stakeholders perceived project processes and outcomes. We began our inquiry with three key research questions (Fig. 8.1):

1. How do each of these stakeholder groups (students, instructors, and community partners) position and value engagement work?
2. When there are problems or failures during community projects, how do participants address these breakdowns?

3. What outcomes does engagement work have for students, instructors, and community partners—both collectively, and for individuals?

Photovoice was an appropriate method for this project for several reasons, but initially, we considered it because of its ease when working with participants outside the university. Photovoice provides a large amount of qualitative data with a low time commitment for participants. Ethically, we needed to consider methods that account for the material constraints on our nonprofit partners, who are working full-time and often lack the time and resources to take part in extended research with academics.

Before the study begins, researchers usually pilot, or test, their methods and techniques with a limited group of people. Even on a small scale, pilot testing helps researchers see their methods in action and identify any logistical problems that might arise during the study. We chose to test the photograph prompts and focus group questions with a few people from each participant group (in this case, students, instructors, and community partners). These participants only took pictures for three weeks, then met for focus groups. Thanks to the pilot, we discovered the need to add short, written reflections to the study in order to capture more participant observations. Additionally, we revised the language and order of focus group questions, because some of our pilot participants did not understand them completely (see "Designing the Focus Groups"). We also extended the timeline, to allow for more participant recruitment and to provide participants more time to collect data.

Figure 8.2 is a photo of a mural taken during the pilot study. Initially, we tried to analyze what this image says about engagement on our campus. This picture was taken downtown, so it might tell us that intellectual engagement happens outside traditional classrooms. We could guess that the project had something to do with art or artists, or maybe even the local music scene. However, during the focus group, we learned that this picture was taken because it depicts the collaboration between several groups involved in the community project, including:

- artists who collaborated to create this specific mural;
- the city that funded and permitted the project;

Fig. 8.2 Colorful mural in downtown area. Pilot study photo, Michaela Cooper, 2015

- the community partner who organized this public art project;
- and the students who developed a mobile walking tour of all these new pieces of public art.

Without conducting focus groups with the participant who took this photo, we might have never fully understood their project, or the large network of stakeholders that were involved. In follow-up interviews and focus groups, participants often discuss the people, places, and objects that are implicated but not necessarily visible in their photos.

Based on the pilot test, we redesigned the research instruments and broke our study up into two phases:

- **Phase One**: Participants take photos and submit short, written responses (approximately 150 words) that are meant to provide updates on the project or reflections on their photos, throughout the duration of the community project.
- **Phase Two**: Participants are invited to take part in a focus group with other participants from their stakeholder groups (instructors with other instructors, students with other students, and community partners with other community partners).

Toward the end of Phase One, we reviewed the collected materials and adapted our focus group questions to respond to the initial data. This allowed us to ask both general and specific questions during Phase Two. In this final focus group, we also provided participants with the images that they had taken throughout the study.

Remember: images can be difficult to understand on their own. That is why this method requires other data in addition to photographs. This data often comes from written reflections, interviews, and focus groups. If you utilize this method in your own research, it is important to consider what kind of supplementary data you want to collect, as well as how and when you plan to collect it. Ultimately, our design was meant to gather multiple types of data across a span of time, culminating in a highly interactive focus group where participants could actively reflect on their experiences in the study.

For participants, though, it all begins with the prompts they receive at the beginning of their data collection. The prompts that researchers put forth frame the entire study for participants. Prompts have a huge impact on the kinds of data you collect and even on how invested participants become in the research. With this in mind, we suggest crafting photo and reflection prompts with attention to the various ways in which participants might interpret what you will ask them. Also, consider how changing the language or phrasing of these prompts may change the kinds of data that they will gather.

Keep in mind that prompts should be short and direct. You need participants to feel confident that they know what you are asking them to respond to. You should also aim for open-ended questions that allow participants to interpret their experiences in a variety of ways. Simple, direct prompts can still lead to very complex and interesting data.

Again, we highly recommend that researchers pilot test these prompts on others, even informally, to find out how people interpret the questions. For example, our first draft of prompts was simple, direct, and open-ended:

1. What does community engagement look like?
2. What does service-learning look like?

However, by piloting these questions and asking others to critique them, we found that they were too vague.

Additionally, the terminology of the two questions was confusing to many participants. As engagement scholars, we are aware of the subtle differences between terms like "service-learning" and "engagement". Service-learning is a model that emphasizes student learning processes and often manifests as volunteerism linked to a class and written reflections, or larger class projects as "a place for collaborative inquiry with the students and community partners."[11] On the other hand, the term "community engagement" refers to the more general notion of engaging with people or organizations outside the university in some capacity. These terms are nuanced and often overlap. We assumed that different participants would identify with one or the other, which is why we originally chose to use both terms. We realized during our pilot that, for nonscholars, using both terms is unnecessarily confusing, because participants spend more time wondering what the difference is or worrying if they are supposed to understand the difference, than documenting their experiences.

We reworked the prompts so they included a suggested quantity and time scale ("as many photos as you would like each week") in order to provide some guidance for participants. The final prompts are still open enough to allow photo-takers to look at the topic from a variety of different angles, but they are more clear and concrete than the previous set. This revision made it easier for participants to respond confidently to our questions with their photos. The final prompt we settled on was:

> Throughout the semester, we'd like you to take photos that describe your community engagement work. Please take as many photos as you would like each week. Some suggested ideas to get you started are below.
>
> 1. What does a "day in the life" of your community engagement project look like?
> 2. Have you had any major successes or obstacles to overcome during the project?
> 3. Are there any people, places, or things that have affected your experience?

[11] Ellen Cushman, "Sustainable Service Learning Programs," *College Composition and Communication* 54, no. 1 (2002): 40–65.

After finalizing our prompts, we moved on to participant recruitment. Recruitment was a large concern for our study, since we were working with three distinct groups who were geographically and institutionally dispersed. When we designed the study, we wrote a general recruitment email that could be sent to instructors, students, and community partners. Since instructors set up their community engagement projects and serve as the link between students and community partners, we started by sending our recruitment email to the listserv of instructors teaching the classes on which we were focusing. Once those who wanted to participate contacted us, we set up a time to come to their classes and speak to their students in person. When we visited classrooms, we followed the script of the email we had composed and asked instructors to step out of the room, to ensure students that their participation in the study would not affect their grades in the class, since the instructor would not know who participated and who did not. We also reached out to their community partners via email, to request their participation in the study. Because of the three groups, recruitment required a multipronged approach and a fair amount of time, so we got started at the beginning of the semester—even if the community engagement project did not actually start until much later in the term.

When we started working on our study, we decided that a semester timeline would be appropriate, since our campus runs on a 16-week semester schedule, and that would provide our participants with plenty of time to take photos. For us, the semester roughly broke down this way: We spent the first 3–4 weeks of the semester recruiting and setting up the file system for participants to submit their photos, which allowed participants the time to get settled into their projects. Then, throughout the majority of the semester (Weeks 5–12), participants were taking photos and submitting reflections to their folders. Every two weeks, we sent reminders via email, which was frequent enough that they did not forget, but not so frequent that they got annoyed with the messages.

It is important to note that since different instructors structured their projects according to different needs and timelines, participants contributed photos at different times during the duration of the semester. Some uploaded a mass of photos and narratives between weeks 6 and 9, while others uploaded a couple each week; this depended upon where they were in their projects. Periodically, we would look over the data and take notes on the participant-generated data, keeping these in mind as we thought about our focus group questions.

Because community engagement projects tend to wind down along with the semester, we reached out to our participants during weeks 13 and 14, to ask if they would participate in our focus groups. We scheduled these sessions for the last two weeks of the semester. After the focus groups were held, we assembled all of the data from throughout the semester and began to look for common themes among different stakeholder groups, different types of data, and different approaches.

We recruited participants from our total participant population and the majority of our photo-takers agreed to participate. We were concerned that a single focus group which included students, teachers, and community partners would create a power differential that inadvertently silenced certain people or skewed participants' responses in the focus group. For example, students might feel pressured to alter their opinions, knowing an instructor was sitting next to them. Because of this, we administered separate focus groups for students, teachers, and community partners.

As each participant entered the room, we handed them their stack of photos, which we had printed prior to the focus group. It was important for us to have printed, rather than digital copies, so that participants could see all their photos at once. They could also create different narratives, by organizing them in different ways as we asked them questions during the focus group. We felt that this gave them space to reflect on their experiences, since they were able to consult all of their data.

When writing focus group questions, it is important to understand that the order in which questions are presented can make a big difference in how participants respond. We began with a short task of arranging images, which allowed participants to take some time to review their own photos. The initial question you choose will frame the entire line of questioning, so it is key not to begin with anything too difficult or probing. After the initial icebreaker question, the rest of the questions should build upon one another, advancing in cognitive difficulty or emotional investment, depending on the research you are doing. Each participant should be given ample time to answer each question before moving onto the next. This helps researchers to be sure that no single person does most of the talking. Be sure to end on a final question that helps your participants ease out of what can sometimes be a mentally or emotionally intense hour. It is also a good idea to allow participants to give feedback on the research, or to give them the space to voice any additional opinions or concerns that the questions did not address.

Our Focus Group Questions:

1. Arrange your own images from most significant to least. Tell us a little about why you chose to take this first, most significant image.
2. And the least significant—what prompted you to take this picture?
3. What kinds of images do you think your students/instructors/the community partners would capture if they were doing this study?
4. What do you think your pictures reveal about the nature of community engagement work?
5. What, if anything, do you wish you had known going into this project?

Our strategy positioned the photos as memory aids, to help participants think about their perceptions of engagement projects over the course of the semester. The images also served as jumping-off points, for deeper insight into their experiences during the study. More than that, for participants whose voices often are not heard, or are inhibited or shy, the images became evidence for them to speak authoritatively to researchers, and to each other, about the meaning that they derived from their work.

The ranking questions (#1 and #2) led us to quite a bit of unexpected data: participants had fascinating reasons for valuing photos in different ways and even took the opportunity to tell us about photos they *wish* they would have taken. For us, some of the most surprising discussions were of the images not taken because of a dead phone, a shot that was gone in the blink of an eye, or forgetfulness. These revealed just as much useful data as the photos that were present.

Finally, after all the data was collected, we began coding the photos, along with the other textual and discursive data collected throughout the study. We identified emergent themes, and also the threads of information that attended to our original research questions. Though we discovered a wealth of complex information overall, some of the most crucial findings arose from what participants valued during the collaborative projects. We found that community partners put a lot of emphasis on student expertise and that they highly valued students as innovators. One of the key reasons that community partners chose to participate in engagement work with the university was to gain access to students' ideas, not merely to have extra help on the work that community organizations were already doing, as we had originally suspected based on the current literature.

We also unearthed some tensions between student objectives and instructor goals. While many of the students in this study outwardly focused on the end goals—the final deliverables they would turn in—as being the most important work of these projects, they also took several pictures of work as a process, such as images of group work and screenshots of text messages discussing the projects. This tension is revealing because writing instructors strive to communicate the importance of the writing process, but teacher lore tells us that students really only value the end product. Clearly, though, the line between how process and product are valued remains blurry for students. Additionally, we found that many instructor participants appreciated the mutable nature of engagement projects, hoping it would help students experience the ways that projects emerge and fluctuate in real-world writing tasks. Partners valued this plasticity as well. However, students often struggled to navigate projects that were in flux, as opposed to traditional writing assignments which were outlined clearly on a static assignment sheet. The convergence of these themes gives us insight into some of the roadblocks that engagement projects face and into what different stakeholders value. By considering these diverse perspectives, we will be better equipped to design and implement engagement projects that successfully attend to the goals of all these groups.

DISCUSSION: TAKEAWAYS ON METHOD

Photovoice invites us to consider the roles of researchers and participants, and especially the interplay between these two roles in navigating research situations. Further, the method is particularly well-suited to community-based research, because such applications illuminate relationships between institutions and local communities. In addition to its value for interrogating the relationships implicit in research, this method is intuitive, allowing students of various levels to both conduct and engage in the research.

After completing two semesters of this photovoice study, we learned quite a bit about the value of the method, including its ability to illuminate previously hidden processes, the importance of supplementary data, and the value of building narratives through photos. As participants

arrange photos, they create narrative threads that bring to light perceptions of engagement work. The activity also helps participants to organize their thoughts and to communicate them in the group. Participants
not only describe the photos they also take into account the contexts,
histories, and relationships that surround and impact their understanding
of the images.[12]

The act of taking pictures, beyond just how we use them to elicit
focus group answers, is a meaning-making endeavor, and can reveal a
great deal on its own. When texts are framed and presented as photos,
it changes how we think about context and process. Photos might also
focus on the mundane—what participants see as uninteresting or unimportant aspects of their experiences. But photos of everyday practices can
be invaluable because they allow you to get a glimpse into the private
and routine experiences of participants.

Further, asking participants to arrange their photos in various ways
allows them to recognize a multitude of themes, insights, and narratives
emerging from their images. Discussions during focus groups also help
participants realize how their own understanding progresses over the
course of the project, as they reflect on their reasoning behind including certain pictures in their collections. For example, although we
expected mostly pictures of face-to-face meetings, several of our participants included screenshots of their writing and research practices. The
inclusion of these photos suggested the importance of this often-invisible
background work, and we were able to ask participants about the role of
this work in the progression of the larger project.

We also learned that while the participant photographs are undoubt-
edly the cornerstone of a photovoice study, the images alone lack context, and the contexts are very important for understanding the larger
implications of findings. Therefore, it is important to provide ample
opportunities for participants to explain and reflect on their photos
through the inclusion of written narratives, interviews, or focus groups.

Having multiple sources and kinds of data is particularly important
when you are highlighting the opinions and voices of your participants.
As we have noted, photovoice data is gathered locally from the ground
up. This makes it useful when studying multiple, local perspectives

---

[12]Darrin Hodgetts, Kerry Chamberlain, and Alan Radley, "Photographs Never Taken
During Photo-Production Projects," *Qualitative Research in Psychology* 4, no. 4 (2007):
263–280.

Fig. 8.3 Students gather around a service dog-in-training. Pilot study photo, Erin Brock Carlson, 2015

instead of top-down approaches to knowledge making. People are able to document their lives and the problems in their environments to make arguments for change, rather than depending on outsiders or institutions to make decisions for their community. The photos can also highlight or uncover relationships between individuals, communities, and institutions. For example, Fig. 8.3 depicts classroom excitement surrounding an in-training service dog who was attending the class that day. Though this is a simple picture at first glance, it represents the partnership between the University and the Indiana Canine Assistant Network (ICAN). It also depicts the engagement work of the individual student, since the student focused on this work and his collaboration with the ICAN for his own project. The image revealed not just a moment of joy, but to the researchers, it brought to light a valuable partnership between students, the campus, and the ICAN, for which many students volunteer.

Images are particularly persuasive evidence when arguing for the importance of social justice efforts and other initiatives to improve the quality of life for citizens.[13] Images, in addition to being visually stimulating, can often evoke a great deal of emotion, through identification or association. Additionally, because we operate so often in digital, highly visual spaces, we perhaps respond more earnestly to visual evidence. Photovoice combines visual and textual data as evidence of lived perspectives on the world—perspectives that often resonate with others. As such, photovoice is well-positioned to work toward social and political reform.

Although photovoice is most often deployed when working inside communities that are local to researchers and is useful in gathering a community around a specific issue, this method is also useful if researchers do not have direct physical access to participants. For instance, if you are working with participants in distant locales or those who are geographically widespread, as is the case with research conducted in digital spaces and online, then photovoice is a good methodological choice. For example, the near-worldwide ubiquity of cell phones capable of taking photos means that researchers can use this method to engage participants from around the globe, including participants in the Global South, indigenous communities, and online spaces.

Because most people carry a phone and regularly take pictures, participants are often already experts in this data collection method. Participants know how to take photos, so the method positions them as user-experts and allows them to take the role of participant researchers. Most people are accustomed to sharing photos digitally, whether by SMS, social media, email, or storage platforms (both web-based and application-driven). Therefore, participants do not need extensive training in the collection method. Additionally, participants can collect data at their leisure, with minimum effort or time investment, resulting in low start-up costs for researchers. Again, these characteristics make photovoice an effective choice when working with communities that have little time and money to dedicate to participating in research.

[13] Heather Castleden and Theresa Garvin, "Modifying Photovoice for Community-Based Participatory Indigenous Research," *Social Science & Medicine* 66, no. 6 (2008): 1393–1405.

CONSTRAINTS AND CONSIDERATIONS

Though relinquishing researcher control of data collection has many benefits, it is also important to consider the problems that may arise. Participants might interpret your prompts in a variety of ways, causing them to veer far from the original goals of your inquiry. At the other extreme, participants might be overly concerned with the expectations of researchers, which affects what pictures they take. Additionally, people will forget to take pictures, so sending reminders periodically is important. For example, even though we sent reminder emails every two weeks, we still had participants tell us, at the end of the semester, that they often forgot to take photos at key times during their project.

Because photovoice provides surprising and very diverse data, you likely will not know what you will get until you see what participants have generated. This makes creating coding strategies ahead of time difficult and requires a lot of time toward the end of a study rather than evenly distributed throughout it. This delay also means that the expectations researchers bring into the study may be challenged, even at the very end of a study; this requires a level of flexibility from researchers.

The method also raises some important ethical considerations. Photovoice is unique because it is inherently linked to social justice and to an ethics of representation that focuses on how marginalized people are represented by others. When using any research method, you must think about the overall power dynamics of your study, as well as more immediate issues like participant safety and data security.

Most research entails an imbalance of power between researchers and participants. Research can easily become a colonizing force if we, as "outsiders," impose our worldview onto "insider" participants, especially when we do not value the knowledge of those whom we study. Wielding representations of others from an outsider position of power can become a kind of symbolic violence against already vulnerable or disenfranchised communities of people.

Because photovoice emerged out of health research—which has been a major driver of the codes that govern ethical research practices across disciplines—ethical considerations are embedded in the technique. It is grounded in "respect for autonomy, promotion of social justice, active promotion of good, and avoidance of harm."[14] Photovoice research

---

[14] Caroline C. Wang and Yanique A. Redwood-Jones, "Photovoice Ethics: Perspectives from Flint Photovoice," *Health Education & Behavior* 28, no. 5 (2001): 560–572.

should focus on ways that communities can use these photos as evidence to enact and change policies, and have the power to participate in their own governance. As a researcher, you are asking those who are normally acted upon to make narratives, tell stories, and voice concerns about the world around them. Because participatory action research (PAR) also involves voicing concerns to governing bodies, photovoice and PAR paired together can empower people to incite action and change on issues related directly to their lived reality.

Photovoice invites participants to challenge external representations of their lives and communities, upsetting the traditional research process that positions researchers as the authorities on interpretation. Participants are not seen as *subjects* (or, perhaps in some cases, *objects*), but as active coresearchers that collect and interpret data from their own perspective. This lowers the chances of researchers inadvertently or carelessly misrepresenting the knowledge work of participant communities.

It is also important to consider that participants, especially in vulnerable groups, might take and discuss photos in the way they think *you* want them to, rather than in the way that *they* want to. People often conform to our expectations of them, especially in research situations. As a result, it is crucial that you consider ways to move participants out of this mindset. Otherwise, you may end up with homogenous sets of images, which fail to capture the nuances and complexities of everyday life—which is the most interesting data of all.

With any research that involves human experience, participant privacy is always a top concern; it is especially sensitive when we ask people to bring us snapshots of their intimate, daily lives. Because this method asks participants to take photos on their personal devices, and often to transfer them digitally to a research repository, data security should be a top priority. We have to consider not only physical privacy and safety, but also data privacy because it could affect participants' online identities and personas.

Consider the following tips to ensure that your participants' data are secure:

- Submit your research protocol through your university's IRB before beginning the study, and include plans for secure data transfer and storage.
- Choose a secure repository to which participants can send or upload their photos from their phone. Focus on storage

platforms that make photo transfer as secure and easy as possible for participant-researchers.

- De-identify your data as quickly as possible by separating personal or identifiable information, like names, from the data; pay attention to all metadata attached to files and photos, which are the elements in the file information that are obscured unless you purposefully look for them.
- Depending on the nature of the data, do not ask participants to send data through email, social media, or any avenue where their data can be easily traced back to them or their online personas.

You must examine your specific participant population when considering all the various issues of privacy and safety. Protecting digital identities should be a concern of all studies, particularly studies that work with online communities or digital data collection and storage. Additionally, because of the emancipatory nature of this method, photovoice studies often focus on vulnerable and disenfranchised populations, as well as on sensitive and private situations. We cannot stress enough that safety and privacy must always be the highest priority, especially when working with these groups.

It is also important that you train participants to value the privacy of other people before they begin collecting data. Instruct coresearchers to avoid taking pictures with people's faces in them, or pictures of private places, such as nonparticipants' homes. The very thing that makes data collection easy—pictures of participants' situated experiences—means that photos are often of private lives. There are laws protecting intrusion into private space and the use of people's likenesses, even in public. You must consider how to deal with participant-generated images that contain the faces of nonparticipants and how to guard against privacy intrusions, especially when research will be shared through official channels like scholarly journals or shared informally without the consent of the subjects in participants' photos.

Conclusions and Applications

In the realm of qualitative research techniques, photovoice is a relatively young method. Therefore, the nuances of procedural steps and applications continue to develop, as more and more researchers employ photovoice in diverse fields to answer various types of research questions.

As you begin to work with this method, you might find other ways to reimagine or tweak protocols in light of your own research questions and participant populations.

Since photovoice is a method that places a great deal of power in participants' hands, it is imperative to consider the needs of your participants in order to design your study so that it complements their everyday practices. Attention to this value will ultimately provide you with the highest amount of participation and the most authentic data. The role of mobile technology in this practice opens up avenues to pursue research questions and participants even when you are physically distant from your participants, further expanding the realm of possibilities for this method.

Photovoice is closely related to ethnographic and autoethnographic methods because it offers participants the opportunity to depict experiences on their own terms. This method requires researchers to really think about the role of the participant in research studies by considering how they approach the study, what power they hold in the study, and what effects they have on the course of the research.

This method is flexible enough to use for a variety of different research situations. We contend that photovoice is best suited for participatory research, which positions participant knowledge and experience as integral to understanding both the questions that we pose and the answers to those questions. We are situated in a net of ideologies that influence our worldviews and our research; we always enter research projects with preconceived ideas of their outcomes. We can never truly step outside of our own perspectives. This is also true for our participants. However, if, instead of feigning objectivity, we can open a space for a multiplicity of voices in this kind of qualitative research, it may help us find richer meaning in the complexities of everyday life.

REFERENCES

Castleden, Heather, and Theresa Garvin. "Modifying Photovoice for Community-Based Participatory Indigenous Research." *Social Science & Medicine* 66, no. 6 (2008): 1393–1405.

Catalani, Caricia, and Meredith Minkler. "Photovoice: A Review of the Literature in Health and Public Health." *Health Education & Behavior* 37, no. 3 (2010): 424–451.

Fusco, Caroline, Fiona Moola, Guy Faulkner, Ron Buliung, and Vanessa Richichi. "Toward an Understanding of Children's Perceptions of Their

Transport Geographies: (Non)active School Travel and Visual Representations of the Built Environment." *Journal of Transport Geography* 20, no. 1 (2012): 62–70.

Hodgetts, Darrin, Chamberlain, Kerry, and Alan Radley. "Photographs Never Taken During Photo-Production Projects." *Qualitative Research in Psychology* 4, no. 4 (2007): 263–280.

Holtby, Alix, Kate Klein, Katie Cook, and Robb Travers. "To Be Seen or Not to Be Seen: Photovoice, Queer and Trans Youth, and the Dilemma of Representation." *Action Research* 13, no. 4 (2015): 317–335.

Sullivan, Patricia. "Participating with Pictures: Promises and Challenges of Using Images as a Technique in Technical Communication Research." *Journal of Technical Writing and Communication* 47, no. 1 (2017): 86–108.

Wang, Caroline C. "Photovoice as a Participatory Health Promotion Strategy." *Health Promotion International* 13, no. 1 (1998): 75–86.

Wang, Caroline C. "Photovoice: A Participatory Action Research Strategy Applied to Women's Health." *Journal of Women's Health* 8, no. 2 (1999): 185–192.

Wang, Caroline C. "Who Knows the Streets as Well as the Homeless? Promoting Personal and Community Action Through Photovoice." *Health Promotion Practice* 1, no. 1 (2000): 81–89.

Wang, Caroline C. "Youth Participation in Photovoice as a Strategy for Community Change." *Journal of Community Practice* 14, no. 1–2 (2006): 147–161.

Wang, Caroline, and Mary Ann Burris. "Photovoice: Concept, Methodology, and Use for Participatory Needs Assessment." *Health Education & Behavior* 24, no. 3 (1997): 369–387.

Wang, Caroline C., and Yanique A. Redwood-Jones. "Photovoice Ethics: Perspectives from Flint Photovoice." *Health Education & Behavior* 28, no. 5 (2001): 560–572.

Yi-Frazier, Joyce P., Katherine Cochrane, Connor Mitrovich, Michael Pascual, Emil Buscaino, Lauren Eaton, Neil Panlasigui, Bailey Clopp, and Faisal Malik. "Using Instagram as a Modified Application of Photovoice for Storytelling and Sharing in Adolescents with Type 1 Diabetes." *Qualitative Health Research* 25, no. 10 (2015): 1372–1382.

CHAPTER 9

Digital Media, Conventional Methods: Using Video Interviews to Study the Labor of Digital Journalism

Tai Neilson

Online interviews extend the tools of qualitative research and facilitate new types of data and research outputs. They allow researchers to reach geographically dispersed populations, reduce some burdens on participants, and still facilitate necessary relationships and rapport between interviewer and interviewee.[1] What follows is a methodological treatise and a guide to conducting online interviews in the Digital Humanities.

---

[1] Susie Weller, "Using Internet Video Calls in Qualitative (longitudinal) Interviews: Some Implications for Rapport," *International Journal of Social Research Methodology* 20, no. 6 (2017); Sally Seitz, "Pixilated Partnerships, Overcoming Obstacles in Qualitative Interviews via Skype: A Research Note," *Qualitative Research* early online publication, 16, no. 2 (2015): 229–235; Hannah Deakin and Kelly Wakefield, "Skype Interviewing: Reflections of Two PhD Researchers," *Qualitative Research* 14, no. 5 (2014); and Naomi Hay-Gibson, "Interviews via VoIP: Benefits and Disadvantages within a PhD Study of SMEs," *Library and Information Research* 33, no. 105 (2009).

T. Neilson (✉)
Macquarie University, Sydney, NSW, Australia
e-mail: tai.neilson@mq.edu.au

© The Author(s) 2018
l. levenberg et al. (eds.), *Research Methods for the Digital Humanities*,
https://doi.org/10.1007/978-3-319-96713-4_9

It is based on observations from my study of digital journalism in New Zealand and the United States. I outline the benefits and limitations of interview methods using digital tools as part of a Digital Humanities approach.

This chapter is animated by a set of concerns about the field, its methodological commitments, and digital media. My central question is: how are interview methods best adapted to digital contexts? First, I ask how research methods such as interviewing, which have been extensively codified in the social sciences and marketing, can be salvaged by and for critical Digital Humanities. To answer this question, I focus on reflexive and critical approaches that can inform a wide range of interests. Second, I pose the question: how should interview methods be rethought in light of changes facilitated by digital media? Digital media provide new opportunities for recruiting participants and conducting interviews, and allow us to develop multisite and transnational studies. They also facilitate types of archiving, analysis, and collaboration that, up until recently, have largely been limited to quantitative research. Third, because my research focuses on digital journalism, I ask: how can interview research be adapted to study technological and economic changes in the **culture industries**? I contend that Digital Humanities researchers can benefit from sustained analyses of labor in the fields that we study and reflections on the labor involved in the research process. I pose provisional answers to these questions using my own work as a case study and guide to conducting online interviews. Further, I draw on the work of exemplary researchers and educators to indicate some new directions for interview research in the Digital Humanities.

Interviews are most suited to investigating individuals' experiences and attitudes. They can elicit detailed accounts of people's lives and the meanings, reasons, and contexts of their actions.[2] They are effective when participants are invited to tell their own stories in their own words. For instance, I interviewed a journalist who worked for a now defunct newspaper in the United States before taking a job as a correspondent for a newswire service. He expressed the anxiety he and his colleagues felt as pension plans were frozen, friends were made redundant, and the paper underwent a merger before replacing its print operations with an anemic online edition. He provided personal narratives about his

[2] Seitz, "Pixilated Partnerships, Overcoming Obstacles in Qualitative Interviews via Skype."

biography, day-to-day work, colleagues, concerns, and aspirations. He also described his experiences of technological changes such as the implementation of a new content management system to govern workflow. His interview helped me to address the central challenge of my research, which was to express the experiences of journalists and to theorize them in relation to broader economic, political, technological, and cultural struggles.

Interviews for the Digital Humanities

Interviews are a fixture of qualitative research in the social sciences and humanities. Yet, there may be some controversy over whether they can be a part of a Digital Humanities approach. In response, I suggest that interviews produce textual data, they are fundamentally interpretive, and are opened to new potentialities through video link-up applications, textual analysis software, digital archiving, and web hosting. Interview methods need to evolve to meet the new opportunities and challenges of Digital Humanities.

Interviews are also well established among practitioners in marketing, health, and other fields. In Media Studies, pioneering work by Paul Lazarsfeld and Elihu Katz used interviews to study messages and audiences.[3] These studies attempted to test short-term "effects" of media content and "laws" about how messages are diffused. They often considered the interviewer a neutral expert tasked with uncovering the truth or laws of media and communication. In Sociology, interview techniques were formalized by members of the Chicago School of Sociology. Their interactionist approach emphasized the ways that people develop shared definitions of reality through social interaction. In research that focused on urban populations, they came to theorize interviews as sites of meaning-making between interviewers and interviewees, but these studies remained largely divorced from questions of inequality and political struggle.[4] Cultural Studies and other fields at the intersection of the social sciences and humanities continue to practice reflexive and critical interview methods.

---

[3] Elihu Katz and Paul Lazarsfeld, *Personal Influence: The Part Played by People in the Flow of Mass Communications* (New York: Free Press, 1955).

[4] Lana Rakow, "Commentary: Interviews and Focus Groups as Critical and Cultural Methods," *Journalism & Mass Communication Quarterly* 88, no. 2 (2011).

Qualitative researchers are now more likely to acknowledge that interviews are not neutral or objective. Participants' answers are context-specific and reflect complex and sometimes contradictory perspectives. As such, the role of researcher is not to simply find an existing "truth" by applying the right techniques. Anselm Strauss and Juliet Corbin's (1998) *The Basics of Qualitative Research: Techniques and Procedures for Developing Grounded Theory* and Thomas Lindlof and Bryan Taylor's (2011) *Qualitative Communication Research Methods* provide instructive approaches to reflexivity in qualitative research.[5] In particular, this chapter is informed by Strauss and Corbin's "grounded theory." In their view, research is a process of developing and testing understandings, interviews are communicative contexts through which meaning is negotiated, and researchers should aim to build theory that can shape practice.

Reflexive research entails navigating power relations and inequalities that are manifested in the interview context and sensitivity to broader social stratifications. Cultural Studies scholars exploring issues of race, gender, and class find interviews useful for understanding the experiences and interests of different communities. For instance, Peter Lunt and Sonia Livingstone argue that interviews in feminist methodological traditions aim to undermine the "masculine paradigm" and establish the "egalitarian power relations implied by the notion of inter-view."[6] Nonetheless, this does not simply mean accepting the perspectives of interviewees. Researchers should not take "common sense" perspectives and assumptions for granted.[7] Rather, it is their role to question and sometimes challenge interviewees' assumptions. This can involve asking interviewees to "unpack" common sense claims or provide specific examples. Researchers can also ask interviewees to read and respond to research findings. In the later stages of my research, I incorporated some of my preliminary theses into the interviews and asked interviewees how they correspond to or differ from their experiences.

---

[5]Anselm Strauss and Juliet Corbin, *Basics of Qualitative Research: Techniques and Procedures for Developing Grounded Theory*, 2nd ed. (Thousand Oaks, CA: Sage, 1998); Thomas Lindlof and Bryan Taylor, *Qualitative Communication Research Methods*, 3rd ed. (Thousand Oaks, CA: Sage, 2011).

[6]Peter Lunt and Sonia Livingstone, "Rethinking the Focus Group in Media and Communications Research," *Journal of Communication* 46, no. 2 (1996): 80.

[7]Strauss and Corbin, *Basics of Qualitative Research*, 98.

Interviews are suited to answering specific types of questions—questions related to individuals' biographies, experiences, and opinions. If the researcher is interested in demographics or the most common views held by a large population then in-depth interviews are not the right method. If the researcher wants to know about policies or industry statistics then, again, there are likely to be more effective ways of seeking answers. Interviews are time intensive; they require a lot of work in the development stage, setting up and conducting interviews, transcribing and coding, analysis, and writing. Nonetheless, interviews can be deeply rewarding, and the affordances of digital media entail new opportunities for reflexive and critical interview research.

DIGITAL MEDIA AND ONLINE INTERVIEWS

The relationship between qualitative research and digital media is more complex than simply providing new "tools" for researchers to incorporate into existing methodologies. The use of digital media has changed our work processes as researchers, academics, and students. They have also transformed other industries and the lives of many of our research participants.

Researchers in the Digital Humanities may find that the objects we study and the people we need to interview are increasingly geographically distributed. In my own research, I used Skype's video link-up service to speak with journalists over a large geographical area. I spoke to interviewees from my two national case studies without incurring the costs and time involved in international travel. I also spoke with people working in smaller towns and large urban centers, which expanded my access to a range of experiences and perspectives. As cultural industries become increasingly global, researchers can use communication technologies to explore these connections.

Digital communication also enables easy interview recording. I audio recorded my interviews, which allowed me to transcribe and relisten to them during the analysis and write-up processes. I also used NVivo software, which allows users to import transcripts, audio, and video for the purposes of coding. In addition to the considerable cost, NVivo and other off-the-shelf computer assisted qualitative data analysis software (CAQDAS) pose difficulties related to sharing coded data in a nonproprietary way. Nonetheless, they greatly improve the speed, ease, and searchability of coding for individual researchers and research teams.

Some qualitative researchers are beginning to archive their interview recordings and transcripts so that they may be accessed by other researchers or students. Universities and national research institutions such as the Australian Research Council (ARC) and the UK's Economic and Social Research Council have an interest in archiving qualitative data. Infrastructure like Qualidata and the Australian Qualitative Archive (AQuA) have been set up to facilitate archiving.[8] Archiving qualitative data raises a number of epistemological, ethical, and practical questions. For example, in my own research, I was unable to make my interview data available to other researchers because of issues related to anonymity. But, these concerns are not insurmountable if researchers consider opportunities to archive and share data at the beginning of their research design. This is a particularly promising area for interview research in the Digital Humanities.

INVESTIGATING THE CULTURE INDUSTRY

Interviews can be used to study workers' experiences across the cultural industries. In particular, there is a long history of ethnographic research on the experiences, attitudes, and practices of journalists. In 1972, Gaye Tuchman used participant observation to investigate journalists' opinions and practices regarding objectivity.[9] Later that decade, Herbert Gans' (1979) ethnographic work untangled some of the professional standards, values, and pressures that determine what journalists consider news.[10] More recently, David Domingo and Chris Paterson (2008 and 2011) continue to demonstrate the strengths of ethnographic methods for understanding journalism in their two collections of essays about digital newsrooms.[11] However, Christian Anderson attests that "as news production decentralizes, traditional methods of exploring the behavior

---

[8] Alex Broom, Lynda Cheshire, and Michael Emmison, "Qualitative Researchers' Understandings of Their Practice and the Implications for Data Archiving and Sharing," *Sociology* 43, no. 6 (2009): 1164.

[9] Gaye Tuchman, *Making News: A Study in the Construction of Reality* (New York: Free Press, 1978).

[10] Herbert Gans, "Deciding What's News: Story Suitability," *Society* 16, no. 3 (1979).

[11] Chris Paterson and David Domingo, *Making Online News: The Ethnography of New Media Production*, 2nd ed. (New York: Peter Lang, 2011).

of journalists 'at work' grow ever more problematic."[12] Many news organizations have dispersed or outsourced tasks to different locations and companies. A lot of journalistic work is conducted outside of "brick and mortar" newsrooms by freelance journalists, contractors, and citizen journalists. These spatial and temporal changes in the organization of news work require us to rethink our methodologies.

Interviews are well suited to studying distributed workplaces and transnational industries. In Journalism Studies, they allow researchers to reach a range of actors in different institutional settings and investigate the changing contexts and processes of news production. My research included thirty-seven in-depth interviews with news workers in the United States and New Zealand. My respondents had a range of experiences in the industry working for different types of organizations (commercial, public, and nonprofit) and in different media (newswire, print, television, radio, and online). Many also had experience as freelancers. Including such a broad range of perspectives led to some difficulties in delimiting the size of the study, but it also meant that I could account for complexity and variation in the news industry. In addition to exploring diverse qualitative experiences, I situated journalists' experiences within more structural changes related to technologies, markets, and national cultures.

A methodological concern for my research was how to navigate the relationship between journalists' experiences and agency, and the political economic structures that shape their industry. I used the scholarship on **digital labor** to frame my research questions and theorize my findings. Issues of digital labor are significant for journalism, the cultural industries, and the work we do in the Digital Humanities. Digital labor requires new skills and forefronts the "information content" of commodities.[13] These changing forms of production include new contexts for work and have resulted in precariousness for creative workers.[14] Recently, ambitious studies have used interviews to study digital labor. Through

---

[12] Ibid., 153.

[13] Maurizio Lazzarato, "Immaterial Labor," in *Radical Thought in Italy: A Potential Politics*, ed. Paolo Virno and Michael Hardy (London, UK: Routledge, 1996).

[14] Nick Dyer-Witheford, *Cyber Proletariat: Global Labour in the Digital Vortex* (Chicago, IL: University of Chicago Press, 2015); Trebor Scholz, *Digital Labor: The Internet as Playground and Factory* (Florence: Taylor & Francis, 2012); and Michael Hardt and Antonio Negri, *Multitude* (New York, NY: Penguin, 2004).

extensive interviews with European workers, Bettina-Johanna Krings, et al. (2009) find many digital laborers are working harder to meet tighter deadlines and working longer hours to keep up with demands.[15] Digital Humanities researchers should be sensitive to labor issues, not just in their area of study, but the work of others who contribute to their research including programmers, designers, IT specialists, lab technicians, librarians, archivist, and others who make Digital Humanities projects possible. Research tends to be the shared accomplishment of a range of actors.[16]

PROCEDURE

Interview procedures and tools differ depending on each researcher's goals and the population being studied. But, all interviewers will likely undertake research design, recruit interviewees, conduct interviews, analyze their data, and write up or otherwise present their findings. If the researcher adopts a grounded theory approach, then these components of the research process will overlap and intertwine. To illustrate the different procedures involved in interviewing, I draw examples and insights from my own research on digital journalism. The majority of my thirty-seven interviews were conducted via internet video services, but I also conducted some via phone and in-person. I analyzed the transcripts on a rolling basis and supplemented interviews with the analysis of industry statistics and reports.

Research Design

Before initiating research design, it is necessary to have a strong understanding about the topic of study and what has already been written about the topic. This requires the researcher to describe the topic and define its key features and context. Based on the research area and prior reading, it is possible to develop original and answerable research

---

[15] Bettina-Johanna Krings, Linda Nierling, Marcello Pedaci, and Mariangela Piersanti, *Working Time, Gender and Work-Life Balance* (Katholieke Universiteit Leuven, Higher Institute of Labour Studies, 2009), 37, http://www.itas.kit.edu/pub/m/2009/krua09a_contents.htm.

[16] Noortje Marres, "The Redistribution of Methods: On Intervention in Digital Social Research, Broadly Conceived," *Sociological Review* 60, no. 1 (2012): 140.

questions. I read widely in at least two large areas of scholarship before embarking on my interview research: Journalism Studies and the Political Economy of Digital Media. I was interested in differences between large and small national news markets and mixtures of public and commercial media, so I selected the United States and New Zealand as national case studies. While my interests lay in the economic and technological changes that were taking place in the news industry, I did not want to look at industry data and make sweeping claims. I wanted to learn about how journalists experience these changes and how they transform their daily work processes. As such, I posed the following questions:

Research Question:

1. How are journalists in New Zealand and the United States experiencing the economic and technological changes that shape their work?

Subquestions:

a. What are the trends impacting news production and how do they differ between the United States and New Zealand?
b. How are changing editorial policies and forms of employment shaping digital news production?
c. How are journalists trying to maintain control over their work and improve their working conditions?

My research questions shifted a little over the course of the research as my participants helped me refine the project. I decided that interviews were the most effective method for answering these questions, but I also knew that they would not suffice. I needed to analyze industry reports, professional publications, employment statistics, government regulations, and pay close attention to news sources about the rapidly changing state of the media in both countries. My questions also determined the populations from which I recruited participants and the interview questions I asked. I discuss these elements in more detail below, but it is important to create and document these questions during research design.

Developing and documenting your research questions, procedures, and recruitment material is often a requirement for getting permission to conduct research. If you are conducting research as a university student or staff member then it is likely that you will need to gain institutional approval before beginning interviews. Permission is usually granted by ethics committees: in the United States these are called Institutional Review Boards (IRB) and New Zealand has Institutional Ethics Committees (IEC). My institution required that I submit a description of the project, an explanation of how I would minimize any risks to my participants, my recruitment material, and interview questions. Templates for gaining informed consent from your participants are available online and through research institutions. While ethical concerns may arise throughout research, it is important to prepare for them during the design phase. Ethical issues in online research can include challenges identifying participants' identities and navigating the differences between public and private information online.[17] The researcher should have documentation ready before beginning recruitment, and consent and ethics should be ongoing concerns.

Recruitment

Your research questions will determine who you need to interview, but you will also need to consider issues of access. For instance, are people in your population likely to take the time to speak with you? Can you ensure, with a reasonable degree of certainty, that the interviews will not subject you or your interviewees to undue risks? Digital communication tools entail a number of benefits for researchers looking to recruit interviewees, but also require researchers to consider new procedural and ethical issues. I recruited participants using publicly listed email addresses on news websites, emailed staff from journalists' organizations and unions, posted notifications in relevant social media groups, and asked interviewees for referrals. All of these methods yielded participants. I developed slightly different recruitment material for each country, different organizations, and personalized emails.

Ted Palys and Chris Atchison note that "modern network technology and communications are designed explicitly for the rapid transmission of information among and between members of distinct social networks."[18] Network sampling techniques using digital media are useful

---

[17] Deakin and Wakefield, "Skype Interviewing."

[18] Ted Palys and Chris Atchison, "Qualitative Research in the Digital Era: Obstacles and Opportunities," *International Journal of Qualitative Methods* 11, no. 4 (2012): 352–367.

for recruiting participants even among marginalized, stigmatized, or isolated people. In online social networks, participants can vouch for the researcher and the project to help recruit others and prospective participants will also appraise the project by investigating your online profile, past work, and communicating with one another.

Using the grounded theory approach means that recruitment is an ongoing process that will likely only be completed when you decide that your data is rich and varied enough to sufficiently answer your questions. I used a type of **purposeful sampling** called **maximum variation sampling**. That is, I intentionally recruited journalists from each country with different amounts of experience in the industry who worked for different types of organizations and media, and in a variety of work arrangements. When I had spoken to a number of similar participants (for instance, journalists working full-time at New Zealand radio organizations), I directed my recruitment efforts elsewhere. Transcribing and analyzing interviews throughout the research process helped me to determine which types of journalists I still needed to speak with. I concluded recruitment of interviewees in New Zealand and the United States when my research questions had been thoroughly addressed and interviews ceased to contribute significantly new data. Strauss and Corbin term this **saturation**.[19] I decided that I had reached saturation after thirty-seven in-depth interviews.

Interview Questions

Interview questions are designed to elicit answers to your central research questions. However, they need to be far more concrete, avoiding any theoretical abstractions or specialist concepts. For instance, my central question about how journalists are experiencing changes in their industry is broken into prompts for journalists to talk about their work and some of the issues they face:

- Can you take me through the process of researching and publishing a story from start to end? You can describe a specific story that you see as representative or discuss the general process.
- What are the main professional concerns that you and your colleagues discuss?

[19] Strauss and Corbin, *Basics of Qualitative Research*, 158.

The first question asks journalists to provide a narrative account in their area of expertise and allows me to ask for further explanation. The second does not prejudge which concerns are most prescient for my participants and allows them to draw on past experiences and conversations. It is good practice to have an experienced researcher read and comment on your questions. You may also be able to try out the questions in a pilot study. My pilot interviews included two informal interviews with journalists that I knew personally. I asked them to tell me if my questions were difficult or unanswerable, so I could edit them before conducting more formal interviews. My initial **interview schedule** included eleven questions and some possible subquestions. My interviews were semi-structured, so my questions changed depending on the stage of the project and whom I was speaking with. Sometimes they even changed during the interview. The interviews ran from 45 minutes to almost two hours depending on the time and detail that interviewees were willing to provide.

Conducting Interviews

This section describes how the process of conducting interviews is shaped by the use of online audio/video link-up services. Participants who are recruited online are likely to have an account or have the ability to create one. Free audio/video link-up applications that use the Voice over Internet Protocol (VoIP) such as Skype, FaceTime, and Google Hangouts are well suited for remote interviewing and their growing popularity increases this utility. Many universities pay for subscriptions to video calling software, which may have better quality connections and more functionality for group video conferencing or recording. Either way, researchers should be aware of the terms of use for the services they employ and investigate issues related to data security. These technologies are a cost-effective tool to bolster existing qualitative methods and facilitate new types of research.

Online video services reduce some of the logistical concerns related to face-to-face interviews, but instantiate new technical issues. Researchers should do everything possible to secure a high quality, sustained connection, and minimize disruptions.[20] Audio quality can impact the transcription process and is particularly important if you plan to archive or share

---

[20]Weller, "Using Internet Video Calls in Qualitative (Longitudinal) Interviews," 8.

the audio files. During my interviews, audio problems required me to ask some participants to repeat or explain points that were initially inaudible. The researcher should also prepare an appropriate space in which to conduct the interview and be prepared with their questions, a notebook and pen, and the recording software or hardware primed, before the scheduled start of the interview. Inevitably, issues will arise. For instance, I scheduled one interview on a Saturday morning after difficulties finding a time when the participant was available. The interviewee was taking care of two grandchildren while trying to respond to my questions. Unfortunately, the resulting data was disjointed and sprawling. Creating an appropriate environment for the interview reduces some of these obstacles.

The process of establishing rapport in an online interview can differ from in-person situations. It begins in advance of the interview through email exchanges, allowing for questions about the process, or sharing your online profile. Suzie Weller (2017) observes that supportive interchanges at the beginning and closing of online interviews may include a quick discussion about the quality of the connection and the framing of the video in addition to the usual greetings and informal discussion. There are some impediments to building rapport in video interviews. For example, eye contact can be difficult to maintain because of the position of the screen and camera, and audio delays can lead to confusion. However, mediated communication can be experienced as less daunting or formal and reduce the "pressure of presence."[21] My participants opened up about their work lives; one participant, in particular, described her experiences in male-dominated rural newsrooms and the precarity of her current editing job. As such, I organized a follow-up interview toward the end of my study to enquire about her ongoing concerns and recent changes. There is no reason why digital interviews should be more detached, formal, or limited than their offline counterparts.

Transcription and Coding

The affordances of CAQDAS are increasingly making coding a multimedia and collaborative process. Yet, there are still problems and limitations with proprietary software. Before transferring their data to a

---

[21] Ibid., 11.

CAQDAS platform and **coding**, most interviewers transcribe their inter-views. Transcription can be the most labor-intensive part of interview research, and one hour of an interview normally requires 4 to 6 hours to transcribe. Palys and Atchison note that transcription software is now available to speed-up the process, including: Dragon Naturallyspeaking (DNS), IBM ViaVoice, MacSpeech, Microsoft Windows Speech Recognition, Philips SpeechMagic, Sphinx, and VoxForge.[22] In addition, CAQDAS such as NVivo now have options to upload and code audio and visual files. Researchers are developing ways to effectively code with-out transcribing entire interviews.

Coding is the procedure for identifying concepts and relationships in data, which can then be organized into categories and theory. During coding, data are broken into constituent parts: key terms or phrases that relate to opinions, actions, processes, objects, or events.[23] These instances are grouped into categories, and researchers create definitions to ensure consistency and aid in collaborative work. Irena Medjedovic and Andreas Witzel (2008) propose that qualitative researchers begin sharing data with codes and category schemes to make the process more transparent and to facilitate secondary analyses.[24] This is an area where Digital Humanities approaches to archiving and sharing data can extend and transform traditional qualitative research. Open source software solutions may be required to share coded data among research communities and facilitate rich and interactive archives.

Coding occupies an intermediary position between raw data and theory. For instance, I found that the term "engagement" was used by journalists during my interviews to describe their actions and interactions with online audiences. I then adopted engagement as a concept for understanding how journalists interpret and place limits on changes in their work. I placed discussions of engagement within the context of structural relations, such as the relationship between journalists and audiences, and critical theories of labor and digital media.[25] Researchers

---

[22] Palys and Atchison, "Qualitative Research in the Digital Era."

[23] Strauss and Corbin, *Basics of Qualitative Research*, 68.

[24] Irena Medjedovic and Andreas Witzel, "Secondary Analysis of Interviews: Using Codes and Theoretical Concepts from the Primary Study," *Historical Social Research* 33, no. 3 (2008).

[25] Tai Neilson, "'I Don't Engage': Online Communication and Social Media Use among New Zealand Journalists," *Journalism* 19, no. 4 (2018): 536–552.

using the grounded theory approach may work both **deductively** and **inductively**. In this case, I worked inductively by grouping qualitative instances together to reduce some of the complexity of raw data and provide a framework for understanding similar occurrences. In contrast, working deductively means using concepts established by other researchers to understand instances in your data. Integrating both of these approaches, researchers can move back and forth between raw data, coding, and evolving theoretical concepts.[26] Hence, the processes of coding, theorizing, and writing up should overlap. Further, Digital Humanities approaches include archiving and circulating research products that result from each of these processes.

THEORIZING AND "WRITING UP"

Digital Humanities scholars are experimenting with new venues and methods for presenting research. Terry Flew (2008) argues that digital media challenges the structural breaks between producers and consumers, design and critique. He observes, the "critique of existing systems happens through design such as open source software, open publishing, citizen journalism and participatory media systems."[27] In the Digital Humanities, for example, practitioners who have identified gaps in access to historical records and literary sources build and host public archives (see Rissam in this volume), and those focusing on interactivity and performance have constructed alternative ways to explore research findings (see Hunter in this volume). Making cultural objects available to a wider public or to other researchers is a commendable pursuit. Nonetheless, I believe it is necessary for digital humanists to pose and answer explicit research questions and theorize their practices (for more on the roles of "making" and "interpreting" in the Digital Humanities see Matthew Gold's excellent edited volume *Debates in the Digital Humanities*). In this section, I present findings from my research and indicate ways that scholars using digital interviews may choose to present their own work.

My interview, research, and findings are organized around my set of thesis questions. Foremost, I set out to ask how journalists in New Zealand and the United States are experiencing the economic and

---

[26] Strauss and Corbin, *Basics of Qualitative Research*, 46.

[27] Terry Flew, *New Media: An Introduction*, 3rd ed. (Melbourne: Oxford University Press, 2008), 41.

technological changes that shape their work. I broke this question into its constituent parts related to (1) differences between my national case studies, (2) changes in news production processes and journalists' professional concerns, and (3) how journalists are imposing some control over their work. My findings do not attempt to derive direct causal relationships; for instance, I do not argue that changes in journalism are the result of new technologies. Rather, I find a number of factors that interviewees discuss in different combinations and consider how they come together to shape the context of news production and journalists' experiences. Similarly, Strauss and Corbin suggest that the result of qualitative research "is much more likely to be a discussion that takes readers along a complex path of interrelationships, each in its own patterned way, that explains what is going on."[28]

Conducting digital interviews with New Zealand and US news workers allowed me to establish differences in the experiences of interviewees between and within each country. Comparisons between the media systems of New Zealand and the United States required additional political economic research because the two national media systems are characterized by differences in market sizes, media policies, and political cultures. In New Zealand, publicly owned broadcast and digital media has a large role, while in the United States nonprofit news media play a supportive role in an otherwise highly commercialized news industry. News production and circulation is increasingly globalized as media corporations, technologies, and content traverse political and cultural boundaries. As such, journalists in both countries shared concerns about redundancies, the quality of news media, shrinking budgets, and media consolidation. The affordances of digital interviewing allowed me to make comparisons between the two national case studies.

I identified two prominent ways that journalists describe changes in their work processes and categorized these as "extension" and "intensification." These concepts are present in other labor scholarship, which allowed me to consider how my data can and cannot be explained by existing theory. First, journalists discuss needing to be "always on" or to "work until the job is done." The gross extension of working hours, facilitated by technology, can be subsumed under Karl Marx's concept

---

[28] Strauss and Corbin, *Basics of Qualitative Research*, 130.

of absolute surplus value extraction.[29] Journalists' work is also extended qualitatively, in ways that blur distinctions between news and marketing, work and leisure. Here, scholarship in the critical Digital Humanities including Trebor Scholz's work on digital labor is instructive. Second, journalists described ways that their work is intensified through managerial directives, online publishing deadlines, and **content management systems** that standardize and streamline work processes. Myriad commentators argue that the value of immediacy in digital journalism is detrimental to the quality and accuracy of news.[30] My interviews provide a detailed account of how immediacy is operationalized by news organizations and demonstrate how journalists experience and react to these demands.

Critical approaches to Digital Humanities should be directed toward challenging unequal power relations. I found that journalists in both countries are trying to impose control over their work processes and conditions through unions. In addition to unions at legacy media organizations, unionization votes in digital newsrooms are a small, but significant, development in labor relations. Drawing on my interview data, I provide concrete steps toward securing better conditions for news production. One such step is the creation of publicly available guidelines for online engagement. More broadly, I argue that labor activism must address the identities and interests of professional journalists and connect their campaigns to other digital laborers and audiences.

Digital Humanities scholars have a range of options for how to present or publish research. Some interviewers archive their data to facilitate secondary research or to provide pedagogical resources. Louise Corti, Andreas Witzel, and Libby Bishop (2005) are strong proponents for archiving and sharing qualitative data, including interviews, for the purposes of secondary analysis.[31] That is, so that researchers can pose different questions in the analysis of existing qualitative data sets. Contributors

---

[29] Karl Marx, *Capital: A Critique of Political Economy* (London: Penguin, 1976).

[30] Megan Le Masurier, "Slow Journalism," *Journalism Practice* 10, no. 4 (2016): 439–447; Neil Thurman and Anna Walters, "Live Blogging–Digital Journalism's Pivotal Platform?" *Digital Journalism* 1, no. 1 (2013); and Alfred Hermida, "Twittering the News: The Emergence of Ambient Journalism," *Journalism Practice* 4, no. 3 (2010).

[31] Louise Corti, Andreas Witzel, and Libby Bishop, "On the Potentials and Problems of Secondary Analysis. An Introduction to the FQS Special Issue on Secondary Analysis of Qualitative Data," *Forum: Qualitative Social Research* 6, no. 1 (2005).

to their special journal edition propose ways of anonymizing interviews for secondary analysis, using open source CAQDAS to share coding, and creating searchable qualitative data archives. For instance, Harry Van den Berg (2005) developed a large interdisciplinary project to rea-nalyze interview data from different theoretical and methodological per-spectives. In addition to these approaches to secondary analysis, digital humanists can publish interview data as a pedagogical resource.[32] Ping-Chun Hsiung (2016) created an interactive archive and guide using a selection of her interview transcripts to teach qualitative research meth-ods. Her courseware, called "Lives & Legacies: A Guide to Qualitative Interviewing," includes 39 interview transcripts and even some of her coding to emphasize that "there is no singular 'right' way of coding."[33] The project emphasizes pedagogical principles that challenge linear con-ceptions of qualitative research, promote hands-on learning, demystify research processes, and destigmatize mistakes. These cases incorporate Digital Humanities approaches to sharing and presenting data, while posing explicit research questions and theorizing the process.

Conclusion

Inherent in my approach are two of my hopes for the future direction of the Digital Humanities. First, digital humanists can pose specific ques-tions and theorize their work to integrate making and critique, practice and theory.[34] Second, Digital Humanities approaches need a reflex-ive approach to labor in the topics we study and the research process itself. Interviewers can produce new types of data and research outputs. Nonetheless, these new opportunities should not come at the expense of rigor or critical analysis. Digital Humanities projects often set out to archive or represent historical or artistic content without posing or answering specific research questions. Making cultural objects availa-ble to a wider public or to other researchers is a commendable pursuit.

[32] Harry Van Den Berg, "Reanalyzing Qualitative Interviews from Different Angles: The Risk of Decontextualization and Other Problems of Sharing Qualitative Data," *Forum: Qualitative Social Research* 6, no. 1 (2005).

[33] Ping-Chun Hsiung, "Lives & Legacies: A Digital Courseware for the Teaching and Learning of Qualitative Interviewing," *Qualitative Inquiry* 22, no. 2 (2016): 135.

[34] Fitzpatrick in *Debates in the Digital Humanities*, ed. Matthew Gold (Minneapolis: University of Minnesota Press, 2012): 13.

However, critical research is also a process of probing difficult theoretical and practical issues. This requires explicit research questions that are embedded in existing theories and critical practices. It also means that digital humanists need to engage with the vast array of critical theories that are already available among the humanities.

Digital media are facilitating the transformation of industries such as journalism, the lives of many of our research participants, and our own work. I found that journalists are experiencing the extension and intensification of their work. We can extend this emphasis on technology and labor to understand changes taking place in universities and research institutions. Digital technologies enable us to engage new participants and audiences, but they are also accompanied by expectations that researchers curate online profiles and self-monitor the reach or impact of our work. Hence, we may reflect on how we, as humanities researchers, experience new technologies and economic changes, and how we maintain control over our work processes and conditions.

REFERENCES

Broom, Alex, Lynda Cheshire, and Michael Emmison. "Qualitative Researchers' Understandings of Their Practice and the Implications for Data Archiving and Sharing." *Sociology* 43, no. 6 (2009): 1163–180.

Corti, Louise, Andreas Witzel, and Libby Bishop. "On the Potentials and Problems of Secondary Analysis. An Introduction to the FQS Special Issue on Secondary Analysis of Qualitative Data." *Forum: Qualitative Social Research* 6, no. 1 (2005): 1–7.

Deakin, Hannah, and Kelly Wakefield. "Skype Interviewing: Reflections of Two PhD Researchers." *Qualitative Research* 14, no. 5 (2014): 603–616.

Dyer-Witheford, Nick. *Cyber Proletariat: Global Labour in the Digital Vortex*. Chicago, IL: University of Chicago Press, 2015.

Flew, Terry. *New Media: An Introduction*. 3rd ed. Melbourne: Oxford University Press, 2008.

Gans, Herbert. "Deciding What's News: Story Suitability." *Society* 16, no. 3 (1979): 65–77.

Gold, Matthew K. *Debates in the Digital Humanities*. Minneapolis: University of Minnesota Press, 2012.

Hardt, Michael, and Antonio Negri. *Multitude*. New York, NY: Penguin, 2004.

Hay-Gibson, Naomi. "Interviews via VoIP: Benefits and Disadvantages Within a PhD Study of SMEs." *Library and Information Research* 33, no. 105 (2009): 39–50.

Hermida, Alfred. "Twittering the News: The Emergence of Ambient Journalism." *Journalism Practice* 4, no. 3 (2010): 297–308.

Hsiung, Ping-Chun. "Lives & Legacies: A Digital Courseware for the Teaching and Learning of Qualitative Interviewing." *Qualitative Inquiry* 22, no. 2 (2016): 132–139.

Katz, Elihu, and Paul Lazarsfeld. *Personal Influence: The Part Played by People in the Flow of Mass Communications.* New York, NY: Free Press, 1955.

Krings, Bettina-Johanna, Linda Nierling, Marcello Pedaci, and Mariangela Piersanti. *Working Time, Gender and Work-Life Balance.* Katholieke Universiteit Leuven, Higher Institute of Labour Studies, 2009. http://www.itas.kit.edu/pub/m/2009/krua09a_contents.htm.

Lazzarato, Maurizio. "Immaterial Labor." In *Radical Thought in Italy: A Potential Politics,* edited by Paolo Virno and Michael Hardy, 132–146. London, UK: Routledge, 1996.

Le Masurier, Megan. "Slow Journalism." *Journalism Practice* 10, no. 4 (2016): 439–437.

Lindlof, Thomas, and Bryan Taylor. *Qualitative Communication Research Methods.* 3rd ed. Thousand Oaks, CA: Sage, 2011.

Lunt, Peter, and Sonia Livingstone. "Rethinking the Focus Group in Media and Communications Research." *Journal of Communication* 46, no. 2 (1996): 79–98.

Marres, Noortje. "The Redistribution of Methods: On Intervention in Digital Social Research, Broadly Conceived." *Sociological Review* 60, no. 1 (2012): 139–165.

Marx, Karl. *Capital: A Critique of Political Economy.* London: Penguin, 1976.

Medjedovic, Irena, and Andreas Witzel. "Secondary Analysis of Interviews: Using Codes and Theoretical Concepts from the Primary Study." *Historical Social Research* 33, no. 3 (2008): 148–178.

Neilson, Tai. "'I Don't Engage': Online Communication and Social Media Use Among New Zealand Journalists." *Journalism* 19, no. 4 (2018): 536–552.

Palys, Ted, and Chris Atchison. "Qualitative Research in the Digital Era: Obstacles and Opportunities." *International Journal of Qualitative Methods* 11, no. 4 (2012): 352–367.

Paterson, Chris A., and David Domingo. *Making Online News: The Ethnography of New Media Production.* 2nd ed. New York: Peter Lang, 2011.

Rakow, Lana F. "Commentary: Interviews and Focus Groups as Critical and Cultural Methods." *Journalism & Mass Communication Quarterly* 88, no. 2 (2011): 416–428.

Scholz, Trebor. *Digital Labor: The Internet as Playground and Factory.* Florence: Taylor & Francis, 2012.

Seitz, Sally. "Pixilated Partnerships, Overcoming Obstacles in Qualitative Interviews via Skype: A Research Note." *Qualitative Research* 16, no. 2 (2015): 229–235.

Strauss, Anselm, and Juliet Corbin. *Basics of Qualitative Research: Techniques and Procedures for Developing Grounded Theory.* 2nd ed. Thousand Oaks: Sage, 1998.

Thurman, Neil, and Anna Walters. "Live Blogging–Digital Journalism's Pivotal Platform?" *Digital Journalism* 1, no. 1 (2013): 82–101.

Tuchman, Gaye. *Making News: A Study in the Construction of Reality.* New York: Free Press, 1978.

Van Den Berg, Harry. "Reanalyzing Qualitative Interviews from Different Angles: The Risk of Decontextualization and Other Problems of Sharing Qualitative Data." *Forum: Qualitative Social Research* 6, no. 1 (2005).

Weller, Susie. "Using Internet Video Calls in Qualitative (Longitudinal) Interviews: Some Implications for Rapport." *International Journal of Social Research Methodology* 20, no. 6 (2017): 1–13.

CHAPTER 10

Building Video Game Adaptations of Dramatic and Literary Texts

E. B. Hunter

This chapter offers a method for adapting a dramatic or literary source into a short video game. Building a video game adaptation of a dramatic or literary text reflects a growing interest in practice-led humanities research, especially within the field of theatre studies. This method also demonstrates how Digital Humanities research can move beyond documentation and preservation to open up critical possibilities for the humanities through making as an **epistemology**. Making a video game adaptation of a play or other literary text is an example of what design and **pervasive computing** scholar Matt Ratto calls "critical making."[1] In a critical making project, the site of knowledge creation is the *process* in conversation with a discipline's scholarly research. The following sections explain how adapting a source text into a video game can allow a

---

[1] Matt Ratto, "Critical Making: Conceptual and Material Studies in Technology and Social Life," *Information Society* 27, no. 4 (2011): 252–260, https://doi.org/10.1080/01972243.2011.583819.

E. B. Hunter (✉)
Northwestern University, Evanston, IL, USA
e-mail: ebh@fabulab.us

© The Author(s) 2018
l. levenberg et al. (eds.), *Research Methods for the Digital Humanities*,
https://doi.org/10.1007/978-3-319-96713-4_10

researcher to illuminate themes, character insights, or plot elements with new emphasis. As an example, I use *Something Wicked*, a video game adaptation of William Shakespeare's gory, witchy tragedy, *Macbeth*. The game was built by Fabula(b), the theatre and computer science lab I started at Northwestern University, and it enacts an epic battle described in Act 1, Scene 2 of *Macbeth*.

When incorporated into a classroom setting, this research method aligns with an approach known in learning sciences as a **constructionist pedagogy**.[2] In this chapter, I describe a constructionist approach whereby individuals or teams make a video game as a complement to traditional humanities research. In addition to thinking through a text by adapting it into a video game, users of this methodology can create projects for public use. Particularly in a classroom setting, this potential public impact can create a sense of investment and encourage researchers to exert more effort and engage in a more substantive analytical interrogation than they might when writing a traditional research paper disconnected from a practical application. Educators and artists have long held the belief that people learn more when they are emotionally invested in a subject; this connection has recently been supported by neuroscience research.[3]

This method could be conducted using a range of game genres and authoring tools; as such, the steps below are not intended as a comprehensive list of tools and technologies. Instead, I focus on the process of thinking about a source text by using the actions, decisions, and rules that characterize the video game medium. Although I provide examples from *Something Wicked*, which is a combat, 2D side-scroller, the method described herein could work for any game genre. The steps below address readers who may not have significant game-building, technological, or learning sciences experience.

---

[2] Seymour Papert, *Mindstorms: Children, Computers, and Powerful Ideas* (New York: Basic Books, 1980).

[3] Jessica Lahey, "To Help Students Learn, Engage the Emotions," *New York Times*, http://well.blogs.nytimes.com/2016/05/04/to-help-students-learn-engage-the-emotions; Helen Immordino-Yang, *Emotions, Learning, and the Brain: Exploring the Educational Implications of Affective Neuroscience* (New York: W. W. Norton & Company, 2016).

As a result, video game specialists may find some of my descriptions broad. This chapter concludes with a short reading list for those interested in a more specialized exploration of the theoretical and practical dimensions of video **game design**.

ORIGINS

The method of adapting a dramatic or literary text into a video game derives from my theatrical work directing site-specific productions of Shakespeare's plays at Sloss Furnaces National Historic Landmark, a restored blast furnace in Birmingham, Alabama. My company staged **"walking showcases,"** which were composed of short Shakespearean scenes set in unusual locations, such as the site's underground tunnels and cavernous machine rooms. Lifting these familiar scenes out of the context of a full play and out of traditional theatrical architecture opened up space for more robust audience participation. At the blast furnace, patrons hissed at Richard III, gave up their drinks to Puck, and even spontaneously charged down the 50-yard Sloss cart path after Henry V, shouting "England, Harry, and Saint George!" Audience members regularly commented that they had never understood Shakespeare so well, they did not realize the plays were so fun, and they felt like they were part of the story. Post-show conversations often engaged deeply with the text.

Live theatre does not scale, so I began using the medium of video games to approximate some of the outcomes I noticed in the walking showcases—namely, increased **comprehension, critical thinking**, and **affinity**—in a format scalable to a broader public. Because much of my directorial experience is in staging Shakespeare's plays, and because his plays are in the public domain, I began with an adaptation of a scene from *Macbeth*. This adaptation, *Something Wicked*, has been successful as a research project in two important ways: (1) early informal feedback shows that players' affinity and comprehension increase through playing the game, and (2) the design and building process demanded I analyze a text I already knew quite well with a very different strategy. *Something Wicked* led to the formation of Fabula(b), where I lead a team to use emerging interactive technologies—like video games—to think digitally about dramatic and literary works. The method below provides a step-by-step guide to using this approach. It is important to note that, while the technological elements of my lab's projects are engineered by paid professionals,[4] industry-grade production values are not requisite for adapting a play or literary text into a video game.

ETHICAL ISSUES

Building a video game with limited resources raises basic copyright issues for digital content. Teams should familiarize themselves with attribution, fair use, and other applicable laws for non-original digital assets they find online, many of which will not be royalty-free. This project also raises questions of design ethics. Like all design, digital technology is not neutral. As an example, consider the cautionary tale of a 2016 online beauty pageant, Beauty.AI. Billed by its creators as an attempt to arrive at a technologically determined, "impartial perception"[5] of beauty, the competition's judge was **artificial intelligence** (AI). AI uses **algorithms**— sets of instructions or rules, written in computer code—to "teach" a machine to quickly evaluate a number of parameters. After thousands of photo submissions from the public, the "impartial" AI robot selected winners who were almost all light-skinned people. Far from an "impartial perception," this result happened because the engineers programmed the algorithms with a data set that included only a few photographs of dark-skinned people.[6] Thanks to its algorithms, the Beauty.AI robot quickly "learned" to reject dark-skinned faces. I include the Beauty.AI lesson to emphasize that *people* designed the algorithms that powered the contest robot. Robots do not impartially judge *anything*. Whether researchers

---

[4] *Something Wicked*, the lab's first project, was made possible by a crowdfunding campaign. Crowdfunding campaigns are complex and time-consuming, and beyond the scope of this chapter. Any teams considering crowdfunding should research the process thoroughly. Major sites like Indiegogo and Kickstarter offer suggestions and tutorials, and alternatives to these sites crop up frequently.

[5] "Beauty.AI Announces the First International Beauty Contest Judged by an Artificial Intelligence Jury," *PRWeb*, November 19, 2015, http://www.prweb.com/releases/2015/11/prweb13088208.htm.

[6] Sam Levin, "A Beauty Contest Was Judged by AI and the Robots Didn't Like Dark Skin," *The Guardian*, September 8, 2016, https://www.theguardian.com/technology/2016/sep/08/artificial-intelligence-beauty-contest-doesnt-like-black-people.

build advanced AI or a simple Twine story,[7] they should consider accessibility, representation, and bias in their design.[8]

WHEN TO USE THIS METHOD

Adapting a literary or dramatic source into a video game encourages interdisciplinary research questions that are largely qualitative, thereby providing an effective way to promote critical engagement with a source text. Users do not need any prior experience with digital platforms—as the guide below demonstrates, this method foregrounds the process of thinking about a source in terms of decisions and player engagement, not technological specifications. Similarly, this project does not require specialized technology beyond internet access and a computer or smartphone. As Step 5 notes, many free or low-cost entry-level game creation tools already exist. In a classroom, this method could serve as an alternative to the traditional research paper, because it generates a complex demonstrable outcome with usability outside the class.

Game builders might ask: "what arguments does my video game make about the themes, plot points, or rule systems in my source text?" *Something Wicked*, for example, argues that Macbeth lives in a world where backstabbing and violence are rewarded. The game makes this argument by setting up rules that reward players for stabbing enemies in the back and penalize players for not killing enough enemies.

Instructors using the method might ask: "does the constructionist approach of building a videogame adaptation enhance students' ability to closely read and critically analyze a source text?" Having assigned myself the task of building a *Macbeth* adaptation, I can confirm my own knowledge of the play increased considerably. Even more exciting, however, is that *Something Wicked* players report combing through Act 1, Scene 2 to see if they can figure out how the game turns the dialogue's imagery into mechanics.

---

[7]Twine is a free, online, and easy-to-use tool for nonlinear storytelling. Links to Twine and other game-building tools appear at the end of the chapter.

[8]"The Bias Blind Spot and Unconscious Bias in Design," *The Interaction Design Foundation*, accessed October 3, 2017, https://www.interaction-design.org/literature/article/the-bias-blind-spot-and-unconscious-bias-in-design.

While this method also works well for nondramatic literary text, it is of particular relevance for plays, because the leap from traditional literary to dramatic analysis can be challenging. For plays, building a video game adaptation foregrounds the distinctions between these two modes of qualitative analysis—video games, like plays, are spatiotemporal arguments. "Thinking with" a video game adaptation foregrounds research questions about dramatic elements like timing, bodily presence, and production choices embedded in dialogue. Creating a classroom-use guide for each game with an accompanying bibliography would also allow users to generate secondary source research activity.

The timeline for this method requires at least several weeks. Building even a short game can be a considerable undertaking, especially for teams new to the process. However, teams with a compressed timeline could follow the step-by-step guide to write a game proposal instead of building a working prototype. Similarly, builders without access to digital technology might create a paper-based game adaptation. Creating a non-digital or even hypothetical version of a game-like adaptation can encourage substantive critical analysis.

STEP-BY-STEP GUIDE

This step-by-step guide is addressed directly to the researcher(s) building the game. As with any recipe, read the entire guide before starting the first step.

Step 1: Write a Beat Sheet

Video games are action. In this regard, they are similar to screenplays, and screenplays should only include descriptions of what can be filmed. A director cannot film "the clown was sad," because this description contains no actions. But a director can film "the clown wept so loudly that a flock of birds fled from the nearby tree" and then three lines of dialogue. However, unlike a screenplay, video games are also a set of possible decisions—should I pick up the red pill or the blue pill in *The Matrix: Path of Neo*? Should I shoot this Big Daddy in *BioShock* or run from it? Whether the team decides to build a first-person shooter or a text-based journey, basing a game's mechanics on the decisions that are in the source text itself will give the adaptation authenticity. These decisions reflect the values of the characters making them and the ethos of the larger **story-world**. Distilling the source text into a list of plot points—its **beat sheet**, to borrow another film business term—will clarify these moments of action and decision.

To make the beat sheet, reread the source and list every point in the narrative where a decision happens that influences the action of the overall narrative.[9] It is also helpful to include the reason for each decision, with a line or a page number from the source text to support each claim. Make a beat sheet for the entire source, not just the section to be adapted—there may be important decisions late in the source narrative that should inform the game. Depending on how long the source is, it might be more efficient to cover only the major plot points, but this document should encompass the entire narrative.

How We Did It

For *Something Wicked*, this document was especially important because not everyone on the team was familiar with Shakespeare's language. The complexity of Shakespeare's language can obscure simple moments of action and decision. I found the process of translating *Macbeth* into decisions a new way of engaging with the text. For example, in Act 1, Scene 7, Macbeth changes his mind and does not want to kill Duncan. However, after Lady Macbeth harangues him, he reverses his decision. Digging into the text to sort out which lines reveal the reasons behind his changes of mind gave the team a much clearer picture of the actions that incentivize Macbeth. I would argue that these lines show that Macbeth does not have a moment of virtue—he just does not want to get caught. Once Lady Macbeth convinces him they will not get caught, he is back to being pro-regicide.

To emphasize this dimension of Macbeth's character by using the tools of a video game, we interpreted "not wanting to get caught" as "sneakiness," and brainstormed the actions people in the violent world of a medieval Scottish battlefield might take to demonstrate sneakiness. Thus was born the game mechanic of backstabbing. We made backstabbing more desirable than a front attack by attaching more "rage"

---

[9]David Ball, *Backwards and Forwards: A Technical Manual for Reading Plays* (Carbondale and Edwardsville: Southern Illinois University Press, 1983).

points to a backstab attack. We also gave players a "rage superhit" that activated a smoking sword once enough rage points had been accumulated. Is it likely that a player will connect backstabbing directly to Act 1, Scene 7? Probably not, but as we learned from creating the beat sheet, this moment is just one of many plot points where Macbeth demonstrates—through actions and his spoken rationale for his decisions—that he is pretty sneaky. We condensed all those moments from the source text into one potent game mechanic to create an authentic, action-oriented representation (backstabbing) of a larger, important theme in the play (duplicity). This design mechanic derives from moments in the play beyond the one battle we represent. Making a beat sheet for the full source text is time well spent.

Step 2: Identify What the Game Will Illuminate

Because adapting a source into a video game requires substantial effort, the next step is to determine which of the source narrative's plot points and themes the game will illuminate. This design choice sets up the game's central argument. The game makes an argument for the importance of specific plot points/themes by including some elements and excluding others. A fast-paced war or adventure story like *Macbeth* might seem easier to transfer to the video game format, but even a quiet, contemplative source narrative includes action. Even in Samuel Beckett's absurdist play *Waiting for Godot*, things happen because Didi and Gogo *decide* to keep waiting instead of leaving. In essence, stories are a set of things that happen because characters make choices.

How We Did It

With *Something Wicked*, we wanted to illuminate the character and world values established by the battle described in Act 1, Scene 2. Thus, *Something Wicked* argues for the importance of nuances embedded the scene. I have noticed in teaching, directing, and writing about *Macbeth* that this battle description is often confusing to readers, actors, and audience members. But this scene is important—these lines inform audiences that in Macbeth's world, bloody violence is normal. More importantly, these lines tell audiences that even in this bloody world, Macbeth's character is extra violent and it is this extra violent nature that earns him social esteem. If readers or audience members do not catch these nuances before Macbeth shows up on stage, their understanding of the play will be skewed by a twenty-first century value system. Because *Something Wicked* uses an action-heavy, text-minimal design to foreground Act 1, Scene 2's importance, the game also addresses ways in which Shakespeare's complex language contributes to contemporary audiences' difficulties understanding the scene's nuances.

Step 3: Set the Production Timeline

Concepting, building, testing, and releasing a video game, even with experienced programmers like the ones who engineered *Something Wicked* can take a while. Once a set of plot points and themes stand out as the most important elements to include, determine the available production timeline. Figure 10.1 offers a potential 15-week timeline. Adjust the weeks as needed, but keep each step. Some developers build games in "game jams" over a weekend, but these scenarios typically involve designers and programmers well-versed in their chosen technology. Teams new to game building might want a timeline of at least 8–10 weeks. Even if the game is a side project, the accountability of a deadline and a public audience expecting to see the game helps keep production on track. The remaining steps explain the milestones listed in the chart.

How We Did It
The famous Iron Triangle of design dictates that, while clients want every project to be fast, cheap, and good, they can only pick two of these attributes. I wanted higher production values for the game than I could

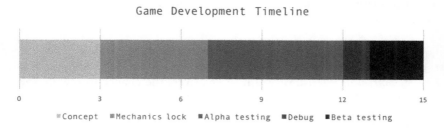

Fig. 10.1   15-week timeline

achieve with my technical expertise. But my timeline was too short to work with coders who might have done the project for free to improve their experience with Unity, the free (but complex) engine many game developers use. Thus, from the Iron Triangle of fast, cheap, and good, I picked fast and good, and ran a **crowdfunding campaign** to fund skilled builders with the computational experience I needed. *Something Wicked* was not part of a class, so our production timeline was longer than a semester, at eight and a half months. However, I needed to show the game at academic conferences and a museum exhibit, so the team still had a hard deadline for finishing.

Step Four: Brainstorm the Design

If the team is new to thinking about video games as digital narrative, spend some time researching games that use the tools of the medium to approach story in different ways. Games like *Blackbar, Heavy Rain, Papers Please, Halo, Undertale, McDonald's Videogame,* and *Curtain* are current examples of ways to manage the relationship between player, decisions, and the unfolding story and/or world values they present. Some of these games deal with violent or upsetting subject matter, so please read their respective content warnings before playing. Do not be intimidated by the slick art and animation of these titles; for this step, the way each game handles story decisions matters more than production values. Deciding on a game's overall design or "high concept" can take a few different paths. Here "design" does not yet include visual aesthetics or sound, which will come later. Keep in mind that every design choice translates into labor for someone on the team, whether in code that has to be programmed, an asset that has to be drawn or recorded, or an animation that has to be rigged. Start with some or all of the questions below.[10]

1. How close will the game stay to the source narrative? Will the game narrative be **railed** in order to follow the source, like *Something Wicked*, or will it offer players the chance to rewrite the story, like *Elsinore*, in which players are Ophelia, trying to prevent *Hamlet's* storyline from happening?

[10] Jesse Schell, *The Art of Game Design: A Book of Lenses* (Amsterdam: Elsevier, 2010).

2. Will players control an **avatar** through the game? If so, which character will it be, and will the game be first- or third-person **perspective?**

3. How will the game integrate text? Through the **interface? Cut-scenes?** A **tutorial?** By using symbols and images to represent ideas described in the text?[11]

4. What does "winning" mean in this game?

5. What are the rules of this storyworld, both in terms of the physical laws of nature and in terms of a value system?

6. What actions should be incentivized, and what **mechanics** will the game include to allow the player to make decisions by following the value system of the source text?

How We Did It:
Something Wicked addressed these questions through a series of design meetings in our early concept weeks:

1. The central design goal for *Something Wicked* was to use a railed narrative to stay close to Shakespeare's text, because the game is a practice-led complement to the theoretical side of my research. In that research, I consider live scenarios like theatre productions, or Disney theme parks, or political rallies. In these scenarios, producers tell the audience two competing things: audience interactivity is vital, but the audience cannot impact the story. So, the audience feels part of the story in a meaningful way that has nothing to do with changing that story. One of the reasons I built *Something Wicked* was to see how this quality operates in a new media environment. The four levels of the game thus follow the story beats of the battle described in Act 1, Scene 2.

2. Another design goal was for players to respond to some of the same world constraints that affect Macbeth, so *Something Wicked's* players control only a Macbeth avatar. Third-person perspective is generally simpler to engineer, and as simpler generally translates to faster and cheaper, it was the design choice that worked best for our parameters.

---

[11] Marvin Carlson, "Semiotics and Its Heritage," in *Critical Theory and Performance*, ed. Janelle G. Reinelt and Joseph R Roach (Ann Arbor: University of Michigan Press, 2010), 13–25.

3. *Something Wicked* visualizes textual imagery with art assets like hearts, sparrows, and hares; the game also features lines from the play in the pregame tutorial. We opted not to include a voiceover, because we did not want an actor's voice to overwrite the player's interpretation of Shakespeare's lines.

4. "Winning" in *Something Wicked* does not mean that Macbeth wins in the end. It means that the player follows the rules established by the game's mechanics. Our mechanics not only incentivize violent actions, they also necessitate violence if a player wants to keep the game going.

5. Though Shakespeare's *Macbeth* features witches, the scene *Something Wicked* enacts does not include supernatural beings. Our animations generally follow recognizable laws of physics (i.e., they cannot fly, and they do not float or transform into other creatures). In terms of a value system, the game requires that players behave violently—stabbing waves of enemies—in order to keep playing.

6. To demonstrate the storyworld's value system, we incentivized backstabbing. Players can choose to kill an enemy from the front and receive X rage points from stepping in the enemy's blood, or they can choose to roll past enemies and stab them from behind to earn 2X rage points from a bigger blood spatter. We engineered the waves of enemies to become too much to manage with only front kills, so players' success in the game depends on their ability to more closely approximate Macbeth's values of duplicity and backstabbing.

7. To balance our timeline and production costs, and to scope down the number of art and animation assets the game would need, *Something Wicked's* mechanics are limited compared to a commercial off-the-shelf (**COTS**) game. Among the more noticeable actions Macbeth can perform are to stab, roll, run, and stand still. While he can cause damage to enemies, he cannot damage the game's environment: i.e., he cannot smash the portcullis at the game's start, and he cannot kill Banquo, the nonplayable character (**NPC**) who follows him. Players can restore Macbeth's heart meter, but they cannot change his weapon.

Step Five: Choose a Platform

Recommending specific game-authoring tools is beyond the scope of this chapter, other than the short list that appears at the end. Free or low-cost consumer-grade digital storytelling tools are released so frequently that what seems cutting-edge today will be clunky or defunct within the year. More important for this step is to gauge the skill level and available time of everyone on the team, and assign responsibility for tasks accordingly. Do not worry if nobody has built a game before, because many authoring tools are designed for true beginners to pick up quickly. Others, like the Unity or Unreal engines, have a steep learning curve even with their respective online tutorial communities.

After evaluating the team's resources (timeline, skill level, and financing), compile a few search terms that describe the design choices from the previous steps. Use these terms to search online for current game-authoring tools that other independent developers are using to build similar games: "easy text-based game creator," "easy location-based game editor," or "free side-scroller game tool" might be a good start. Because so many different game builders exist, the remaining steps do not cover the technical aspects of any one authoring tool. Instead, they cover the main steps of the overall design process. Online troubleshooting suggestions and tutorials for specific issues exist for most game creation tools.

How We Did It

We chose the tools each team member already knew well. Our artist/animator built all the art assets in Adobe Photoshop and exported them to Spine, an animation tool that was designed specifically for 2D games. Spine integrates nicely with Unity, the free game engine the programmers used to write the game's code. Our music director also used a tool that integrates nicely with Unity—Digital Performer—to build the game's music score and sound effects.

Step Six: Scope It Down

Scope the project down to the smallest possible game that adapts the smallest possible element from the source text, but that still demonstrates an important theme or concept. Scoping the game down includes narrative focus as well as art and animation style. For example, 2D animation is generally simpler than 3D animation to engineer, and plain text screens are simpler than animated 2D. If your team is embarking on their first game building project, the process will likely take longer than anyone anticipates. A small, simple game, elegantly designed and thoroughly

Fig. 10.2 *Something Wicked's* 2D aesthetic

tested, promotes a better quality of research into the source text than does an unwieldy, unfinished grand concept. A small, working game can always be expanded in the future with more features or updates.

How We Did It

Once my team looked at the timeline and available resources, we scoped the game down to the two waves of enemies and two boss battles that Act 1, Scene 2 describes. To simplify the engineering, we also chose a 2D visual aesthetic (Fig. 10.2). Our flat, puppet-like art and animation thus became a stylized design choice instead of a limitation.

Step Seven: Brainstorm a Visual Style

This step can begin much earlier, but if it has not, now is the right time to start finding visual inspiration. Remember, a strength of the video game medium in adapting a source text is that games foreground the *actions and decisions* that drive the source text. The art assets should round out this focus, not eclipse it.

Collect an online folder or mood board of visual art, movies, games, or other images that capture an aesthetic that might work for the game. Once the game has a clear visual style, it can be helpful to settle on one key image for inspiration. As I discuss below, our key image helped us craft game mechanics and solve design challenges. While any image can serve as informal inspiration, be sure to research and follow all copyright, derivative, fair use, or other relevant laws before using non-original images or artwork in the actual game build. Instructions for creating original digital art assets and animation is another complex topic beyond the scope of this chapter, but, as with game-building tools, many free or low-cost, consumer-grade options exist for creating video game art and animation.

How We Did It

Because we knew flat, puppet-like art and animation would save time and budget, we compiled inspiration images of other flat animation styles that captured the dark aesthetic we wanted. Early examples included the animated films *The Secret of Kells* (2009) and *The Adventures of Prince Achmed* (1926), the artist Henri Matisse's paper collages, and the video game *Apotheon* (2015), which has visuals inspired by ancient Greek urns. These early images led one of the designers to research medieval storytelling scrolls because *Macbeth* is set in medieval Scotland. This brainstorm led us to *Something Wicked's* main visual inspiration, the Bayeux Tapestry.

The Bayeux Tapestry depicts the 1066 Battle of Hastings, and its 231 feet of embroidered battle scenes and simple environmental pieces were an ideal inspiration for our game. In addition to providing us with a visual touchstone, the Bayeux Tapestry informed many of our mechanics. Because the medium of cloth has its own rules and affordances, thinking about how the tapestry itself would behave helped us solve design challenges. It also helped us create elements like bloodstains that dry and stain the cloth, and sear marks from Macbeth's sword, which, as Shakespeare's play says, "smoked with bloody execution." (Act 1, Scene 2, line 20)

Step Eight: Lock Mechanics

Before dropping in art assets, get the game's basic rules and interactions working properly. Use rough shapes to approximate any elements of the game that will eventually be art and make sure the core mechanics behave as needed. Additional mechanics might be added later, but the first major hurdle in programming is to establish the game's central interactions.

How We Did It
Some of the basic rules of interaction for *Something Wicked's* avatars include: (1) avatars can walk forwards and backwards; but not through one another; (2) only Macbeth can roll past another avatar; (3) Macbeth and Banquo can cause damage to the enemies, but not to each other; (4) enemies can cause damage only to Macbeth; and (5) all avatars can stab. Before we added art and animations, the programmers used simple rectangles to test and perfect these rules of interaction.

Step Nine: Add Art

With this step, the game begins to look and feel much more complete. Because the previous step set up placeholders for eventual art assets, this step amounts to dropping those assets in and making the elements aesthetically consistent. Most of the game authoring tools available online will have instructions for importing finished art.

How We Did It
To avoid any copyright issues, we built all the assets in *Something Wicked* from scratch: fonts, background, avatars, environmental pieces, music, and sound effects. Even within our design, which is sparse compared to many 2D side-scrollers, creating all these elements from the ground up was a substantial undertaking. Because the programmers could use placeholders as they engineered the mechanics, the production timeline was rarely dependent on completion of any given art asset; we were able to keep adding and testing mechanics as the programmers finished them, and then replace the placeholders with art assets when they were ready.

Step Ten: Playtest Alpha Versions

Making changes to basic mechanics is much easier earlier in the production process, so as soon as the game reaches the **alpha stage**, start playtesting it. An ideal alpha playtester is a gamer who is also familiar with the source text. If these candidates are limited, recruit gamers who do not know the text, rather than non-gamers who do know the text. Playing an unfinished game can be unproductively confusing to players who are unfamiliar with video games, regardless of how well they know the source text. Because they know what a game should feel like, gamers are more likely to give feedback that can be addressed with another alpha build. It is helpful to have fresh eyes on major new builds, so try to keep some playtesters in reserve throughout the testing process.

Playtest early and often to make sure the game is recognizable as an adaptation of the source, especially after adding new mechanics. In terms of research insights, the alpha testing stage can be a powerful opportunity to test the legibility of the game's argument with players who might not know the source well. In the design process, similar to the rehearsal process in theatre, it is easy to lose sight of what will register with an audience and what will be too nuanced.

It is tempting to explain all the mechanics to a new playtester, but explanations will hide the game's design flaws. Simply set up the game without a preamble and provide a feedback survey. Effective feedback surveys do not measure whether the player is smart enough to understand the game's links to its source text. Rather, effective feedback surveys measure the game's ability to telegraph these links. In other words, effective questions measure what *actually* registered with the player, not what the development team hopes players will see. With this goal in mind, avoid questions like "what do you think the birds mean?" A question about birds reminds players the game had birds, so there would be no way to know if the player missed the birds altogether while playing. More effective questions are "what did you pay attention to in the game?" or "what was the most/least satisfying aspect of the game?"

How We Did It

Once we locked the mechanics and had art for the Macbeth avatar, we began playtesting alpha builds of *Something Wicked*. We adjusted major game mechanics after these early playtests, like the bottom border's hearts, which indicate how much damage Macbeth has sustained. Our feedback questions helped us flag an early design flaw that plagued these hearts. Our first iteration of a damage meter was a line of big hearts in the bottom border of the frame. This damage meter was obvious to the development team because we had spent so long debating the best visual before deciding on hearts.

However, in answer to our feedback question, "did any information seem missing?" our gamer playtesters noted that they kept looking for a way to measure Macbeth's damage level—and these were experienced gamers, who knew to look for a damage meter. When our experienced gamers did not make the connection that the big hearts represented Macbeth's damage level, we knew we needed to come up with a more legible representation. With the game's current, smaller hearts, Macbeth's remaining "heart level" is much more legible. But we would have missed this flaw until it was too late to change it, if a leading feedback survey question had asked, "what did the hearts mean?" Phrased this way, the question would have reminded players of the hearts and made the connection for them.

Step Eleven: Debug and Release the Beta

A common refrain in game design is that games are not finished so much as they are abandoned. A game can always be improved, but at some point the team needs to release it. After the major mechanics and assets are in, after a few rounds of alpha playtesting and adjustments, spend the remaining production timeline playing the game over and again to catch any **bugs** that arise. By the beta stage, there is less opportunity for adding major research insights. This step is comparable to the syntax and proofreading stage of completing a research paper. However, unlike proofing a research paper, it is hard to estimate how long debugging will take. In a video game, one tiny misplaced command or typo in the game's code can cause major mechanics to stop working. Finding a bug might take five minutes or it might take five hours. Once the game is reasonably debugged and non-gamer players can navigate it, call it a **beta** and release it to the world.

How We Did It

Fabula(b)'s programmers describe effective debugging as looking for a lost object in a house: the fastest way to find it is not to wander aimlessly. Instead, retrace steps from the last known location and then thoroughly search different sections, one at a time. One particularly stubborn *Something Wicked* bug cropped up when the programmers changed the color of Macbeth's sword to demonstrate he is about to unleash a rage superhit. After one of the programmers made the change, the color disappeared if Macbeth got too close to the enemies. To find and fix the bug, the programmers first made a copy of the existing build and archived it, in case debugging caused more problems. Then they discussed what they added that might have altered the code for the sword. Next, they made sure the sword's code and sequential order were correct. Then they adjusted every variable affecting the sword until they found the problem.

Bonus Step: Write a Classroom Use Guide

Video games are meant to be played. And as an adaptation of a play or a work of literature, games can promote a close reading of the source, as players try to figure out how to play better. Video games can also encourage critical thinking, as players enact the plot points and themes the game showcases, and debate whether the game is authentic to its source. But not every instructor knows how to incorporate a video game into a lesson plan. A classroom-use guide can help an instructor integrate the game effectively and quickly, without having to rewrite the curriculum. Consider providing 2–3 sentence directions that address questions like "What is this?" "Why do I need this?" "What do students need?" and "How long will it take?" A guide might also include a list of discussion questions that ask players to identify plot points based on the game's presentation or imagine elements they would have designed differently.

CONCLUSION

Thinking about a literary or dramatic text by adapting it into a video game results in a meaningful, widely usable Digital Humanities research project that can demonstrate a deep critical engagement with the source. This method encourages a close reading of the source and a coherent distillation of themes and plot, and it can be accomplished with minimal technological experience and access. These qualitative research findings will be evident in the game itself. The game can also serve as a platform for representing traditional and supporting scholarly research data.

As I noted in Step 2, one of the arguments *Something Wicked* makes is that Shakespeare's complex language is often a barrier to understanding the play. A robust cottage industry exists around helping people decode this language[12] as a first step to understanding and enjoying the plays.[13] *Something Wicked* takes an alternative approach inspired by the

---

[12] Perhaps the best-known contemporary example of "translating" Shakespeare's language is the No Fear Shakespeare series, which provides Shakespeare's "original" dialogue on the left side of the page, with a version on the right in "the kind of English people actually speak today." "No Fear Shakespeare: Shakespeare's Plays Plus a Modern Translation You Can Understand," accessed October 6, 2017, http://nfs.sparknotes.com/.

[13] A longer explanation of the impossibility of an original, authoritative Shakespearean text is beyond the scope of this chapter. Intrigued readers should begin with Stephen Orgel's excellent *Authentic Shakespeare and Other Problems of the Early Modern Stage* (Florence: Taylor & Francis, 2013).

recent scientific evidence linking emotion and learning outcomes. The game proposes that people will be more intrinsically motivated to decode Shakespeare's language if they understand the storyworld and become emotionally invested in it *before* they encounter the language. Our early results support this hypothesis.[14]

However, an unexpected insight we learned in our alpha testing was that people are emotionally attached to Shakespeare's "original" text even if they are simultaneously confused and frustrated by its complexity. They wanted to see the words written on the screen. We were hesitant to overshadow the action of the game with full lines, so we built a tutorial section that shows each of Macbeth's available moves with its inspiration line in the top border above the avatar. We also included the full text of Act 1, Scene 2, in a separate screen, to encourage players to analyze the full text in order to figure out the game's connections.

References

Ball, David. *Backwards and Forwards: A Technical Manual for Reading Plays.* Carbondale and Edwardsville: Southern Illinois University Press, 1983.

Bizzocchi, Jim, and Joshua Tanenbaum. "Mass Effect 2: A Case Study in the Design of Game Narrative." *Bulletin of Science Technology & Society* 32, no. 5 (2012): 393–404.

Bloom, Gina. "Videogame Shakespeare: Enskilling Audiences Through Theater-Making Games." *Shakespeare Studies* 43 (2015): 114–119.

Bogost, Ian. "The Rhetoric of Video Games." In *The Ecology of Games: Connecting Youth, Games, and Learning*, edited by Katie Salen, 117–140. Cambridge: MIT Press, 2008.

Carlson, Marvin. "Semiotics and Its Heritage." In *Critical Theory and Performance*, edited by Janelle G. Reinelt and Joseph R. Roach, 13–25. Ann Arbor: University of Michigan Press, 2010.

Cutting, Andrew. "Interiority, Affordances, and the Possibility of Adapting Henry James's *The Turn of the Screw* as a Video Game." *Adaptation* 5, no. 2 (September 2011): 169–184.

Flanagan, Mary. *Critical Play: Radical Game Design*. Cambridge: MIT Press, 2009.

---

[14] My favorite informal feedback was from two ten-year-olds who happened to be on-site during a playtest. They informed us that, though they had not yet read any of Shakespeare's plays, they did know his name. After playing *Something Wicked*, they told us they did not realize Shakespeare plays would have "awesome fighting."

Gee, James Paul. "Good Video Games and Good Learning." *Phi Kappa Phi Forum* 85, no. 2 (2005): 33–37.

Immordino-Yang, Helen. *Emotions, Learning, and the Brain: Exploring the Educational Implications of Affective Neuroscience.* New York: W. W. Norton & Company, 2016.

Jenkins, Henry. "Game Design as Narrative Architecture." In *First Person: New Media as Story, Performance, and Game,* edited by Noah Wardrip-Fruin and Pat Harrigan, 118–130. Cambridge: MIT Press, 2004.

———. "Ethics and Game Design: A Conversation (Part One)." *Confessions of an Aca-Fan.* Last modified August 5, 2010 and Accessed May 8, 2017. henryjenkins.org/2010/08/ethics_and_games_a_conversatio.html.

Lahey, Jessica. "To Help Students Learn, Engage the Emotions." *New York Times.* http://well.blogs.nytimes.com/2016/05/04/to-help-students-learn-engage-the-emotions.

Levin, Sam. "A Beauty Contest Was Judged by AI and the Robots Didn't Like Dark Skin." *The Guardian,* 2016. https://www.theguardian.com/technology/2016/sep/08/artificial-intelligence-beauty-contest-doesnt-like-black-people.

Novak, Peter. "Shakespeare in the Fourth Dimension: *Twelfth Night* and American Sign Language." In *Remaking Shakespeare: Performance Across Media, Genres and Cultures,* edited by Pascale Aebischer, Edward J. Esche, and Nigel Wheale, 18–38. New York: Palgrave Macmillan, 2003.

Orgel, Stephen. *Authentic Shakespeare and Other Problems of the Early Modern Stage.* Florence: Taylor & Francis, 2013.

Papert, Seymour. *Mindstorms: Children, Computers, and Powerful Ideas.* New York: Basic Books, 1980.

Ratto, Matt. "Critical Making: Conceptual and Material Studies in Technology and Social Life." *The Information Society* 27, no. 4 (2011): 252–260.

Salen, Katie, and Eric Zimmerman. *Rules of Play: Game Design Fundamentals.* Cambridge: MIT Press, 2004.

Schell, Jesse. *The Art of Game Design: A Book of Lenses.* Amsterdam: Elsevier, 2010.

———. *The Art of Game Design: A Book of Lenses.* 2nd ed. Boca Raton, FL: Taylor & Francis, 2015.

"The Bias Blind Spot and Unconscious Bias in Design." *The Interaction Design Foundation.* Accessed October 3, 2017. https://www.interaction-design.org/literature/article/the-bias-blind-spot-and-unconscious-bias-in-design.

Related Links

Construct 2 (drag-and-drop tool for HTML5 2D game): www.scirra.com.

FreshAiR (location-based, augmented reality stories and games): www.playfreshair.com.

Indiegogo crowdfunding site: www.indiegogo.com.

Kickstarter crowdfunding site: www.kickstarter.com.

Scratch (simple, intuitive beginner's programming language for stories, games, and animations): www.scratch.mit.edu.

Something Wicked: www.fabulab.us.

Twine (interactive, nonlinear stories): www.twinery.org.

CHAPTER 11

Virtual Bethel: Preservation of Indianapolis's Oldest Black Church

Zebulun M. Wood, Albert William,
Ayoung Yoon and Andrea Copeland

This chapter will offer a basic introduction to the principles behind three dimensional (3D) imaging, modeling and representation of spaces and objects, and how these can be used in research, and teaching and learning. We will present a local heritage community-based research project. The class project involves students' hands-on learning to produce complete 3D models and visualizations at the Media Arts & Science Program in School of Informatics and Computing (SoIC) at Indiana

Z. M. Wood (✉) · A. William · A. Yoon · A. Copeland
Indiana University – Purdue University Indianapolis, Indianapolis, USA
e-mail: zwood@iupui.edu

A. William
e-mail: almwilli@iupui.edu

A. Yoon
e-mail: ayyoon@iupui.edu

A. Copeland
e-mail: ajapzon@iupui.edu

© The Author(s) 2018
l. levenberg et al. (eds.), *Research Methods for the Digital Humanities*,
https://doi.org/10.1007/978-3-319-96713-4_11

University—Purdue University Indianapolis (IUPUI). Our experience has been overwhelmingly positive in terms of the knowledge gained by the team and the goodwill generated in our community. Our intention is to help Digital Humanities researchers embark on 3D modeling and virtual reality recreations of physical spaces.

The Virtual Bethel experience presented several challenges to our team from which we will share lessons that are likely to be useful to other virtual recreation projects. The following lessons will be unpacked throughout the chapter: first, working on a community-based heritage project takes a considerable investment of time regarding relationship and trust building. Second, individuals cannot accomplish a project of this magnitude working alone, rather, a large team of diverse highly skilled individuals is required. Third, partnerships are essential to meet the range of skills needed and to share the considerable technology costs. Lastly, and most importantly, respect for the **intangible cultural heritage** of the people involved needs to be reflected in the virtual recreation. Above all else, we want our community partners to feel respected by the rendering of their cultural heritage when they and others experience Virtual Bethel.

BETHEL AME CHURCH OF INDIANAPOLIS

Bethel is the oldest African American church in the city of Indianapolis and was once a vital part of a thriving African American community in the heart of the Indiana Avenue Jazz District. The Church was founded in Indianapolis in 1836, and its archive documents a shared heritage and a living community. Over its 180 years of existence, the Bethel AME Church has played a vital role in the Underground Railroad, the founding of the National Association for the Advancement of Colored People (NAACP) in Indiana, the founding of the first formal School for Black Children in Indianapolis, and the development of the African Methodist Episcopal Church in the United States. In the 1960s and the 1970s, the development of the Federal interstate highway system and of IUPUI displaced many members of the community over the course of just a few decades. Where the church was once surrounded by the homes and businesses of its members, high-end condominiums now encroach on the tiny parcel upon which the crumbling brick building stands and IUPUI's five-story School of Informatics and Computing, where the authors work, looms across the street.

For the past three years, Andrea Copeland worked closely with Olivia McGee-Lockhart, the Bethel AME Church of Indianapolis' **Keeper of History**, church archivist and historian. Their common goal is to preserve and make accessible the church's archive dating back to the 1850s. The oldest items in the archive include handwritten journals, letters, and other evidence that the church was a station on the underground railroad. This archive came to Copeland's attention only because one of the School's alumni was a member of the church and sought her help. Unfortunately, many community archives are similarly discovered by happenstance as there are no connections to bridge marginalized groups to formal support structures. To lessen the role of chance in whose history is preserved, methods for creating connections between resource-rich institutions and history's underrepresented groups are desperately needed. These connections can help to realize more inclusive historical representations. Virtual reality projects such as the one described here produce excitement, as evidenced by the local TV news station's interest in the project.[1] That excitement can be used to focus needed attention on the diverse preservation needs within a community.

Given the social and economic influences in downtown Indianapolis, Bethel's membership has dwindled, and the majority of its parishioners are now elderly. Over time, the church building suffered physically and, with increasingly limited resources, repairs became unlikely. Selling the building and relocating the church became the best option for sustaining the 180-year-old congregation. The church was sold for several million dollars in fall 2016 and will become a hotel in spring 2017. Moving forward, the congregation is already building a new church in another part of the city. The 3D virtual representation of the church's sanctuary is now a significant part of local history documentation. Perhaps more importantly, it allows the cultural heritage of this community to remain accessible in a "tangible" form to be celebrated, learned from, connected to, shared with others, and passed on to future generations.

Local heritage institutions have played an important role in this project, which will continue going forward. The church's archive now resides at the Indiana Historical Society and through a partnership with the IUPUI library, the archive has been digitized. The images created in

---

[1] Nick McGill, "Indy's Oldest Black Church Get 'Digital Restoration'," last modified February 23, 2017, http://fox59.com/2017/02/23/indys-oldest-black-church-gets-digital-restoration/.

support of Virtual Bethel constitute a digital archive of over **60,000** files. Now that considerable documentation of this church's history is accessible, our next challenge is to bring the digitized archive into the virtual space. By representing the church's sanctuary we will create new opportunities for learning and research.

As the development of this project has taken an organic path that has evolved over several years, we have gained valuable insight that can be applied to similar cultural heritage challenges. The displacement of this congregation brought about through **gentrification** is a phenomenon facing communities all over the United States. Projects such as this one can not only provide historical preservation, but also raise awareness about what is being lost from our collective cultural heritage experience due to gentrification.

CREATING VIRTUAL SPACES—IT TAKES A VILLAGE

Virtual reality utilizes 3D content, the creation of images, spaces, and animations to implement fully digital-virtual recreations of historical artifacts and spaces. Experiencing spaces in virtual and mixed realities provides an impactful, contextual, and immersive environment for learning history and conducting research with digital artifacts. Use of virtual reality (usually built on **game engines**) is expanding in Digital Humanities as a research and education tool. Entire spaces can be replicated to allow users to immerse themselves in places that no longer exist due to time, historical events, or inaccessibility. Taking an interdisciplinary and technological approach allows for new experiences and research questions to be asked of those historical materials and experiences. The threats to artifacts, documents, and buildings representing diverse cultural pasts are ever-present and our work here begins to look at ways to preserve the experiential aspects inherent in static representations of the past.

A Media Arts & Science team-based course in 3D production/visualization served as the production lab for this project. The course is designed to include work with community partners to provide students with real-world, context-driven, hands-on learning opportunities. The course focuses on the creation of high-end, broadcast-quality animations through team-based learning. Students develop skills in areas related to production in a 3D project. These include preproduction skills such as story concept and development, script writing, research, conceptual drawing, storyboarding, animatics, and project management. Production skills are explored in 3D asset creation, time management, file management, sound, and title sequences. Post-production processes include final rendering issues, movie creation, and formatting for various playback devices.

Our experience working with students and community partners provides methods for developing 3D technology-based Digital Humanities projects while developing interdisciplinary research collaborations and capacity for community engagement. Students and faculty work with archival documents and physical artifacts/spaces to learn methods to represent that history using new media technology. Further, they worked with heritage professionals, historians, and community experts. The Media Arts faculty, Zebulun Wood and Albert William, work in conjunction with Ayoung Yoon and Andrea Copeland, faculty from the Department of Library and Information Science which is also in SoIC, as well as faculty in the History, Geography and Anthropology departments in the School of Liberal Arts. This project illustrates the need for cross-campus department collaborations to develop Digital Humanities projects of magnitude. The well-documented Virtual Harlem project provides another example of how important interdisciplinary collaborations are for historical virtual recreations.[2]

Copeland and Yoon are leading the local cultural heritage project involving the Bethel AME Church of Indianapolis. They partnered with Wood and William, who teach courses in 3D/visualization, for the purposes of extending research and curriculum initiatives. This project provides the opportunity for students to use digital arts technology to preserve and represent physical objects and spaces as well as to engage audiences in the exploration of history through new media. 3D virtual technology is used to preserve an important historic space that will no longer exist owing to gentrification, redevelopment, and changes in the city's use of its landscape. The virtual representation of the church's sanctuary now provides a vessel to engage audiences in the history of the Bethel church as well as the history of African Americans in Indianapolis. Like other virtual history projects, we want to replicate or translate a historic experience for modern audiences in a way that engages them bodily

---

[2] James J. Sosnoski, Patricia Harkin, and Bryan Carter, *Configuring History: Teaching the Harlem Renaissance Through Virtual Reality Cityscapes* (New York: Peter Lang, 2006).

and emotionally.[3] We believe this sanctuary is worthy of our efforts because of its historical significance, but also because of the injustice to the community brought about by gentrification. We are hoping that others will take an interest and think differently about the changes they see around them.

COMPETENCIES FOR RESTORING 3D SCANNED STRUCTURES

The technology, skills, and human resources needed to build virtual environments are considerable. Without the contributions of students in a Media Arts and Science program and a lab dedicated to these types of projects, the digital preservation would not have been possible. The discussion that follows regarding the course and the competencies illustrates the depth of knowledge needed for Digital Humanities projects of this magnitude. Given that you might not be fortunate enough to have numerous talented media arts students available to you, this section will help you determine what skills are needed for your own project and who, exactly, you need to partner with.

Our 3D team production class allows students to work as a group and emulates the collaborative efforts found in the media and animation industry. Students should have a number of prerequisites completed, including intermediate courses in **3D modeling, texturing** and **lighting**, and **animation**. The goal of the course is to bring students together to work on a common project. Students are encouraged to bring their existing knowledge and specialty (modeling, unwrapping, shading, lighting, game engines, or development) to the table, and also to investigate new skill sets they may be interested in or that are needed to facilitate the success of the production.

Through teaching this course for several years, we have found that students are drawn to this class for a number of reasons. It allows them to work together on a single project synergistically. Students can apply their existing skills and also find ways to pursue other interests they may not have yet explored. It teaches them team dynamics and helps foster group activity. It explains goals that are essential to the success of group

---

[3]Alison Landsberg, "Digital Translations of the Past: Virtual History Exhibits," in *Engaging the Past: Mass Culture and the Production of Historical Memory* (New York: Columbia University Press, 2015): 147–176.

work: communication, leadership, organization, and accountability. Past class assessments have provided us with feedback that the experiences students receive in this class are different to their regular class work, that they relish this experience, and that the overall result is a very satisfying academic exercise. You will need to identify project partners that have technical skills as well as "soft skills," e.g., communication, time management, and team-based problem-solving.

At the beginning of class, we assess student skills and strengths, and build the team according to this assessment and the project goals. We carefully look at the abilities needed and often recruit students that we feel can benefit from the class and can contribute to specific portions of the project as it develops. We encourage and expect leadership from within the group. Based on our course design, we encourage you to assemble a team that focuses on the strengths of each individual and structure the project so that all team members can easily interact with one another. We encourage you to create a communication system that is easiest for them to use; many times students have opted to use Facebook. A cloud-based file sharing and storage system called IU Box is utilized for file sharing, reference, and communication between the team and stakeholders.

Knowledge of the subject matter is, of course, critical to the success of the project. We challenge the students to research any new topics on their own. We also provide supplementary material on the course's online course management software, CANVAS. Knowing the history of the subject, or the background of the story gives you a more vested interest in the success of the program. Fostering relationships with community members and working to develop an understanding of their history facilitates more respectful and valuable intangible cultural heritage projects.

Digital Preservation Pipeline

In the fall semester of 2016, our class was presented with the opportunity to recreate the historic Bethel AME Church in Indianapolis. We felt that a virtual reality experience that utilized 3D models and textures would be a powerful way to tell the story of this church. We also felt this opportunity for community engagement was a perfect fit for the class. Any chance for our students to interact with the community is a positive experience on all accounts. We presented them with this possibility in the first class meeting and it was met with great excitement. Students

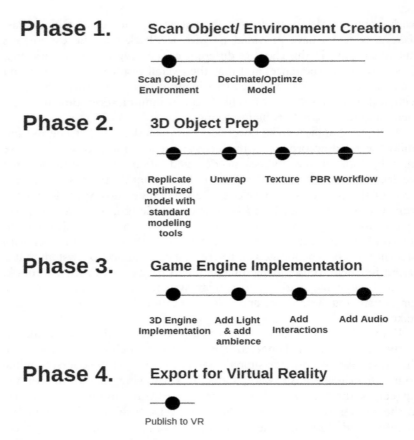

Fig. 11.1   Scan to VR data pipeline

felt this was a meaningful use of their skills and time, and were excited that they were working to give back to the community. Figure 11.1 provides an overview of the technical processes associated with each phase of development.

During our second class meeting, all students and faculty visited the church to take **reference photographs** and to experience the space we would recreate. On a warm, late afternoon with sunlight streaming through the stained glass windows, we spent over two hours exploring every corner of the church. We took approximately 2000 high-quality photographs to use as reference models and textures that would go into the VR. Additionally, we utilized a GigaPan robotic camera system to capture images that were stitched together to form highly detailed panoramas of the interior, ensuring there was not an inch of the space missed; a Ricoh Theta camera was also used to capture low-resolution 360° images. All of these photographs were cataloged, archived, and used to help recreate the digital space. Measurements of some structures were also taken for use as a scale reference.

Before the start of the semester, laser scans of the interior of the Bethel AME church were created by Online Resources, a local 3D scanning company, and the data were given to us to use in our project. 3D scanning can be utilized for many applications and is not limited to room-scaled objects. It is becoming a common tool to preserve the likeness of objects both large and small. This data set of 8 scans was approximately 10 GB and contained 39 million polygons. To review the data, we decimated the scan with Pixologic's Zbrush 4r7 plugin to reduce the polygon count to approximately 800,000 polygons. Tests were done to see what the scanned data looked like using the Unreal 4 game engine outputting to an HTC Vive VR system. Based on these tests, it was apparent that the students would need to rebuild the interior of the church digitally because the scanned data contained many holes, the polygon mesh was not clean, and the high polygon count made it impractical for real-time VR. While these data were to scale and detailed, it was incomplete and unsuitable to use without considerable modifications. We recognized it as an excellent reference resource to speed up our modeling workflow. One of the first steps we took to develop the church interior involved exporting the scanned data into Unreal and scaling it correctly. This allowed us to compare the experience of the digital space and the real Bethel sanctuary. We noted heights of objects (like a pew during reference photography) and then compared them to measurements of the same object in the VR template. The team agreed on a realistic scale for the pews, organ, piano, and second floor early in the project.

Students used Autodesk Maya 2016 as the software to model all the assets. The scanned data was brought into Maya and scaled to its proper dimensions for use as a template. Objects that had been measured by students were used as references. Then, the scanned model was brought to its proper relative scale based on unit settings in Maya. This data set was used as a reference to build all the components for the interior of the church.

To give an example of this workflow, we can look at the creation of the church's pews. For the most part, the pews were all the same design but differed in size and orientation. By using the scanned data and the reference photographs, our modeler was able to determine the basic shapes of each part of the pew to scale and build a simple base model. We needed to be cognizant of the number of polygons that this model contained so that it would show enough detail, but not be so high as to hinder the Unreal 4 engine when it was brought to VR. Once this model was completed satisfactorily, with necessary technical considerations of polygon count and overall topology, it was used to populate the environment by duplicating and adjusting the scale and position of each pew to match the scanned church model.

Similar processes were completed to construct all elements of the environment. The church's primary structure of the walls, floor, and ceiling was built. The stairs, balcony, the pulpit, choir lofts, and the pipe organ was among the many pieces that were created. All assets were built to adhere to technical standards that would allow them to function optimally in VR.

The team reviewed, critiqued, and assessed each asset as it was created. Production meetings were held at the beginning of each week's class in a conference room, instead of our usual classroom to focus on each asset and consider the broader context of the project as a team. Each student's work was reviewed weekly by the team; concerns were addressed as needed, then tasks were allocated to move forward. Students sign weekly contracts so that everyone knows expectations and deadlines. We stress that others are relying on their progress and adherence to mandatory deadlines. Production meetings were followed by visits to the IU Advanced Visualization Lab to view the advances in the VR environment with the tools we are designing. Then, there was time for all members to interact, work, and receive instructions on techniques that were necessary to further progress. As we neared completion, several Bethel congregants and the church's pastor visited to see our progress. This was an inspiring visit for all involved, as the students saw the impact of their work on the visitors and understand the project's cultural significance.

As students completed assets, a spreadsheet was updated with progress. As digital models were completed students began unwrapping the 3D objects, so they could be textured using Allegorithmic's Substance Painter. This process applied materials and colors to the 3D models to

Fig. 11.2 A photo of the original church

impart a sense of realism. A pipeline was developed to simplify the identification of particular materials and a library was created for students to access materials. As models were painted, texture maps were exported for use in the Unreal 4 VR.

After all models had materials applied to them and had been added to Unreal, various processes were used to optimize the scene; these included critically testing the textures to see if there were errors, adding lighting to the scene to simulate light coming through the windows, optimizing navigation controls, and creating teleportation to navigate in the environment.[4]

Figures 11.2 through 11.3a–c, visually illustrate the development process. Figure 11.2 is a photograph of the church's sanctuary. Figure 11.3a is a screen capture showing the original 3D LIDAR scan inside of Epic's Unreal game development engine. In Fig. 11.3b, the 3D model has been recreated by students using a 3D modeling technique known as retopology (simplifying and creating efficient geometry for real-time rendering and animation). Lastly, in Fig. 11.3c the sanctuary appears fully textured, shaded, and rendered dynamically ready for virtual reality.

---

[4]Rachel Davidson and Tyler Jackson, "Project Progress Video," last modified February 2017, https://vimeo.com/209509528.

Fig. 11.3 The digital modeling process. **a** Laser scan model provided by Online Resources, Inc., **b** Recreated 3D model of Bethel AMC from 3D laser scan, and **c** A fully lit and textured Virtual Bethel shown in Epic's Unreal game development engine

IMPLICATIONS FOR TEACHING AND LEARNING IN DIGITAL HUMANITIES

Team learning is the key to the design of the project. Students hold themselves and their peers equally accountable in their respective roles, for meeting deadlines, responsibilities, and reassigning tasks. Week contracts commit them to achieving goals on behalf of the team/project. Furthermore, when working in a team in which all members contribute separate files into the same project requires the diligent management of file dependencies and naming conventions, because it is easy to save over, replace, or misplace someone else's work. Cloud-based project folders and structures have helped this class considerably when dealing with versioning issues. Communication skills are developed that span from interpersonal collaboration to formal project documentation.

Service learning is the element which connects the team to communities outside of the university. The community partner becomes the students' client and their payment is the chance to make a difference. At IUPUI, an important goal is to connect our students' expertise to unique applications of knowledge through service and engagement, which can benefit the community. The Virtual Bethel project exemplifies this IUPUI staple and demonstrates the value of our students' skillsets beyond video game and film entertainment.

IMPLICATIONS FOR RESEARCH IN DIGITAL HUMANITIES

In March of 2017, we received a New Frontiers in the Humanities Grant from IUPUI to create the Virtual Bethel Learning Sanctuary and to build an image archive.[5] At its core, Virtual Bethel Learning Sanctuary exemplifies a new, multifaceted approach to preserving and experiencing cultural digital heritage. This project will bring diverse historical evidence (documents, photos, oral histories, video, etc.) together in one place, thereby transcending the walls of the institutions that contain each of the component parts. The combination of archival artifacts and documents with virtual reality, which is inherently participatory, extends the functionality and impact of online exhibits of cultural materials which are overwhelmingly static in nature. Interaction and immersion within virtual environments

[5] Zebulun Wood, "New Frontiers Proposal Video," last modified October 2016, https://vimeo.com/187085145.

and archives enable innovative research and learning with primary sources. However, this will present further challenges and pose new questions about what narrative is told, who tells it, how it is told, and how those decisions impact the experience of participants in the virtual learning space. Public history digital collections and sites have been criticized for their lack of critical evaluation in terms of how the projects are experienced by their users.[6] This next phase will allow us to explore research questions related to public perceptions of value in digital historical experiences and what kinds of learning take place in virtual spaces.

Further, this project contributes to research in digital preservation. The combination of 3D modeling with virtual reality technology for historic preservation is a recent innovation.[7] As such, the project will contribute to the development of standards and best practices for the management and preservation of virtual reality data. Learning from game and software preservation research, this project addresses core preservation concerns when developing the Virtual Bethel Learning Sanctuary that can be suitable for long-term preservation and use. Future research will continue to explore methods for preserving complex interactive, multilayered digital object virtual reality data, and technological requirements for rendering.

Given the diversity and sophistication of the equipment used to generate images for the Virtual Bethel project, the research advances knowledge in image archiving **data curation**. Making the Virtual Bethel "construction documents" archive (60,000+ files) open access might well be unprecedented, and certainly is not the norm. This will allow others, without the vast technological resources of SoIC to explore 3D modeling and virtual reality. The archive will also document virtual reality technology and development in the years 2016–2017 to support future research in this area.

Our experience illustrates that local community-based Digital Humanities projects are resource and time intensive. The level of coordination

---

[6]Fien Danniau, "Public History in a Digital Context: Back to the Future or Back to Basics?" *BMGN: Low Countries Historical Review* 128, no. 4 (2013).

[7]Kyriacos Themistocleous, "Model Reconstruction for 3D Vizualization of Cultural Heritage Sites Using Open Data from Social Media: The Case Study of Soli, Cyprus," *Journal of Archaeological Science: Reports* 14 (2017); Belen Jiménez Fernández-Palacios, Daniele Morabito, and Fabio Remondino, "Access to Complex Reality-Based 3D Models Using Virtual Reality Solutions," *Journal of Cultural Heritage* 23 (2017).

needed among faculty, community members, and students is considerable. The relationships that underpin this project were developed over years. The course was team taught and enrolled 12 students resulting in an instructor to student ratio of 2:6. The technology investment is significant given the lab space, equipment, and software needed to teach, create, and research in this area. The costs are high, but hopefully we have illustrated that the benefits are significant as well. In addition to creating a powerful learning environment for our students, this project has benefitted the research agendas of several faculty, preserved an important part of Indiana history, and provided a framework from which to approach future projects.

Acknowledgements Special thanks to **Online Resources, Inc. for 3D scan of Bethel's sanctuary:** Without the Scan of Bethel Sanctuary we would not have had an ideal reference of the space to rebuild for VR. JD Schaumburg of Online resources recalls the amount the day of scanning: "5 hours of scanning and it took about 3 hours of computer crunching time to merge the High Res files to the low res files. Yes we can upload the High Res scans to the IU box. They are about 1 GB to 1.5 GB for each scan, and we have 8 total scans." Online Resources can be found at http://www.onlineresourcesinc.com/. We'd also like to thank **Advanced Visualization Lab (AVL), UITS, IUPUI.** Without the AVL team we could not have compared Unreal and Unity Game engines. In the end, both engines are entirely capable of Digital Preservation of spaces for Virtual Reality. Thanks for your wisdom and advice Mike, Jeff, Chauncey. Tyler you are at the heart of this project's success. Advanced Visualization Lab can be found at https://rt.uits.iu.edu/visualization/avl/.

APPENDIX: HARDWARE AND SOFTWARE

Hardware:

HTC Vive Virtual Reality Kit
Compatible PCs
Surphaser—3D Scanner (property of Online Resources, Inc.)

Software:

Retopologizing of the Scan
Pixologic Zbrush
3D Modeling Software Used

Autodesk Maya
3D Unwrapping Software Used
Autodesk Maya & Headus UV Layout Pro
3D Texturing Software Used
Adobe Photoshop
Physically Based Rendering Texturing Software Used
Allegorithmic Substance Painter & Designer
Game Engines Used
Epic Unreal Engine
Unity Game Engine for comparison

REFERENCES

Danniau, F. "Public History in a Digital Context: Back to the Future or Back to Basics?" *BMGN: Low Countries Historical Review* 128, no. 4 (2013): 118–144.

Davidson, R., and Tyler Jackson. "Project Progress Video." Last modified February 2017. https://vimeo.com/209509528.

Jiménez Fernández-Palacios, B., Daniele Morabito, and Fabio Remondino. "Access to Complex Reality-Based 3D Models Using Virtual Reality Solutions." *Journal of Cultural Heritage* 23 (2017): 40–48.

Landsberg, A. "Digital Translations of the Past: Virtual History Exhibits." In *Engaging the Past: Mass Culture and the Production of Historical Memory.* New York: Columbia University Press, 2015.

McGill, N. "Indy's Oldest Black Church Get "Digital Restoration." Last modified February 23, 2017. http://fox59.com/2017/02/23/indys-oldest-black-church-gets-digital-restoration/.

Sosnoski, J., Harkin, Patricia, and Carter, Bryan. *Configuring History: Teaching the Harlem Renaissance Through Virtual Reality Cityscapes.* New York: Peter Lang, 2006.

Themistocleous, Kyriacos. "Model Reconstruction for 3D Vizualization of Cultural Heritage Sites Using Open Data from Social Media: The Case Study of Soli, Cyprus." *Journal of Archaeological Science: Reports* 14 (2017): 774–778.

Wood, Z. "New Frontiers Proposal Video." Last modified October, 2016. https://vimeo.com/187085145.

CHAPTER 12

Code/Art Approaches to Data Visualization

J. J. Sylvia IV

This chapter introduces a code/art approach to data visualization. Though coding has received increasingly greater amounts of attention within the field of Digital Humanities, it has primarily focused on more traditional types of visualizations such as charts and graphs. However, the **iteration** that is possible through **generative design** affords more artistic approaches. Casey Reas and Chandler McWilliams[1] claim that particular programming languages afford specific opportunities. In much the same way that a carpenter would select particular tools and a particular wood depending on the project, programming languages require similar careful selection. I use p5.js as the language of choice for this chapter because it is a free, open source language specifically designed for beginners, artists, and educators. It is a very accessible language that allows one to quickly begin creating dynamic content on the screen, even with very little previous programming experience.

---

[1] Casey Reas and Chandler McWilliams, *Form Code: In Design, Art, and Architecture* (New York: Princeton Architecturel Press, 2010).

J. J. Sylvia IV (✉)
Fitchburg State University, Fitchburg, MA, USA
e-mail: jsylvia3@fitchburgstate.edu

© The Author(s) 2018   211
l. levenberg et al. (eds.), *Research Methods for the Digital Humanities*,
https://doi.org/10.1007/978-3-319-96713-4_12

My project, *Aperveillance: Watching with Open Data*, serves as the case study for this chapter. Through a web-based visualization, I take an artistic approach to data visualization that is afforded by iteration and generative design. Whereas a more traditional approach to data visualization would seek to answer questions or create clearer explanations through the process of visualization, my work instead aims to provoke further questions about the societal tensions between surveillance and privacy. My research question in light of this goal is: How can the artistic combination of disparate sources of publicly available data make clear the societal tensions between safety, surveillance, and privacy? A Digital Humanities approach to this research question can make these tensions more immediately present and real to a viewer by drawing them into the activity of surveillance as a participant.

ETHICAL ISSUES

Ethical issues related to code/art data visualizations mirror many of the larger ethical concerns of working with data in general. First, the data that one uses should be both reliable and verifiable to the furthest extent possible. In other words, any data used for a visualization should come from a trustworthy and accurate source, otherwise the visualization that is created from the data will be similarly misleading or inaccurate. This is especially important for artistic visualizations because it is often harder for viewers of the visualization to verify the accuracy of the data than it would be in a chart or graph. Because artistic visualizations offer different ways of seeing data, the underlying data can often be harder to quantify. While this other way of seeing data is an important benefit of artistic visualizations, it should also underscore the importance of beginning with accurate data.

Determining the reliability of data is often a difficult process, however, one indicator for quality is the source of the data. For example, data from open government sources, such as the City of Raleigh—Open Data initiative that I used for my project, is likely to be more reliable than data from unknown or unofficial sources on the web. Although you will be creating artistic projects, these visualizations can be persuasive, thus it remains important to use valid data for that persuasion.

The other major ethical issue concerns protecting the privacy of those who may be represented in the data. Although all reliable data sources will have anonymized their data before making it accessible to the public, the vast amount of data that now exists means that it is increasingly likely that multiple data sources can be combined together in order to identify seemingly anonymized individuals. For example, in 2006, America Online released 20 million anonymized search queries from that year. Despite this anonymization, reporters from *The New York Times* were able to cross reference the queries and identify a particular user's search queries.[2] Additionally, if you collect information, even from public sources, there may be ethical problems with displaying that data in new ways. For example, a 2010 Harvard Facebook study and a 2016 release of data collected from public profiles on the OKCupid dating website both raised ethical concerns. Even though the information in these studies was publicly accessible, the arrangement of the data in a new way can draw extra attention to the data and put it a new context that was never intended by the user who originally posted it.[3] In other words, consent was not given for this particular use of the data. Collecting, formatting, and then using data in new ways changes its context and, if your data contains information about individual people, this is an issue for which extra care should be taken.

When academic researchers collect their own data, the context in which the data will be used must be approved by the participants before the data gathering process can begin. The protection and restriction of confidential data must be clearly elaborated and approved by review boards at universities. However, private corporations do not face the same ethical scrutiny and users often agree to allow carte-blanche use of their data by simply accepting the Terms of Service when they sign up for an account with a particular site or application. Users frequently approve these terms without reading them thoroughly, or at all. Because of these vastly different approaches to collecting and using data, academics must pay particular care to ethics when using data that they have not personally collected, especially if such data has been collected by a private company.

[2]Viktor Mayer-Schönberger and Kenneth Cukier, *Big Data: A Revolution That Will Transform How We Live, Work, and Think*, First Mariner Books edition (Boston: Mariner Books, Houghton Mifflin Harcourt, 2014).

[3]Michael Zimmer, "OkCupid Study Reveals the Perils of Big-Data Science," *Wired*, May 14, 2016. Accessed April 12, 2017, https://www.wired.com/2016/05/okcupid-study-reveals-perils-big-data-science/.

WHY USE A CODE/ART APPROACH TO VISUALIZATION?

In teaching p5.js as part of both classes and Digital Humanities related workshops, I have developed a better understanding of the strengths and weaknesses of a creative coding approach. First, the artistic nature of p5.js affords the opportunity to create data visualizations that offer a high level of affective impact, which is the often emotional or visceral transformation that one experiences in reaction to a new experience. Viewers are more often engaged with an artistic visualization than they would be with a chart or graph. All data visualizations are engaging, but creative code approaches afford the opportunity to open spaces for questions by allowing the viewer to be an active participant in the process. In other words, the meaning of a particular visualization may be somewhat ambiguous in a way that asks more questions than it answers. Viewers may be able to ask their own questions about ethics or meaning based on their reaction to a visualization.

Said another way, traditional visualizations aim to render complicated data in a way that it is easily understandable at a glance. A bar chart, for example, can make fluctuations in income across a span of years quickly recognizable in a way that looking through a larger spreadsheet of numbers would not. A bar chart, though commonly visualized using computer software, is still something that could easily be created by hand. I could fairly quickly recreate a bar chart using a piece of paper and a pen. Coding approaches to visualization unlock techniques that would be either impossible or highly infeasible by hand. Both the generative nature of coding—the ability of the computer to run through thousands of iterations of code per second—and its ability to use multimedia inputs highlight the strengths of this approach.

The generative nature of coding offers the possibility to create elaborate artistic pieces with comparatively little code. For example, the following code, adapted from Casey Reas, Lauren McCarthy, and Ben Fry's introductory text on p5.js, will create a series of kinked lines (Fig. 12.1):

Fig. 12.1 Example of kinked lines

```
for (var i = 3; i < 400; i += 3) {
    line(i, 0, i + i/2, 200);
        line (i + i/2, 200, i*1.2, 400);
}
```

Fig. 12.2 Generative design

These few lines of code can generate over one hundred lines on the screen in a fraction of second (see Fig. 12.2). This generative approach can also be used with various types of data, as a way to influence the iterations that occur, or as data that is displayed to viewers. In addition to data, p5.js facilitates access to images, video, and sound, allowing multimedia to be integrated into and manipulated by the generative process.

This generative design approach can be used in a variety of ways. On the one hand, it might be used to answer difficult design questions. For example, in 2004, NASA engineers used generative **evolutionary algorithms** to design an effective X-band antenna: "Whereas the current practice of designing antennas by hand is severely limited because it is both time and labor intensive and requires a significant amount of domain knowledge, evolutionary algorithms can be used to search the design space and automatically find novel antenna designs that are more effective than would otherwise be developed".[4] In other words, generative design was used to create random antennae that were then tested for effectiveness. The most effective ones were allowed to evolve further until a final most efficient design was derived.

On the other hand, a humanities-based project might raise more questions than it answers. For example, the 2006 exhibit, *Being not truthful*, by Ralph Ammer and Stefan Sagmeister, provokes questions about truth and vulnerability:

> "Being not truthful works against me" is part of a list in Stefan Sagmeister's diary entitled "Things I have learned in my life so far." In the installation *Being not truthful*, this maxim is woven into a virtual spiderweb, which rips if a viewer's shadow touches it; then, bit by bit, the web reconstructs itself. This fragile construction serves as a metaphor for the vulnerability of Sagmeister's aphorism and the effort required to follow it, raising questions about the nature of truth and the value of sincerity.[5]

The movement of those who are viewing the exhibit is incorporated into the project itself, highlighting the possibility of drawing on information from the surrounding environment as part of the project. This type of project does not give us any particular answers—no best design emerges and we do not straightforwardly learn anything about the truth. Instead, we are provoked to ask even more questions about the nature of truth.

One weakness of this approach is that it can actually be more difficult to use than traditional data visualization tools when one is trying to get the same types of results as traditional data visualizations. For instance, when I first introduce these creative visualization projects in classes and workshops, many students immediately think about a variety of charts or graphs that they might create about their text. It is quite possible to do this kind of visualization through a programming language like p5.js, but other tools such as Tableau are able to do this much easier with a wider variety of analytic tools quickly available. Many people who have done past data visualization work tend to default to the same types of questions they would attempt to answer with those tools. For example, I have had

---

[4] Gregory Hornby et al., "Automated Antenna Design with Evolutionary Algorithms," *American Institute of Aeronautics and Astronautics* (2006), https://doi.org/10.2514/6.2006-7242.

[5] Hartmut Bohnacker et al., *Generative Design: Visualize, Program, and Create with Processing* (New York: Princeton Architectural Press, 2012).

multiple students who wanted to analyze the frequency of occurrence for a particular word or words within a text. While this is possible to do with a creative coding tool such as p5.js, there are easier ways of doing this.

Therefore, the major weakness and strength of this approach are related. A creative coding approach is strongest when it is used to create outside-the-box visualizations based on repetition and iteration. However, to use the tools in this way, one must begin by thinking about data sets in a way that differs from traditional data visualization approaches. Creative approaches are less about analysis and more about exploration. They are less about answering questions and more about generating new questions.

STEP-BY-STEP GUIDE

To provide a guide to using a code art approach I will draw examples from my research project, *Aperveillance: Watching with Open Data* (aperveillance.com). This project contributes to the significant body of scholarship on surveillance in the field of Communication and Media Studies, by raising questions about the types of watching that are now becoming increasingly possible with open data. Thus, I coined the term *aperveillance*[6] for my project as a way to distinguish it from more traditional methods of surveillance, which are typically only available to powerful entities like governments or large corporations. My project instead focuses on the type of surveillance that is available to everyone.

Michel Foucault is widely considered a founding figure in the area of surveillance studies, though the area only coalesced as a definite area of study after the 9/11 attack in the United States and the passing of the Patriot Act in its wake.[7] Gary Marx[8] offers a thorough overview of the field, showing how surveillance has shifted as technology has changed. For example, he cites the way that technology has impacted the scale and ease of

---

[6][ap-er-**vay**-lans]*n*. derives from the Latin "*aper*" meaning "open", and "*veiler*" meaning "to watch." In the context of this project, aperveillance means "open watching," or a form of watching with open data.

[7]Michel Foucault, *Discipline and Punish: The Birth of the Prison*, 2nd ed. (New York: Vintage Books, [1975] 1995); Peter Monaghan, "Watching the Watchers," *The Chronicle of Higher Education*, 2006; Kirstie Ball, Kevin Haggerty, and David Lyon, eds., *Routledge Handbook of Surveillance Studies* 1. Paperback ed. Routledge International Handbooks (London: Routledge, 2012).

[8]Gary T. Marx, "Surveillance Studies," in *International Encyclopedia of the Social & Behavioral Sciences* (2015): 733–741, https://doi.org/10.1016/b978-0-08-097086-8.64025-4

routine strategic surveillance. An example of strategic surveillance would be Lantern Laws that required slaves to carry a lantern with them while they were out at night. Technologies such as big data, GPS, ubiquitous cameras, and DNA analysis, on the other hand, have enabled strategic surveillance to become pervasive and less visible, facilitating involuntary participation. For example, a citizen may not even be aware of the extensive system of cameras set up in their city. A primary concern of surveillance is its conflict with expectations of privacy.[9] An emerging practice of sousveillance, or the use of personal devices for recording an activity by a participant who is involved in the activity, considers how one might use devices to monitor those who are doing the surveillance. Aperveillance aims to open a field of questions somewhere between surveillance and sousveillance. What kind of watching is possible with data and images that are publically available?

My first step consisted of using this context to develop a clear research question: How can the artistic combination of disparate sources of publicly available data make clear the societal tensions between safety, surveillance, and privacy? Based on this research question, I began to brainstorm ways to address this question by visualizing data and drawing viewers into the process as an active participant.

This web-based visualization project uses webcam images from Raleigh and the larger North Carolina area that are publicly available. When a viewer loads the project on a personal computer, the code will check to see if there is an accessible camera associated with the computer, such as the camera that comes built-in on most Apple computers. If there is a camera, the code will use that to capture a still image of the viewer that will be randomly included among the other images that have been pulled from the webcams in the larger community. It also uses Raleigh's open crime data to randomly display information about the previous day's crimes, juxtaposed on top of the webcam images. This is intended to provoke questions about the type of watching that we as citizens can do with open data on the web. The inclusion of the image from the viewer's own camera is often disorienting, because it is not immediately obvious that the viewers themselves have been included in the visualization. It also creates confusion about whether their image is viewable to everyone who is accessing the website.

---

[9]Helen Nissenbaum, "Protecting Privacy in an Information Age: The Problem of Privacy in Public," *Law and Philosophy* 17, no. 5/6 (November 1998): 559, https://doi.org/10.2307/3505189.

Fig. 12.3 Aperveillance on display in Hunt Library's code+art gallery at North Carolina State University

Using examples from the programming language p5.js, I demonstrate the potential for using code and algorithms to generate databased visualizations through **repetition, modulation, transformation,** and **parameterization**. This work exists at the intersections of **data visualization, Media Studies, big data,** and **information aesthetics** (Fig. 12.3).

This project uses p5.js, a language based on Processing and created to be accessible to beginners, educators, and artists. The processing language was originally developed for visual artists, with the goal of making coding accessible to a wider audience and promoting software and visual literacy. p5.js builds upon this foundation and extends these goals. However, because it is a JavaScript based language, it is native to the web, and enables the creation of interactive elements directly within a web browser. One important caveat to note is that p5.js is a living and evolving language, which means that some of the functionality may change over time, or most likely, new features and functions will continue to be added to the core functions. These changes should not be cause for alarm, however, as the core functionality has remained the same, and all the updates have been aimed at making development easier and more accessible.

Getting Ready to Code

The first step to creating a code/art visualization is downloading the files needed to begin coding. One example of the changes associated with p5.js is the method used to write the code itself. Early in the development of the language, there was a self-contained editor available from the website. This development environment has been depreciated and instead, users are encouraged to use other software developed to help with coding. There are a wide variety of free and open source options for coding editors, but one widely used example is Brackets (http://www.brackets.io).

Next, you will need to download the p5.js core files, which enable its functionality. To do this, visit http://www.p5js.org and click on the Download tab. You should download the Complete Library, as this contains not only the files that offer the most robust functionality of p5.js, but also a helpful example project. It is worth noting that there is a very early alpha version of an online editor available for p5.js, accessible at https://alpha.editor.p5js.org. This may be the best option for those who are most interested in a quick overview of the language and smaller, simpler projects. At this point in time, larger and more complex projects are most suited for development using the downloaded complete library. After downloading and unzipping the complete library, the following files should be accessible (Fig. 12.4):

Fig. 12.4 p5.js core files

- addons
  - o p5.dom.js
  - o p5.dom.min.js
  - o p5.sound.js
  - o p5.sound.min.js
- empty-example
  - o index.html
  - o sketch.js
- p5.js
- p5.min.js

The p5.js file is the main file that contains the core of the language. p5.sound.js and p5.dom.js add extended functionality. The versions that contain "min" in the file name are compressed to speed up loading times.

In order to view the output of the code, use a web browser to access the index.html file in the empty-example folder. It is set up by default to load the p5 related JavaScript files, but will appear blank if opened in a browser. It is helpful to create a master copy of this file so that you can use it as a template for future projects.

Opening the index.html file in a code editor such as Brackets offers a glimpse of how the p5.js files are loaded and accessed:

The file below (Fig. 12.5) loads the JavaScript files that contain the core functionality of p5.js as well as the sketch.js file, which will contain the code created for new projects. One detail worth noting here is that the first three JavaScript files are being loaded directly from the website cloudflare.com. However, it is also possible to load the files locally, in the same way that the sketch.js file is being loaded. You would simply need to move the other JavaScript files into the same folder as your index.html file.

The last thing to think about is how the public will access your project. Currently, the index.html and sketch.js files are only stored locally on your own machine. This is preferable while you are creating and coding your project, but you will want others to be able to access them more widely when you are done. The simplest option, if you already have web hosting, is to upload these files to your existing server and then access them through the associated URL for your hosting.

Finally, if you open sketch.js using your editor of preference, there is a bare-bones p5.js project ready for creation. The limitations imposed by the format of a book chapter make it infeasible to offer a full introduction to either programming in general or p5.js in particular, but there are many great resources available, including the tutorials on the p5.js website at: https://p5js.org/tutorials/ and the book authored by the creators of the language: *Getting Started with p5.js: Making Interactive Graphics in JavaScript and Processing (Make)* by McCarthy, Reas, and Fry (2015). The remainder of this guide covers how I accessed the data I used and a general overview of how it was visualized using p5.js.

```
<!DOCTYPE html>
<html>
  <head>
    <script
src="https://cdnjs.cloudflare.com/ajax/libs/p5.js/0.5.11/p5.min.js"></script>
    <script
src="https://cdnjs.cloudflare.com/ajax/libs/p5.js/0.5.11/addons/p5.dom.min.js"></sc
ript>
    <script
src="https://cdnjs.cloudflare.com/ajax/libs/p5.js/0.5.11/addons/p5.sound.min.js"></
script>
    <link rel="stylesheet" type="text/css" href="style.css">
  </head>
  <body>
    <script src="sketch.js"></script>
  </body>
</html>
```

Fig. 12.5   Example of index.html file

ACCESSING DATA

This project arose from an assignment created for students in my course *Big Data and the Rhetoric of Information,* in which I challenged students to create a variety of visualizations based on open source data. I was also creating my own project along with them as an example, and I knew I wanted to use local data available from the *City of Raleigh—Open Data* project at https://data.raleighnc.gov.

One of the intriguing visualizations on the site is a map of the previous day's crime incidents. In thinking about visualizations, I also reflected on the large number of webcams in our area, many set up to monitor traffic and/or weather patterns. Although I originally considered trying to match webcams to the locations of crimes, I quickly realized that despite the prevalence of webcams, this would be an infrequent pairing. In addition, simply juxtaposing crime data with the variety of webcams publicly available created its own set of intriguing questions about the type of surveillance the average citizen can perform (Fig. 12.6).

The next step in the project was to access the data associated with the visualization, so I could use it within p5.js. The export function of the website offered several different formats in which I could access the raw data. These included Comma Separated Value (CSV), CSV for Excel, CSV for Excel (Europe), JSON, RDF, RSS, TSV for Excel, and XML. I selected the CSV option and downloaded it directly to my computer, but I also realized that if I right-clicked the link, I could copy the URL

Fig. 12.6   The previous day's crime incidents—city of Raleigh

where the CSV file was accessible on the web. This file is updated once per day at 11 am.

I tried to access and load this CSV file directly within p5.js, but this created an error, likely because server settings prevented this type of access. This can sometimes be a problem with images and other files as well. To work around this, I created an Automater script through macOS that would automatically download the file locally.[10] This was done with the following Automater actions:

1. **Get Specified Finder Items**: here I selected the location of the current version of the file, which resided in my Dropbox folder.
2. **Move Finder Items to Trash**: This deleted the current version identified in the previous step.

---

[10]For more information on Automator for MacOS, see https://support.apple.com/guide/automator/welcome/mac.

3. **Get Specified URLs**: Here I used the URL that I copied above: https://data.raleighnc.gov/ap/views/guyh-emm5/rows. csv?accessType=Download.
4. **Download URLs**: Using this action, I specified that the file should be saved into the same folder as the previous version of the file I had deleted in step 2.

This Automater task deletes the previous day's file and then downloads the most recent version of the crime data, titled Daily_Police_Incidents. csv. I then used the Calendar application on my Mac to automatically run this script once per day. I then created similar scripts for the webcam images I wanted to access. I set this script to run every 15 minutes rather than once a day.

There are a few important caveats about this method. First, downloading these files and saving them to my computer ensures that my application will still run even if the webcam images are temporarily unavailable on the internet. Second, you may have noticed above that I was downloading these images directly to my Dropbox (http:// www.dropbox.com). I have long used my Dropbox as a web server, and hosted my Aperveillance project directly from there. However, this ability to use Dropbox as web server was restricted to paid subscribers only in 2016 and is slated to be eliminated entirely at the end of 2017. Therefore, in the future, it will be necessary to take the additional step of uploading these files to a web server. With the CSV and webcam JPG images now saved to the same folder, I can create the code for my visualization.

CODING

The image in Fig. 12.7 represents the final version of the project as seen in the browser. There are several images from webcams displayed in a grid on the screen, including an image from the viewer's own local camera on the bottom right. Each of these images is placed randomly and updated and moved approximately every 15 seconds. In addition, the randomly placed white boxes contain information about crimes that were committed in Raleigh, including the date and time of the crime, the GPS coordinates where the incident occurred, and the type of incident. The grid is automatically scaled to fit any screen and if the device used to access the page does not have or does not allow access to the local

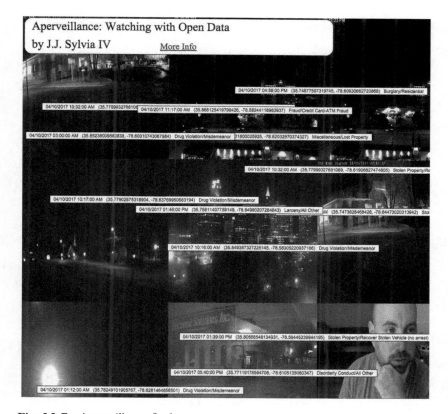

Fig. 12.7 Aperveillance final

webcam, that image will be replaced by another random webcam image from Raleigh.

The full p5.js code needed to create this project is listed below. Though it may look complex for those with little or no coding background, the amount of code required to create this project is quite small. Following the code, I will briefly walk you through how each section works.

The code begins by defining the **variables** (especially **arrays**) that will be used as part of the program. Next, the preload function loads all of the media and other files that will be used within the code.

```
var img = [];
var r3 = 0;
var stats;
var dt = [];
var loc = [];
var desc = [];
var howMany = 0;
var mic;


function preload() {
  img[0] = loadImage("raleigh-640x480.jpg");
  img[1] = loadImage("apex_skycam-640x480.jpg");
  img[2] = loadImage("airport_skycam-640x480.jpg");
  img[3] = loadImage("auburn_tower_ptz-640x480.jpg");
  img[3] = loadImage("wral_gardens-640x480.jpg");
  img[4] = loadImage("durham_skycam-640x480.jpg");
  img[5] = loadImage("truelook_chapel_hill-640x480.jpg");
  img[6] = loadImage("fayetteville_skycam-640x480.jpg");
  img[6] = loadImage("roxboro_skycam-640x480.jpg");
  img[7] = loadImage("wilson_skycam-640x480.jpg");
  img[8] = loadImage("wilimington_ptz-640x480.jpg");
  img[9] = loadImage("hive5-640x480.jpg");
  img[10] = loadImage("HGHPP_1.jpg");
  img[11] = loadImage("current.jpg");
  img[14] = loadImage("ELZBL_1.jpg");
  img[12] = loadImage("carolinabeach-640x480.jpg");
  img[16] = loadImage("201NST.jpg");
  img[17] = loadImage("auburntower-640x480.jpg");
  img[13] = loadImage("RLGSH_1.jpg");
  img[14] = loadImage("current-1.jpg");
  img[15] = loadImage("current-2.jpg");
  img[16] = loadImage("THMSD_1.jpg");
  img[17] = loadImage("current-3.jpg");
  stats = loadTable("Daily_Police_Incidents.csv")
}

function setup() {
  createCanvas(windowWidth, windowHeight);
  var options = {
    audio: false,
    video: true
  };

  capture = createCapture(options);
  capture.hide();
```

```
  var aper1 = createDiv("<font size='6'>Aperveillance: Watching
with Open Data</font>");
  aper1.position(30, 15);
  var aper2 = createDiv("<font size='6'>by J.J. Sylvia
IV</font>");
  aper2.position(30, 65);

  var rowCount = stats.getRowCount();
  for (var i = 0; i < rowCount; i++) {
    desc[i] = stats.getString(i, 1);
    loc[i] = stats.getString(i, 4);
    dt[i] = stats.getString(i, 2);
    howMany++;
    frameRate(0.1);
  }
}

function draw() {

 var aperveillance = createDiv("<font size='5'><a
href='http://www.jjsylvia.com/aperveillance/'>More
Info</a></font>");
aperveillance.position(375, 75);

 for (var y = 0; y <= height; y += 400) {
for (var x = 0; x <= width; x += 400) {
     var index = floor(random(img.length));
image(img[index], x, y, 400, 400);
}
  }
  var theWidth = width / 400;
  theWidth = round(theWidth);
  var r5 = random(1, theWidth);
  r5 = round(r5);
  r5 = r5*400;
  var theHeight = height / 400;
  theHeight = round(theHeight);
  var r6 = random(1, theHeight);
  r6 = round(r6);
  r6 = r6*400;
  image(capture, r5, r6, 400, 400);
  var rowCount = stats.getRowCount();
  for (var i = 1; i < 26; i++) {
    var r4 = floor(random(desc.length));
    var r = random(0, width-400);
    var r2 = random(175, 1900);
```

```
var bWidth = textWidth(desc[r4]);
var cWidth = textWidth(dt[r4]);
var eWidth = textWidth(loc[r4]);
rect(r-10, r2-15, bWidth+cWidth+eWidth+40, 20);
textSize(12);
text(dt[r4], r, r2);
text(loc[r4], r+cWidth+10, r2);
text(desc[r4], r+cWidth+eWidth+20, r2);
}

rect(10,10,830,100,20);
  textSize(45);
}
```

This ensures that the media loads and the code does not encounter an error in middle of executing.

In the set up function, the canvas—where the code will be executed—is created to match the height and width of the window in which it is being loaded. The createCapture code accesses the webcam using options that set it to only access the video feed and not the audio feed. The createDiv functions then create a place to insert HTML, which creates the header that contains the title and byline. Finally, a **for loop** accesses all of the data from the CSV file and stores it in variables so that it can be manipulated with code.

The draw function is used to put the majority of the content onto the screen. The first loop featured in this section selects a random webcam image and places it in the next spot in the grid, sized to 400 pixels wide by 400 pixels high. It does this until the entire screen, or canvas, is filled. The next section of code determines a random grid spot on which to overlay the webcam image from the viewer's own camera, if available. The image is then displayed using the image(capture, r5, r6, 400, 400); code. The majority of the remaining code determines the length of the crime incident data and places it randomly across the canvas in a white rectangle.

The main generative nature of this project involves the random placement of random webcam images in juxtaposition with crime data and the image from the viewer's camera. The positioning of these are changed approximately every 15 seconds to keep the display fresh and to prevent the viewer from being able to dwell too long on the relationship between the placement of the text and the images. However, it would also be quite easy to change the project and, for example, display the most common types of crimes, each sized larger depending on their frequency of occurrence.

The key to an artistic approach such as this is to try to think outside of the normal data visualization approach. In the case of this project, I was less interested in the frequency of any particular crimes—a more traditional data analysis question—and more interested in bigger picture Humanities-esque questions about the nature of surveillance. For example, should we have an expectation of privacy when we are in public places?[11] Aperveillance extends that question to ask who should have access to the data generated by surveillance and what opportunities such data affords when combined in novel or unexpected ways. p5.js allowed me to create a provocative artistic interpretation of that question in a way that a more traditional data visualization tool like Tableau would not. Aperveillance, for example, was displayed in a manner that mimics the aesthetic of rows of footage from surveillance cameras. Such an aesthetic harkens back to Jeremy Bentham's Panopticon.[12] The Panopticon is a circular building designed to serve as a prison. A circular guard tower sits in the middle, with individual cells located in the outer wall. A bright light from the guard tower would enable the guards to see all of the prisoners, but prevent the prisoners from being able to see the guards or even confirm whether or not they were in the tower. Camera-based security systems mirror this aesthetic with rows of televisions that display camera images. The guard sees out through the cameras, but those being observed cannot see the guards or even know if the footage from the cameras is being monitored. This aesthetic is important because the power disparity between the guard and the prisoners emerges through the aesthetic design.

Finally, my index.html and sketch.js files, along with the images and CSV file were made publicly available through my Dropbox. This could also be done by uploading them to a web server. I linked the URL aperveillance.com to the URL for the index.html file in my Dropbox and then anyone in the world could access the program through that URL.

---

[11] Helen Nissenbaum, "Protecting Privacy in an Information Age: The Problem of Privacy in Public," *Law and Philosophy* 17, no. 5/6 (November 1998): 559. https://doi.org/10.2307/3505189.

[12] Jeremy Benthamn, *Works of Jeremy Bentham* (S.l. London: Forgotten Books, [1789] 2015); Michel Foucault, *Discipline and Punish: The Birth of the Prison*, 2nd ed. (New York: Vintage Books, [1975] 1995).

CONCLUSIONS

Code/art projects make use of the iterative nature of generative design. It is this iteration, in part, that affords the possibility of creating artistic data visualizations. This artistic approach allows one to ask different questions than those that could be answered through traditional data analysis. Based on my analysis of qualitative verbal feedback provided by viewers of the Aperveillance project, several conclusions can be drawn. First, many people are unaware of the amount of data that is openly accessible on the internet, and have infrequently, if ever, thought about the consequences of combining multiple data sources. While this accessibility bothered viewers in a general way, they were often unable to connect it to concerns about their own individual privacy. Only upon realizing that a camera was incorporating their image into the project was this connection made. Many viewers were bothered about their unwilling inclusion in surveillance, though this process mirrors the form of much of contemporary technological surveillance. By experiencing their own surveillance as both the surveilled and the one surveilling, viewers were able to articulate questions about the tensions between privacy and surveillance of which they were previously unaware or unconcerned.

While there are a wide variety of languages available to use, p5.js offers an option that is accessible to beginners. My students and workshop participants with little prior programming experience have been able to master the basics of the language within as little as one week. Nonetheless, it is important to consider the goal of your data visualization when selecting the tool, as p5.js can be a more difficult option when trying to complete traditional data visualization analyses.

REFERENCES

Ball, Kirstie, Kevin Haggerty, and David Lyon, eds. *Routledge Handbook of Surveillance Studies* 1. Paperback ed. Routledge International Handbooks. London: Routledge, 2012.

Benthamn, Jeremy. *Works of Jeremy Bentham.* S.l. London: Forgotten Books, 2015.

Berman, Jules J. *Principles of Big Data: Preparing, Sharing, and Analyzing Complex Information.* Amsterdam: Elsevier, Morgan Kaufmann, 2013.

Bohnacker, Hartmut, Benedikt Gross, Julia Laub, and Claudius Lazzeroni. *Generative Design: Visualize, Program, and Create with Processing.* New York: Princeton Architectural Press, 2012.

Eiben, Agoston E., and James E. Smith. *Introduction to Evolutionary Computing,* 1st ed., 2 printing, Softcover version of original hardcover ed. 2003. Natural Computing Series. Berlin: Springer, 2010.

Foucault, Michel. *Discipline and Punish: The Birth of the Prison.* 2nd Vintage Books ed. New York: Vintage Books, 1975.

Hornby, Gregory, Al Globus, Derek Linden, and Jason Lohn. "Automated Antenna Design with Evolutionary Algorithms." American Institute of Aeronautics and Astronautics, 2006. https://doi.org/10.2514/6.2006-7242.

Manovich, Lev. "Info Aesthetics," 2001. http://www.manovich.net.

Marx, Gary T. "Surveillance Studies." In *International Encyclopedia of the Social & Behavioral Sciences,* 733–741, 2015. https://doi.org/10.1016/b978-0-08-097086-8.64025-4.

Mayer-Schönberger, Viktor, and Kenneth Cukier. *Big Data: A Revolution that Will Transform How We Live, Work, and Think.* First Mariner Books edition. Boston: Mariner Books, Houghton Mifflin Harcourt, 2014.

McCarthy, Lauren, Casey Reas, and Ben Fry. *Getting Started with p5.js: Making Interactive Graphics in JavaScript and Processing.* San Francisco, CA: Maker Media, Inc., 2015.

Monaghan, Peter. "Watching the Watchers." *The Chronicle of Higher Education,* 2006.

Nissenbaum, Helen. "Protecting Privacy in an Information Age: The Problem of Privacy in Public." *Law and Philosophy* 17, no. 5/6 (November 1998): 559. https://doi.org/10.2307/3505189.

Reas, Casey, and Chandler McWilliams. *Form Code: In Design, Art, and Architecture.* New York: Princeton Architecturel Press, 2010.

Zimmer, Michael. "OkCupid Study Reveals the Perils of Big-Data Science." *Wired,* May 14, 2016. Accessed April 12, 2017. https://www.wired.com/2016/05/okcupid-study-reveals-perils-big-data-science/.

CHAPTER 13

Research Methods in Recording Oral Tradition: Choosing Between the Evanescence of the Digital or the Senescence of the Analog

Nick Thieberger

In this chapter, I present methods for creating primary research records in ways that can be archived and reused in the future, with a focus on linguistic fieldwork, but with principles that apply across a range of humanities disciplines. Research is stronger if primary data can be accessed and cited so that readers can verify that the source material actually exists and so that they are able to apply their own analysis to it. This relies on the data being deposited and curated in an archive that guarantees access over time. Our research group in Australia is preserving records of intangible cultural heritage[1] in the world's small languages, by building the Pacific and Regional Archive for Digital Sources in Endangered

[1] See for example, UNESCO's page on intangible cultural heritage, https://ich.unesco.org/en/home.

N. Thieberger (✉)
The University of Melbourne and ARC Centre of Excellence for the Dynamics of Language, Melbourne, Australia
e-mail: thien@unimelb.edu.au

© The Author(s) 2018
l. levenberg et al. (eds.), *Research Methods for the Digital Humanities*,
https://doi.org/10.1007/978-3-319-96713-4_13

233

Cultures (PARADISEC.org.au). As the collection grows in size (currently 45 terabytes) and number of languages represented (currently just over 1170) we have to seriously consider the long-term viability of the collection. But the most urgent issue that faces us is to locate and digitise recordings that will not otherwise be preserved. Many of these are field recordings made by past generations of linguists, musicologists and ethnographers, from a time when emphasis was placed on the analysis of the contents of the recordings, not on preservation of the recordings themselves. As we will see, archiving is no longer an end-of-career activity, relegated as it used to be to your retirement or to your executors after you die. Archiving is now central to research methodology, creating citable records that allow research to be contextualised and verified. As Barwick notes, we are turning old ideas upside-down and this means we are training new researchers to think about the quality of the records they produce, including the content, file-naming, formats, metadata, and equipment they use.[2] There is much in all of this work that is applicable more broadly to Humanities research practices.

Our particular focus is on records of small languages for which there is otherwise little information available, and so the work of a linguist recording speakers of the language becomes all the more important. Keep in mind that there are some 7000 languages in the world and that for most of them there are few, if any, records. Thus, making recordings in the course of linguistic fieldwork becomes a critical point at which not only can scholarly work be done, but basic records of performance in another of the world's cultures can be created. The records have intrinsic value for the speakers and their descendants as well as for linguistic research. Hence there is a great responsibility, for linguists who create them, to manage these records properly.

RESEARCH AND ARCHIVING

The research questions for field linguists today focus on what each new language has to tell us about the range of possible variation in the structures and communication strategies involving language. There is a recognition that our own use of our research data will never be exhaustive, and

---

[2] Linda Barwick, "Turning It All Upside Down ... Imagining a Distributed Digital Audiovisual Archive," *Literary and Linguistic Computing* 19, no. 3 (2004): 253–263.

that creating well-annotated and described collections will allow others to continue working with this material. I prepared the data that I created in my research on Nafsan (a language of South Efate, Vanuatu), so that it could be reused by providing a finding aid[3] to provide contextual information about the files. Other researchers are now using this material and focusing in more detail than I did on aspects of the language. They can only do this because I created and archived all the material with future reuse in mind.

Archiving is central to scholarly research. Using archives to locate primary sources is normal research practice, but it is less common for researchers to think of their own work as being an archivable resource. If your work creates new documents (be they textual or media) or touches manuscripts that no one has used or that you are providing with a new interpretation, then that interpretation and those documents need to be made available to the audience you are writing for. Creating well-formed ("archive-ready") research materials makes them reusable, and archiving ensures that you can access your own materials and that others can benefit from work you have done. In order for this virtuous work practice to be achieved, certain steps need to be put in place. These were recently summarised by an international consortium of researchers in the FAIR[4] principles, which suggest that records should be findable, accessible, interoperable, and reusable. While there is a clear case for making good records of small and maybe endangered languages, given the rarity of records for most such languages, the same methods can be applied to most humanities research. There is a logical workflow in making recordings, applying metadata, naming files systematically, transcribing files and so on, so that the files can be archived without much effort on the part of the researcher.[5] As with most Digital Humanities methods, we emphasise reusability of the research materials. For us, this means using uncompressed formats (e.g., tif rather than jpg, wav rather than mp3), providing a good description and getting licenses from the people recorded so that it is clear how the research can be used by others.

---

[3] http://www.nthieberger.net/sefate.html.

[4] https://www.force11.org/group/fairgroup/fairprinciples.

[5] Nicholas Thieberger and Andrea Berez, "Linguistic Data Management," in *The Oxford Handbook of Linguistic Fieldwork*, ed. Nicholas Thieberger (Oxford: Oxford University Press, 2012), 90–118.

The Virtue of Archiving

Fixing a performance, opportunistically captured, as an archival record-ing risks privileging that recording so that it can be seen as providing an authority that it was never meant to have. From an archive's point of view, these are predictable problems in the literature[6] and accepted as the necessary corollary of keeping records. Similarly, we know that archives are extremely partial, representing those with the power to make records and preserve them.[7]

If scholars work with primary materials and use them as the basis for their analysis, then the reader should be able to verify claims by going back to those primary materials. It used to be the case that the (analog) records sat in an office and were only available by visiting the researcher[8] and it is usually still the case that digital records can only be obtained in the same way. New research methods, including archiving, free the original researcher from dealing with such requests and allow her/him to specify conditions under which the materials can be used, that is, provid-ing a licence for their use. A license can be as simple as a statement that the records can be used only for educational purposes. Rather than mak-ing up a range of different licenses, it is easiest to use an existing system, like, for example, Creative Commons.[9] These internationally recognised licenses are flexible and cover a range of options that you, as the crea-tor of the work, can select from. You could think of questions like the following:

- Are you allowed to make copies?
- Did you get a release form from the person you recorded?
- Did the library where you copied them allow you to enrich them and make them available to others?

---

[6] Jacques Derrida, *Archive Fever: A Freudian Impression* (Chicago, IL: University of Chicago Press, 1996); Terry Cook, and Joan M. Schwartz, "Archives, Records and Power: From (Postmodern) Theory to (Archival) Performance," *Archival Science* 2, no. 3–4 (2002): 171–185, http://dx.doi.org/10.1007/BF02435620.

[7] Linda T. Smith, *Decolonizing Methodologies: Research and Indigenous Peoples* (Dunedin: Zed, 1999).

[8] For a humorous but nevertheless accurate portrayal of this situation, see this video pro-duced by the TROLLING (https://dataverse.no/dataverse/trolling) archive in Norway: https://www.youtube.com/watch?v=uEf0cONT9.

[9] https://creativecommons.org/.

- Was the original you made of sufficient quality to allow other users or is it too compressed and poorly captured to be used again?
- Did you make enough backups and have you archived the files?
- Did you give the files you created unique names that allow you to find them again?
- Do you have a description of what is in the files so you do not need to open each file every time you want to look at or listen to it again?

Each of these questions suggests simple issues of data management. Fortunately, there are well-established standards for file formats and data management[10] that linguists can adopt. But even if these files do make it into a curated repository, how long is digital data going to last? There is no proven storage medium, so the key to preservation of data is migration to the next storage system. Given that all research data will need to be properly curated over time, we are confident that national storage infrastructure will soon become the norm and that our collection will become part of that larger effort. Academic institutions will increasingly provide archival storage for primary research data, but you may need to curate your collections in some more temporary solution until a suitable archive is available.

In our experience of working with many legacy collections (those made in the past by retired or deceased researchers), we have learned what it takes to get from an undifferentiated box of tapes to a well-organised collection. If a researcher is still able to provide information about their tapes, archiving them is usually the first time that they compile their notes in an organised way. This creates a catalog that lists enough information for someone else to make sense of the item that they have described. It is very rare for collections of recordings to have even the most minimal metadata or cataloging information. In some cases, in our work on archiving language records, we have preserved tapes for which there is no metadata, but we assume they are worth digitising because of the value of the collection they are part of. At some point, we intend to put this kind of unannotated material online for crowdsourced annotation (see e.g., Zooniverse[11] as a platform for online annotation). An example of a collection of primary records we have worked with was

---

[10] Louise Corti et al., *Managing and Sharing Research Data: A Guide to Good Practice* (London: Sage, 2014), 56.

[11] https://www.zooniverse.org/.

created by Arthur Capell, who was a professor of linguistics and a prolific collector of information in many languages. When he died in 1986, he left many boxes of papers and audio recordings. We put 15,000 pages of Arthur Capell's notes online[12] (but untranscribed) with sufficient metadata to make them locatable and archived the same collection with the same metadata to ensure longevity of access.[13] Another current project is a set of 24,000 pages of manuscripts and typescripts created by the ethnographer Daisy Bates since 1904, which represents information about many Western Australian Aboriginal languages. We are now working to put these page images online[14] with textual versions of some 4000 pages. This is more complex than the Capell project in that it requires typing the manuscript text (and encoding it in XML), but it has the benefit of allowing the text to be searched, always with the ability to see the original page image, so in each of these cases a user can cite the original document which is a necessary step for scholarly practice.

Metadata for Findability

Metadata is the cataloging information about an item that typically includes basic information about what it is, when and where it was made, by whom and with whom. Within the PARADISEC collection, there are hundreds of recordings that have only the information written on their tape covers as metadata. In some cases, this is a single and cryptic word that would clearly have made sense at the moment it was written but is not particularly informative about the contents of the recording for anyone else now searching the catalog. We have improved our methods as an academic discipline since these recordings were made and are in a better position to create materials that we can access ourselves in future. So, if you record someone telling a story or being interviewed, then noting down all these details will help you remember what is on the recording later. For example, at the beginning of a recording, I will say who is being recorded, on what date and where. If I know what they will be talking about I will summarise it here too. This means the recording has some internal identification in case it is separated from other metadata.

---

[12] http://paradisec.org.au/fieldnotes/AC2.htm.

[13] http://catalog.paradisec.org.au/collections/AC2.

[14] http://bates.org.au.

I also take note on paper of what the recording device has named the recording and also note the contents and this will later be typed into the metadata notes I keep for all my files. The archive you will deposit your files with can advise on the metadata they need, so that you can start getting your catalog into the right shape to meet the archive's requirements. For example, each archive has its own notion of what an "item" is and how much information should be provided for each item. Some standard metadata terms (typically modeled on Dublin Core,[15] the librarian's standard) include: "Title" of the item; "Role" of the people involved; "Date" recorded (in a specific format); "Coverage", or what geographic area does it cover; "Content language", or the language used in the item; "Subject language", or what language the item is about (these last two use the ISO-639-3 code for language identification); and, "Roles" of people involved (speaker, singer, writer etc.).

Any files you create in the course of your research should be uncompressed and high resolution to allow them to be used in various ways later on. If you are going to make copies of a manuscript that only exists on paper or microfilm in one library then consider making good quality copies and taking careful notes about the context of the images (the library identifier or the pages and book title), so that you can relate them to the originals later on.

How to Name Files

File-naming is one of the simplest first steps for managing research data and a lack of proper file-naming can result in a loss of data. If you use a device like a camera or recorder then it will typically name files sequentially, often restarting the same names every month (like STE-0023, STE-0024, and so on). You need to change these to a unique name (like 201702-0023 for example) and then never change them again! All of your metadata will then relate to that filename and, when the file is archived, it should ideally retain that name so that you can cite it in the course of your own research. And, the case of the name is critical. If you use uppercase in the filename then the metadata listing of that filename has to be identical. This is because when you copy your metadata to an archive's catalog, the name will be the lynchpin between the

---

[15] http://dublincore.org.

metadata and the file in the archive. A mismatch in case will mean the file is not related to the metadata. The Bates project mentioned earlier includes over 24,000-page images that each needed to be named according to a principle that relates a page back to its original document in the National Library of Australia. In my (2006) PhD dissertation, I was able to cite each example sentence in my grammar back to its source in archival digital audio files and to provide them on a DVD with the book.[16] The archival references will continue to work after the DVD is no longer playable, but only because the same filenames are used in the book as are used in the archive.

All of these methods rely on training new researchers with better methods for recording, annotating, transcribing, and curating their research data. As part of our work, we run regular training sessions in linguistic data management built into normal fieldwork practice. The ability to develop this research infrastructure further depends on the degree to which academic institutions recognise that holding such repositories enhances their prestige and hence requires their support. In our case, it helps that PARADISEC has been listed by the UNESCO Register of Intangible Cultural Heritage for the Memory of the World and has been awarded the European Data Seal of Approval. Our main problem is how to make sure this digital material can be shepherded through the next period and survive the evanescence that otherwise awaits.

As research produces more and more digital material, often of considerable heritage importance, the onus is on the research community to provide long-term repositories for this material. In fact, there is no other choice for preservation of analog recordings but to digitise them. In this chapter, I have addressed key factors in mitigating digital evanescence, so that our precious research materials will survive into the future. When it comes to media recordings, the evanescence of the digital is preferable to the senescence of the analog.[17]

---

[16] Nicholas Thieberger, *A Grammar of South Efate: An Oceanic Language of Vanuatu* (Oceanic Linguistics Special Publication, No. 33. Honolulu: University of Hawai'i Press, 2006).

[17] Also see the UCLA Library's guide to audio archiving: http://guides.library.ucla.edu/ethno/ethnomuc200.

REFERENCES

Barwick, Linda. "Turning It All Upside Down ... Imagining a Distributed Digital Audiovisual Archive." *Literary and Linguistic Computing* 19, no. 3 (2004): 253–263.

Cook, Terry, and Joan M. Schwartz. "Archives, Records and Power: From (Postmodern) Theory to (Archival) Performance." *Archival Science* 2, no. 3–4 (2002): 171–185. http://dx.doi.org/10.1007/BF02435620.

Corti, Louise, Veerle van den Eynden, Libby Bishop, and Matthew Woollard. *Managing and Sharing Research Data: A Guide to Good Practice*. London: Sage, 2014.

Derrida, Jacques. *Archive Fever: A Freudian Impression*. Chicago, IL: University of Chicago Press, 1996.

Smith, Linda T. *Decolonizing Methodologies: Research and Indigenous Peoples*. Dunedin: Zed, 1999.

Thieberger, Nicholas. *A Grammar of South Efate: An Oceanic Language of Vanuatu*. Oceanic Linguistics Special Publication, No. 33. Honolulu: University of Hawai'i Press, 2006.

Thieberger, Nicholas, and Andrea Berez. "Linguistic Data Management." In *The Oxford Handbook of Linguistic Fieldwork*, edited by Nicholas Thieberger, 90–118. Oxford: Oxford University Press, 2012.

CHAPTER 14

A Philological Approach to Sound Preservation

Federica Bressan

Sound recording technology has been around for roughly 150 years. Since Thomas Edison's phonograph in 1877, the techniques and technologies to improve the quality, the bandwidth, the duration of sound recordings, and the portability of recording/playback devices have been evolving and keep being improved today. The result is a diverse coexistence of practices and standards, some of them so obsolete that it is not inappropriate to speak about "media archeology." This chapter will focus on the challenges posed by audio heritage in the Digital Humanities. It will include a guide to support a rational systematization in the field of preservation, because every technical choice or solution has an impact on our perception of preserved objects and, through them, on our understanding of the world. Remembering that sound recording technology has not always been around is a good place to start, because it reminds us that hearing "voices from the past" is a true marvel of our times and a world without them would be a very different place.

F. Bressan (✉)
Ghent University, Ghent, Belgium
e-mail: federica.bressan@ugent.be

© The Author(s) 2018
l. levenberg et al. (eds.), *Research Methods for the Digital Humanities*,
https://doi.org/10.1007/978-3-319-96713-4_14

Keep the Music Playing

In order to understand why the preservation of audio documents should be challenging at all, we need to define **"audio document"** and **"preservation."** Let us begin with the concept of **carrier**. An audio carrier is a physical object designed to store an audio signal. This definition does not say anything about diverse types of carriers or about the complexity of how the signal is stored on them. Tape cassettes, compact discs (CDs), and vinyl records are examples of audio carriers we are likely familiar with. As for "preservation", it is defined as "the sum total of the steps necessary to ensure the permanent accessibility—forever—of documentary heritage."[1] Here, forever means "decades or centuries, or long enough to be concerned about the obsolescence of technology."[2] Imagine you have a sound recording on tape and you want to preserve it, ideally, forever. What can you do? For example, we can lock it up in a safe and come back every other year to check that everything is ok. This works for most objects we have considered worth preserving and makes up much of our shared cultural heritage. There are obvious differences between objects made of paper, wood and stone, but none degrade at the rate of audiovisual carriers, the life expectancy of which can be measured in years or decades. The paradigm of "traditional" cultural heritage, which privileges "preserving the original," has persisted relatively unquestioned.[3] But what is the equivalent for audio carriers? Should we extend the life of a specific tape, because it stores a specific recording? This was in fact the main approach in the early days of preservation, but it did not work because audiovisual carriers are subject to a process of physical degradation that eventually causes the irreversible loss of their content—in a generation's time. The paradigm of "preserving the original" applied to audiovisual carriers is doomed to fail. So, can we find another way?

[1] Ray Edmonson, *Memory of the World: General Guidelines to Safeguard Documentary Heritage* (Paris: UNESCO, 2002), 12. Accessed May 5, 2018. http://unesdoc.unesco.org/images/0012/001256/125637e.pdf.

[2] Margaret Hedstrom, *It's About Time: Research Challenges in Digital Archiving and Long-Term Preservation. Final Report: Workshop on Research Challenges in Digital Archiving* (Washington, DC: National Science Foundation and Library of Congress, 2002).

[3] Dietrich Schüller, *The Ethics of Preserving Audio and Video Documents* (Paris: UNESCO, 2006).

To answer this question, it may be useful to stop and reflect on what the object of our interest is: the tape or the recording? The carrier or the message? The content or the container? Normally it is the recording or, more specifically, what the recording *means* (not the audio signal in itself, but rather a song or a speech represented by the signal). If the recording is not valuable then the carrier may still be the object of desire for some collectors. But, the problem of preservation primarily emerged not because carriers, as such, were at risk, but recordings. We can then agree that the objects of preservation are sound recordings, and that audio carriers are important insofar as they are the physical objects on which sound recordings are stored.

Fortunately, there is something that distinguishes audiovisual carriers from other "traditional" cultural heritage materials, except for written texts: the possibility to separate the content from the container. Leonardo da Vinci's Mona Lisa is intrinsically one with the canvas. There is nothing we can extract from it and move to another canvas. Or, at least, not in the same way in which we can copy or re-mediate a sound recording. An audio carrier is an industrial product and it belongs to, what Walter Benjamin terms, the era of "mechanical reproduction".[4] This means that sound recordings can have a life expectancy independent from the carriers. The carriers fatally degrade, but the content can be copied onto new carriers as the old ones give out. This represents a paradigm shift, from "preserving the original" to "preserving the content", and it raises a whole new set of problems because, according to Ray Edmonson:

> copying is not a value-neutral act; a series of technical judgments and physical acts (such as manual repair) determine the quality and nature of the resulting copy. It is possible, in effect, to distort, lose or manipulate history through the judgments made and the choice and quality of the work performed. Documenting the processes involved and choices made in copying from generation to generation is essential to preserving the integrity of the work.[5]

Therefore, the crucial question of audio preservation is not about the carriers, but about the *process of re-mediating* their content.

---

[4]Walter Benjamin, *The Work of Art in the Age of Mechanical Reproduction* (Frankfurt am Main: Schram Verlag, 1955).

[5]Ray Edmonson, *Audiovisual Archiving: Philosophy and Principles* (Paris: UNESCO, 2004), 14.

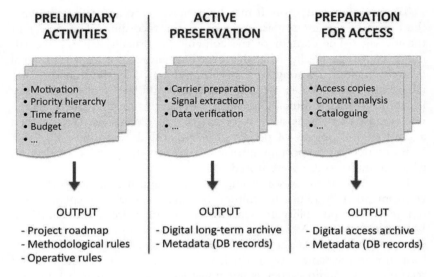

Fig. 14.1 The scheme summarizes the main steps of the preservation process for audio documents

A METHODOLOGY IN THE MAKING

A detailed description of the methodology (theory and practice) for the transfer of audio documents to an all-digital document set would require an extended dissertation. Here, we present the theoretic foundations of the methodology and give a general overview of the fundamental steps, before we focus on some practical examples to show the connection between audio documents and digital **philology**.[6]

Figure 14.1 shows the three fundamental steps of preservation: preliminary activities, active preservation, and preparation for access. Active preservation (as opposed to passive preservation) is the step that is normally identified with the entire process, as it consists of the extraction of the information contained in the original carriers and its encoding onto

[6]For an extended account of existing methodologies see the International Association of Sound and Audiovisual Archives—Technical Committee 05 (IASA-TC 05) (2014), the International Federation of Library Associations and Institutions (IFLA)—Audiovisual and Multimedia Section (2004), Media Preservation Initiative Task Force (2011), and Bressan (2013).

a new medium. We speak of **digitization** when the recording technique of the source carrier is analog and the destination carrier is digital. When the recording technique of the source carrier is digital [for example, when we transfer information from CDs or Digital Audio Tapes (DATs) to Hard Disk Drives (HDD)], we should use the term *re-mediation*, as there is no analog to digital (A/D) conversion of the audio signal.

The goal of the methodology is to make sure that preservation is performed according to rigorous scientific protocols and that a qualitative output is achieved. In this context, we will consider a "qualitative output" that which derives from a working approach that implements philological principles (these principles are elaborated below). Output that is not backed up by documentation of the objective of the action, its limit, or the procedures that have been applied is considered *low profile*.[7] The trans-coding that occurs when the information from the source carrier is extracted and moved to a new carrier has **hermeneutic** implications, because it cannot be performed without creating (or assuming) a *model* of the source.[8] A model requires, by definition, the identification of relevant features. George Brock-Nannestad suggests, "it should be emphasized that selecting features for restoration or preservation in the worst instance means deselection of the rest."[9] Deselection means exclusion from the information workflow and can result in features being discarded from history.

Wrong data (for example, a badly compensated equalization curve) means wrong or misleading output data. The expected final output is a digital collection of data (Fig. 14.1) that represents the audio signal and all the accompanying material of the source carriers; each element in the digital collection is associated to a description (metadata). At a higher level of abstraction, we can define the output as a collection of "objects" associated with descriptions that help retrieve and identify these objects. The objects that are normally included in an audio *preservation copy* are:

---

[7] Giuseppe Gigliozzi, *Introduzione all'uso del Computer Negli Studi Letterari* (Milan: Bruno Mondadori, 2003).

[8] F. Bressan, S. Canazza, T. Vets, and M. Leman, "Hermeneutic Implications of Cultural Encoding: A Reflection on Audio Recordings and Interactive Installation Art," in *Digital Libraries and Multimedia Archives.* Proceedings of the 12th Italian Research Conference on Digital Libraries (IRCDL 2016) (Elsevier, Procedia – Computer Sciences, 2017), 47–58.

[9] George Brock-Nannestad, "The Rationale Behind Operational Conservation Theory," in *Conservation Without Limits: IIC Nordic Group XV Congress,* ed. Riitta Koskivirta (Helsinki, FI: IIC Nordic Group, 2000).

the audio signal, pictures of the carrier, the box and its attachments, a video of the carrier during signal extraction, and a descriptive sheet including codes for data integrity verification (**checksums**). What cannot be directly represented in a digital form (e.g., smell) is thoroughly documented in a description as objectively as possible, hence the need for common vocabularies and reference grids (until maybe in the future we will develop a technology to digitize smell or to recreate it from our description).

COMPUTER SCIENCE: MORE THAN SOFTWARE TOOLS

Reconstructing Audio from a Picture

Photos of Ghosts (also known as Photos of Grooves and Holes or Supporting Tracks Separation) is an innovative method to reconstruct the audio signal from a picture of the grooves on a disc's surface. Overlapping pictures of the disc surface are divided in sectors, the grooves on each sector are identified and rectified thanks to image processing techniques, then the waveform is reconstructed from a unification of the grooves' segments. The touch-free technology allows for the treatment of fragile and even broken disks. The automation of image processing tasks decreases the time and cost of digitization with respect to reading the disc on a turntable. Using this process, a new approach to sound restoration can be envisioned: for example, foreign bodies can be graphically removed from the picture before the audio is reconstructed. Thus, we can obtain clean audio directly from the carrier, instead of applying noise removal filters later. Photos of Ghosts is also inspiring innovative ways to produce preservation copies of phonographic discs: instead of storing the audio signal, we may store a high definition 3D model of the carrier itself and reconstruct the audio as necessary with future and more sophisticated algorithms. It is intriguing to imagine the same approach for magnetic tapes: instead of audio, we would store a "magnetic map" of the tape and the benefits for endangered tapes would be revolutionary.

Remind and Rewind

The preservation of audio recordings with digital technology is predicated upon the disembodiment of the document. All relevant information should be transferred minimizing information loss, nonetheless audio, video, texts, and images collapse in a flow of **unimedia**[10] and will only be accessed through software applications—the sense of touch is lost. Typically, iTunes-like audio players rarely include a functional integration of the accompanying material (images, video, etc.). Remind[11] and Rewind[12] are two applications dedicated to digitized historical audio documents. Besides providing the user with a graphic interface reproducing the original controls of the equipment, they connect audio and metadata in a meaningful way. Reel-to-reel recorders move along the tape linearly, not allowing for random access. Remind preserves this feature in the replica of the control panel, including fast forward and rewind at fast or library wind speed. Conversely, Rewind is the virtualization of a turntable and, like the real-life original, it supports random access. Both applications allow the user to adjust the equalization curves, which are modeled according to the analog original. The video of the carrier during digitization, if available, is aligned with the audio, therefore, eventual defects on the source carrier are easily detectable and associated to the audio stream. Remind and Rewind also support specific features of the historical equipment, such as quadraphonic audio (Remind) and stylus type and weight (Rewind). The uniqueness of these applications resides in the fact that their design is dedicated to digitized audio documents and in that they constitute a step towards future applications that may integrate a philological approach to gestures (loading a disc on the turntable) in VR environments.

Digital Philology: An Emerging Discipline

What is philology? It should not surprise that the meaning of the term philology is obscure to most people who are not directly involved with it for their profession. It normally conjures images of yellowed pages, filled with text that people called philologists spend their life analyzing.

---

[10] Nicholas Negroponte, *Being Digital* (New York: Vintage Books, 1995).

[11] Federica Bressan, Sergio Canazza, Carlo Fantozzi, and Niccolò Pretto, "Tape Music Archives: From Preservation to Interaction," *International Journal on Digital Libraries* 18, no. 3 (2017), 233–249.

[12] Sergio Canazza, Carlo Fantozzi, and Niccolò Pretto, "Accessing Tape Music Documents on Mobile Devices," *ACM Transaction on Multimedia Computing Communications* 12, no. 1s (2015), 1–20.

But, whatever it is, most people know that "it has to do with texts." This association is correct and touches the core of philology. The discipline of philology is applied to different fields, and the definitions found in each field tend to consider specific aspects of the discipline—sometimes leaning towards analytic activities, sometime towards the interpretative ones. The term refers to the critical study of texts, the languages they use, and of methodologies for their historical interpretation. Philology is a foundational form of study; its goals are to resolve issues concerning the nature of textual evidence, so that literary, philosophical, and historical theories based on texts are less likely to be undermined by misdating or misreading of the textual data. Philological studies include such subfields as etymology (principally focused on the development of characters and their semantic basis), paleography (the study of old [Greek: paleo-] writing) and epigraphy (the study of inscriptions [Gr. Epigraphe]), and historical phonology and linguistics. More broadly, philology engages issues of textual history (the lineage of editions behind extant texts) and the mastery of various historical, institutional, and cultural fields that relate to the essential formative environments within which texts were generated.[13]

It should be kept in mind that this definition applies to "traditional" philology, and by all means not to "digital" philology. But, as we will see, digital philology is a new discipline born out of the encounter of two pre-existing areas of study, i.e. philology and computer science (or, textual criticism and information science). It is important to clearly define the contributing areas separately before observing how they merge together. For the purposes of our discourse, we do not need to proceed into the implications of the nature of texts nor the single movements within the history of philology. In its essence, the piece of information that we need to take home is: philology is a discipline that deals with texts, intended as such (written sources) and as entities with a cultural meaning (their interpretation). Particular attention is given to the authenticity and the accuracy of texts.

There are many reasons why the impact of the "digital revolution" on our society is hard to assess (for one, lack of historical distance). Digital technology has become pervasive in all aspects of our life, directly or indirectly. But, not everything that has to do with digital technology has turned into something qualitatively new. Narrowing

---

[13] Class Materials presented by Professor Robert Eno, Indiana University, 2011.

Fig. 14.2 Manually counting words in a text on a digital device does not make you a digital philologist

our scope to our field of interest, "digital philology" cannot be claimed as a new discipline due to the simple existence of digital texts (roughly speaking, a text that can be displayed on a computer screen). Intuitively, we can agree that changing the medium has an impact on the text and on our perception of it. But, pinning down what this impact is, let alone measuring it, is no easy task. Acknowledging that a traditional philologist does not become a digital one just because he reads some texts on his computer screen is a very important starting point (Fig. 14.2). Digital philology is not the discipline that deals with texts displayed on a computer screen. Let's think of art for an obvious example: an electronic reproduction of da Vinci's Mona Lisa does not make it "digital art". Intuitively we may feel that there is something different in the work of a scholar who analyses a text, or a painting, in direct contact with the real object or from a computer screen, but the point is that the questions they ask and the methods they apply are not necessarily different. Scholars involved with textual criticism and other disciplines that rely on literary sources are currently engaged in re-thinking their activity in light of the impact of digital technology on research and education.

"Digital philology" is an expression constituted by two words: so far, we have considered the second. What about digital? Digital refers to the other contributing area of knowledge: computer science. Computer science brings to the table its approach and some of its concepts and methodologies—not only technology. The conceptual principles used to model the world, or the tendency to look at things with different levels of abstraction, are tools of thought that can easily be exported to other domains, and fruitfully so. To summarize, the contribution of computer science comprises: technological tools for quantitative analyses and for sharing *corpora* through a network; and, methods and concepts that inform the theoretical speculation for fostering the development of new tools, in a virtuous loop.

There are three degrees of impact in which computer science can influence or transform the job of a philologist. From the smallest impact (level 1) to the greatest impact (level 3):

- Level 1: the computer performs tasks that could be done by hand.

  - Example: counting words in a text.
  - Benefits: the time needed to perform the task is reduced to fractions of a second; accuracy is virtually optimal (clean data, no bugs in the count algorithm, filter set properly, etc.).

- Level 2: the computer performs tasks that could be done by hand *qualitatively* but not *quantitatively*.

  - Example: counting words in a million texts.
  - Benefit: the task is possible whereas, before it was not (plus, sustainable computational time, and accuracy).

- Level 3: the computer manipulates the data in a way that allows us to ask new research questions. Inspiring examples are found in new research fields such as the neurosciences.

Indeed, Marcos Marín (2001) suggests "what is different is not the quantity, it is the new insights, the new questions that we can ask."[14] From the point of view of how deeply computer science modifies philology by contributing to it, two distinct steps can also be distinguished:

---

[14]F. A. Marcos Marín, "Where is Electronic Philology Going? The Present and Future of a Discipline," in *Proceedings of the First Seminar on Computers, Literature and Philology*, ed. Domenico Fiormonte and Jonathan Usher (Edinburgh: University of Oxford, 2001), 11–22.

1. preparation of the working materials;
2. support to textual criticism (assisted or [semi]automated analyses).

This chapter focuses more on the first point, which is included in the definition of preservation: the way in which inscriptions are photographed and text corpora are transcribed and encoded, as well as the way in which a sound recording is re-mediated, "is crucial for the way in which these research objects will be studied in the future. [...] The creation of digital objects [...] is a crucial part of the humanities research. It is more than just preparation for research."[15]

What has been said so far constitutes a fairly large body of principles, ideas, and observations. But, a good theory is one in which the prescriptions can be implemented in the real world. So, let us examine three examples where some fundamental principles of philology are applied to scenarios frequently encountered in the practice of audio digitization. The true value of these examples does not lie in the practical solution adopted each time, but in the principle that led to the solution.

EXAMPLES OF PRACTICAL IMPLICATIONS OF THE THEORETICAL PRINCIPLES OF DIGITAL PHILOLOGY APPLIED TO SOUND RECORDINGS

Handling audio carriers correctly (applying a set of technical skills) is crucial for their protection, but the compilation of an encyclopedic manual for the treatment of historical sound recordings would be a sterile exercise. The solution to most operational problems encountered in the daily practice of digitization find a natural solution in the frame of an overarching intellectual perspective, based on the notion that audio documents are complex cultural objects of historical value, of which technology represents only one aspect. A parallel with other domains may prove useful again: we are not describing the technique to restore the leg of a Louis XIV cabinet. We are in front of a cabinet and we are asking ourselves the fundamental question: is this just a piece of furniture

---

[15]Wido van Peursen, "Text Comparison and Digital Creativity: An Introduction," in *Text Comparison and Digital Creativity: The Production of Presence and Meaning in Digital Text Scholarship*, ed. Wido van Peursen, Ernst Thoutenhoofd, and Adriaan van der Weel (Leiden: Brill, 2010), 1–27.

or something with an artistic and historical value? The answer will dramatically determine the approach to restoration: if it is just a piece of furniture, we will proceed with the best reparation possible, to optimize stability and robustness. The materials and techniques we choose will only have to fulfill the requirements for stability and robustness. No other external factor will influence the intervention. But, if the cabinet is recognized to have an artistic and historical value, then a lot of external factors will come into play: solidity and robustness will have to be balanced out with stylistic requirements, the choice of materials and techniques will depend on other choices at a higher level—not only the technical level! In this latter case the provocative question "should we replace the leg at all" would represent a valid theoretical position and could result in an answer that nullifies any subsequent questions about the techniques and methods of restoration.

These opposite approaches are theorized in a milestone textbook ([1963] 2005) called "*The Theory of Restoration*" written by Cesare Brandi.[16] Even if this is a book that everybody in the field of preservation and restoration of cultural heritage ought to be familiar with, it certainly did not address audio and video carriers that, in 1963, were far from being recognized as part of the world's cultural heritage. The good news is that the fundamentals of Brandi's theory are still valid, and they can be applied to audio and video documents. So, there is no need to invent a new theory for audio and video documents from scratch: including them in the family of cultural heritage materials allows us to extend the traditional theory and only adapt or integrate the aspects that do not translate to the new context. The bad news is that the exclusion of audio and video documents from the definition of cultural heritage materials has shown an incredible inertia and Brandi's theory is, to this days, hardly applied to audio and video documents, and, hence, necessitates the following examples.

SILENCE/BLANK TAPE

Often, it may happen that a tape has not been fully recorded (i.e. There are portions of tape where no useful signal is present). In everyday language, we would say that there is "nothing" there, or maybe that "there is silence." Digital storage space is expensive and it is reasonable for most

---

[16] Cesare Brandi, *Theory of Restoration* (Florence: Arte e restauro, 2005).

institutions/individuals to decide that keeping "silence" is not a good idea. However, the nature of "silence" as "nothing" (no information) is questionable for a number or reasons. Some reasons concern the informational content of the tape. What we perceive as "silence" may contain useful information on the recording system used to make the recording, on previous recordings (subsequently erased), and most importantly on disturbances possibly present throughout the tape. This information is essential to enhance the performance of the algorithms for noise removal and it can be extracted with existing signal processing tools. As for the future, we cannot foresee the limits of technological evolution but, from past experience, it is reasonable to say that new signal processing tools will become available. The "silence" on the tapes might contain useful information that we are not able to extract today, but maybe we will in the future: if we get rid of the "silence," we will never know.

In addition to considerations related to the informational content of the tape, there is a formal reason, more closely related to the principles of digital philology. The blank portions on a tape can be compared to the blank pages in a book or manuscript. The object of our preservation are the tape and the book as a whole. The "whole" is the cultural entity: the audio and the text are only part of the whole, and we need to preserve every part to maintain the "documentary unity". Removing any part of the whole corrupts the documentary unity and represents a deliberate act of interpretation of the content (meaning), because it requires a decision about what is relevant and what is not. We aim to "save history, not rewrite it," therefore, this kind of interpretation should not be allowed during digitization.[17] At a later stage, an expert may decide that the silent parts are not relevant to the target audience and omit it from the access material, but it will always be kept in the document's preservation copy. This holds true for blank parts of the tape at the beginning, at the end, or in between recordings. Eliminating blank portions from a sound recording is equivalent to ripping pages out of a book. What philologist would approve of this?

Similarly, changing the speed of a recording or eliminating multiple speeds during digitization impose interpretations and lead to the loss of

[17] George Boston, Memory of the World: Safeguarding the Documentary Heritage, a Guide to Standards, Recommended Practices and Reference Literature Related to the Preservation of Documents of All Kinds (Paris, France: UNESCO, 1998). Accessed May 5, 2018. http://unesdoc.unesco.org/ulis/cgi-bin/ulis.pl?catno=112676.

information in preservation copies. Most tape recorders support multiple tape transfer speed rates (some of them are standard values, while some may be custom). This allows a great flexibility in the use of tapes, the duration of which is not pre-determined by its length but depends on the tape transfer speed rate at which the recording is being made. There is nothing to prohibit multiple speeds on the same tape. But, why would someone select different speeds? The most common reason is: the tape was running out before the recording was over. The recording of a live event, unlike that of an interview for example, does not offer the possibility to stop the recording at the end of the tape, turn the tape or take a new one, and resume the recording. Therefore, it is very typical in live recordings (concerts, theatrical representations) to encounter a speed decrease at some point, normally at about two thirds of the tape length. The most likely reason was to make the tape, or rather the recording capacity of the tape, last longer. But, this is not the only probable reason. The quality of the recording is a function of the tape transfer speed rate (as a rule of thumb, "the higher the speed, the better the recording"). Sometimes, field recordings containing spoken parts (interview, introductions) and musical/sung parts (typically folk repertoire, such as ethno-musicological recordings) include alternating speed rates depending on the content: lower speed for the spoken parts, faster speed for the musical/sung parts. The number of speed changes along the same tape can vary from two to twenty, there is no way of knowing this in advance, for example by looking at the tape. And, this is a crucial point: the characteristics of a tape (the recording parameters: speed, track configuration, etc.) are only revealed at playback time (along with some syndromes due to ageing). Therefore, tapes should always be monitored from top to bottom during digitization.

So, what do we do when we encounter a speed change? We have a natural tendency to approach sound recordings as the "final listener," after all, a sound recording is made to be listened to. But we are preserving a historical cultural object, a "whole," that is *not necessarily ready for fruition*. In other words, the material might not be ready to be delivered to our final audience. Our work should be inspired by the UNESCO precept to "save history, not rewrite it," and not by what we think our final user might like.[18] I will elaborate on this below. Our job occurs prior to the preparation of the materials for the public: our goal is to produce a preservation copy that is reliable and complete, so that

---

[18] Ibid.

a variety of future uses are possible starting from this material. Then we may ask: "How do we save this tape, and not rewrite it?" It is not an easy question, because there is a technical challenge standing between us and the content of the tape: for the content to be intelligible, it must be read at the correct speed. Intuitively, we strive to have a single digital file where every section is properly intelligible. This solution satisfies, again, our desire to be the listener of that file. But, if we eliminate the speed differences, which are a characteristic of the tape, we *lose information* in the transfer process. A digital file with no speed changes will either be the result of a real-time speed change at playback (fundamentally impossible to perform accurately for technical and cognitive reasons) or of an editing work after digitization. In either case, the result will not match the source tape, with its "segments" characterized by different tape transfer speed rates.

We must ask ourselves how we can preserve the speed differences and at the same time let the audio be intelligible. A valid answer is: the tape will be read in its entirety as many times as there are speeds encountered on each tape side. Note that it is not as many times as the speed changes, but the speeds themselves. This solution is satisfactory because every digital file will reflect all the speed changes on the source tape, at the cost of having to read the tape multiple times and, of course, storing an equal number of digital files. This can be work and cost-intensive if one of the speeds only appears for a few seconds or minutes, which can be the case. However, from a philological perspective, this approach is sound and defendable. In a way none of the digital files exactly corresponds to the source tape, but in a way *all of them* contain the necessary information to reconstruct it.

This example demonstrates that the ratio between tapes and digitized files is not necessarily 1:1. For tapes with two sides, there will be at least be two digital files. In the case of multiple speed (and non-standard track configuration, a problem we do not tackle in this chapter) we can have N digital files resulting from one tape. The presence of a blank portion of tape may raise additional questions about speed: at what speed was it recorded (if it was recorded)? We said in the previous example that silence can be a precious source of "hidden" information about the recording system and the tape content. So, even reading blank parts at the correct speed is a philological issue.

The final example involves editing. There are many ways in which one may feel tempted to edit a digital file resulting from an A/D conversion.

The whole spectrum of available digital tools offers chances for "temptation." These include enhancement tools (noise removal, frequency boost, etc.) and the possibility to cut and paste audio segments to reconstruct content unity. In either case, the intervention on the digitized file needs to be considered, from a philological viewpoint, an arbitrary act of interpretation. When audio material is prepared for the final users all sorts of interventions are allowed (and the user should be made aware of them), but our attention at this stage goes to the archival material that serves as a reference for preservation purposes. It is *supposed* to be "raw" material, not ready for fruition. Therefore, from a philological perspective, any intervention should be avoided at this stage, rather, the benefits of edits can be realized *at a later stage.*

A softer position on this matter (a viable "middle way") is represented by the possibility to perform reversible modifications *only*, and to document them very well. All compensations and processing, if applied, are based on the capacity for precise counteraction,[19] which means reversibility of each operation and, consequently, on the capacity to trace the original characteristics/values that were modified.[20] When digitizing a sound recording that belonged to our family we may decide to act according to our personal taste: we can go from the digitization to the preparation of a playlist with tracks that were optimized for our ears (matching our needs and aesthetic taste, applying a de-noise or a sound boost for example). But, when digitizing a historical sound recording that belongs to a public archive or a collection that has a clear value for a larger community, we must put ourselves back in the shoes of the philologist who deals with a historical document (a "whole" with a specific meaning in a cultural and social context). Then, all the possible ways to intervene on a digitized audio file should become questionable.

There are parallels between audio preservation and other forms of textual preservation. Removing noise can correspond to correcting a spelling mistake: what historian would allow for that? It is the work of the historian to study the pristine documentary source and build theories

---

[19] Dietrich Schüller, "Preserving the Facts for the Future: Principles and Practices for the Transfer of Analog Audio Documents into the Digital Domain," *Journal of Audio Engineering Society* 49, no. 7–8 (2001): 618–621.

[20] Federica Bressan, "The Preservation of Sound Archives: A Computer-based Approach to Quality Control" (PhD thesis, Sciences Engineering Medicine, Verona, 2013), 34–35. Accessed May 5, 2018. http://samp.dei.unipd.it/proceedings/12_WSa1_01.pdf.

based on all the information it contains. What we consider a spelling error today might have also been an archaic spelling of the same word. What about texts in languages we do not understand? Removing blank pages, re-uniting paragraphs, adding punctuation are all operations that are legitimate in a process of text editing, but they are inappropriate in a context of preservation. The text must be preserved as faithfully as possible, and that includes errors and mistakes. No philologist would want to work on a reworked version of an old manuscript (especially if the re-working has not been thoroughly documented), and the same strict policy should be applied to historical sound recordings. Adopting this policy will result in more reliable audio resources and establish the value of sound recordings as documentary sources.

These are just some examples of possible violation of philological principles in common audio preservation practices. Everything in the field of preservation is the result of a choice. There is no right or wrong as in a mathematical proof, therefore, decisions should be informed and documented. When choosing a treatment for historical sound recordings many approaches are legitimate if they are well documented and they justify every choice in light of philological principles. Ignoring these principles, is also a choice, but one that devalues historical sound recordings as documentary sources. Also, final users (scholars or the public) should develop the awareness and the critical tools necessary to evaluate the material they access and pressure archival institutions to deliver complete and reliable materials.

CONCLUSIONS

The preservation of audio documents is a recent field of study and practice that requires theoretical and technical expertise. The nature of sound recordings poses some unique challenges for digital preservation. Namely, it involves the disembodiment of the physical object in a process that results in an all-digital collection of data. The transfer process requires the identification of the relevant features of the audio documents and their correct trans-coding so that we "preserve history, not rewrite it." As a result historical audio recordings can be made permanently accessibility. Several disciplines are called to contribute to this task, from archival science to computer science to chemistry; their contribution is not limited to the provision of working tools but also concepts and methods that forge a new cross-disciplinary domain.

Digital philology is a new discipline, which emerged from the combination of textual criticism and computer science. Its application to audio documents is particularly important, because these sources are not always perceived and treated with the same philological rigor reserved for printed texts and traditional documentary forms. This chapter provides an introduction to digital philology for audio documents, and some examples where philological principles are reflected in the preservation practice. Preservation is a field where intellectual work is still needed; it is normal that a great wave of technological expansion is followed by a time in which practices are formalized and ordered. It is important that the ongoing technological evolution is accompanied by intellectual work, because the consequences of technical choices reverberate all the way up to the cultural interpretation of documents and influence the way we understand the world. Without rigorous philological principles applied to the preservation of audio documents, we risk leaving poor documentary material.

References

Benjamin, Walter. *The Work of Art in the Age of Mechanical Reproduction*. Frankfurt am Main: Schram Verlag, 1955.

Boston, George. *Memory of the World: Safeguarding the Documentary Heritage, a Guide to Standards, Recommended Practices and Reference Literature Related to the Preservation of Documents of All Kinds*. Paris, France: UNESCO, 1998. Accessed May 5, 2018. http://unesdoc.unesco.org/ulis/cgi-bin/ulis.pl?catno=112676.

Brandi, Cesare. *Theory of Restoration*. Florence: Arte e restauro, 2005.

Bressan, Federica. "The Preservation of Sound Archives: A Computer-based Approach to Quality Control." PhD thesis, Sciences Engineering Medicine, Verona, 2013. Accessed May 5, 2018. http://samp.dei.unipd.it/proceedings/12_WSa1_01.pdf.

Bressan, Federica, Sergio Canazza, Carlo Fantozzi, and Niccolò Pretto. "Tape Music Archives: From Preservation to Interaction." *International Journal on Digital Libraries* 18, no. 3 (2017): 233–249.

Bressan, F., S. Canazza, T. Vets, and M. Leman. "Hermeneutic Implications of Cultural Encoding: A Reflection on Audio Recordings and Interactive Installation Art." In *Digital Libraries and Multimedia Archives*. Proceedings of the 12th Italian Research Conference on Digital Libraries (IRCDL 2016), 47–58, Elsevier, Procedia – Computer Sciences, 2017.

Brock-Nannestad, George. "The Rationale Behind Operational Conservation Theory." In *Conservation Without Limits: IIC Nordic Group XV Congress*, edited by Riitta Koskivirta, 21–33. Helsinki, FI: IIC Nordic Group, 2000.

Canazza, Sergio, Carlo Fantozzi, and Niccolò Pretto. "Accessing Tape Music Documents on Mobile Devices." *ACM Transaction on Multimedia Computing Communications* 12, no. 1s (2015): 1–20.

Edmonson, Ray. *Memory of the World: General Guidelines to Safeguard Documentary Heritage.* Paris: UNESCO, 2002. Accessed May 5, 2018. http://unesdoc.unesco.org/images/0012/001256/125637e.pdf.

Edmonson, Ray. *Audiovisual Archiving: Philosophy and Principles.* Paris: UNESCO, 2004.

Eno, Robert. Teaching materials presented at Indiana University, 2011. http://www.indiana.edu/~p374/c511/C511_4-Philology.pdf.

Gigliozzi, Giuseppe. *Introduzione all'uso del Computer Negli Studi Letterari.* Milan: Bruno Mondadori, 2003.

Hedstrom, Margaret. *It's About Time: Research Challenges in Digital Archiving and Long-Term Preservation. Final Report: Workshop on Research Challenges in Digital Archiving.* Washington, DC: National Science Foundation and Library of Congress, 2002.

IASA Technical Committee. *Handling and Storage of Audio and Video Carriers.* Edited by Dietrich Schüller and Albrecht Häfner. Milton Keynes: IASA Technical Committee, 2014. Accessed May 5, 2018. https://www.iasa-web.org/tc05/handling-storage-audio-video-carriers.

Indiana University Bloomington Media Preservation Initiative Task Force. *Meeting the Challenge of Media Preservation: Strategies and Solutions.* Bloomington: Indiana University, 2011.

International Federation of Library Association (IFLA). "Guidelines for Audiovisual and Multimedia Materials in Libraries and Other Institutions." *IFLA Professional Reports* 80 (2004). Accessed May 5, 2018. https://www.ifla.org/files/assets/hq/publications/professional-report/80.pdf.

Marcos Marín, F. A. "Where is Electronic Philology Going? The Present and Future of a Discipline." In *Proceedings of the First Seminar on Computers, Literature and Philology*, edited by Domenico Fiormonte and Jonathan Usher, 11–22. Edinburgh: University of Oxford, 2001.

Negroponte, Nicholas. *Being Digital.* New York: Vintage Books, 1995.

Schüller, Dietrich. "Preserving the Facts for the Future: Principles and Practices for the Transfer of Analog Audio Documents into the Digital Domain." *Journal of Audio Engineering Society* 49, no. 7–8 (2001): 618–621.

Schüller, Dietrich. *The Ethics of Preserving Audio and Video Documents.* Paris: UNESCO, 2006.

van Peursen, Wido. "Text Comparison and Digital Creativity: An Introduction." In *Text Comparison and Digital Creativity: The Production of Presence and Meaning in Digital Text Scholarship*, edited by Wido van Peursen, Ernst Thoutenhoofd, and Adriaan van der Weel, 1–27. Leiden: Brill, 2010.

CHAPTER 15

User Interfaces for Creating Digital Research

Tarrin Wills

People working in the humanities often do repetitive and structured analyses of texts, images, or other cultural products. Often these processes could be done through digital methodologies, but more often than not, humanities scholars and students choose to do them in a non-digital way, limiting the way their work might be used by others. These choices are difficult to understand for those of us working in Digital Humanities.

The problem can be addressed in part by paying attention to the way **applications** and interfaces are used by humanities scholars to interact with information in their particular fields. Projects can develop methods and interfaces that allow students and researchers to feel comfortable when producing and analyzing data, while maximizing the potential of that data for research purposes. "Skaldic Poetry of the Scandinavian Middle Ages" is a Digital Humanities project that exemplifies small-scale custom interface solutions. This chapter focuses on the technologies and applications that connect scholars who produce data with the data itself, namely, the **user interface** (UI).

T. Wills (✉)
University of Copenhagen, Copenhagen, Denmark
e-mail: tarrin@hum.ku.dk

© The Author(s) 2018
l. levenberg et al. (eds.), *Research Methods for the Digital Humanities*,
https://doi.org/10.1007/978-3-319-96713-4_15

A Short History of UIs and Digital Humanities

In the late 1980s and 1990s graphical interfaces emerged for creating digital documents. In particular, **word processors**, such as Microsoft Word, which displayed a close approximation of the print document being created on screen developed 'what you see is what you get' (WYSIWYG) interfaces. This development rapidly promoted the use of computers in all fields where documents were used and exchanged. Humanities research was no exception, and the technology, which is now ubiquitous, highlights one of the important factors in a successful user interface: it is much easier for a user to create data if they get very accurate and quick feedback on how the data will be displayed and understood. In other words, the WYSIWYG interface not only allows the user to accurately create formatted textual data, but also brings that data as close as possible to what the end-users (their audience) will need to see: the printed page.

Word processors have limitations for working with research data. A researcher could use a word processor to produce a scholarly edition, a dictionary, or a catalogue suitable for print publication, but they would lose much of the information about the structure and meaning of the resource. The kinds of useful information which cannot be retrieved easily from a word processor file might include: a particular version of a text in an edition, dictionary entries organized by part of speech instead of alphabetically, or the cross-references to texts in a catalogue of manuscripts. These situations mean that electronic documents created by word processors are often little better than print publications in terms of exchanging data.

The solution to these problems was to develop standards, such as the Text Encoding Initiative (**TEI**) standards, that would record the semantic information and structure.[1] Data produced using these standards could form the basis of print and electronic publication by using programming languages or style sheets to transform the code into more readable documents or web pages. To do so, the data creator must have a close understanding of a complex technical standard and the ways it can be transformed. TEI and similar standards have been widely adopted and

---

[1] The Text Encoding Initiative (TEI) released its first official standard in 1994, http://www.tei-c.org/About/history.xml.

most users of TEI directly create the (normally) **XML** code themselves, although often with the aid of applications that check the validity of the code. Using these methods the data creator has very close control over the semantics (the meaning of the data), but the trade-off is that the code must be separately processed to make it useful to someone who does not understand it. The main question that this chapter addresses is how to manage and minimize the trade-offs between the integrity and usability of the research data, the needs and methods of the data creator(s), and the needs of the end-users and research field more generally.

THE DATA AND THE USER

This chapter has already mentioned two types of interface for data creation, namely WYSIWYG word processors and editors for producing XML code. These represent extreme ends of the spectrum between data accessibility and integrity. There is (almost) no scholar alive today who is not comfortable with creating a word processor document, so in many ways this technology represents maximum accessibility. **TEI/XML** documents represent the pinnacle of data integrity, combining a well-documented de facto standard with detailed semantic and metadata tagging, but very few scholars end up directly creating research data using such a standard.

Depending on the detail of the information required, the two types of encoding may be exchangeable within a single project. Consider the following: a convention for typesetting transcriptions of manuscripts is to expand abbreviations using italics, e.g.: 'gefn*ir*' (expanding the abbreviation for er/ir in 'geſñ' in a manuscript).[2] TEI might encode this using the expansion tag: 'gefn<ex>ir</ex>'. Someone with knowledge of manuscript transcription conventions but not digital text encoding would be able to correctly interpret the italics, but not the code. Conversely, someone with an XML background but no transcription experience may not understand the italics, but could interpret the code by looking up the TEI standard. The TEI/XML text would ideally be used for archival and exchange purposes. But, a digital transcriber need not necessarily understand this format: if the italics unambiguously represent expansions of

[2] Manuscript 1009 fol. in the Old Royal Collection (GKS), Royal Library in Copenhagen, fol. 2v/22.

abbreviations, they can be transformed at the point of storage into TEI/ XML code and can be retrieved through the interface as italics. Even easier to transform in this way are different types of brackets, which might, within a particular project, indicate expansions, editorial interventions, text supplied from other sources, damaged or difficult sections, and so on.

TEI allows the encoder to include both the abbreviated and expanded form in the above example. If that level of detail is required, where parallel information is encoded at the same point, it becomes much harder to convert between a word processor format and XML. Nonetheless, a user interface might be able to find other ways, such as through a pop-up dialogue, to enter the additional information. The information might then be hidden under normal circumstances, or in print, but available when the user clicks on a word in a web page, for example.

A project might use different methods and standards to give a variety of end-users outputs in appropriate formats. For a digital repository such as the Oxford Text Archive or Menota, the data should be in a standardized, exchangeable format such as TEI. This allows other digital scholars to use the data with reference to a common standard, but without requiring specific disciplinary knowledge to understand the data and its structure. A researcher working in the discipline (e.g. a historian or linguist) may want the data in a traditional format such as a book, or a format which they can print or view on an e-book. Such a format can also be stored in a library without the pitfalls of digital-only archiving. Other researchers may be able to make use of an interface that allows them to query the data, transform it, or combine it in ways that they can use for research purposes. Some projects might have the general public in mind and create an interface which allows the public to access the information in an accessible form. All these types of output can be created from a single data repository, using different techniques to transform the data as necessary.

The skills and interests of the end user are highly diverse, but we can reduce them to four types:

1. Digital specialists without a background in the specific discipline of the project;
2. Discipline specialists with a reasonable comfort level with digital approaches and interfaces;
3. Discipline specialists with a low interest in digital interfaces;

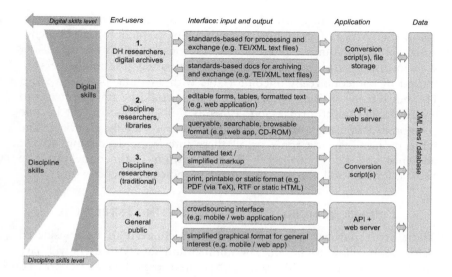

Fig. 15.1 Systems of conversion and skills required for different end-users

4. The general public, who may be interested in accessing the information digitally but who have little or no training in the particular subject.

For each type of user, the interface to the data might be organized in a different manner with an application converting the data from the form used by the project to the form required by the user. This model is shown in Fig. 15.1. (It should be noted that there is no restriction on how input formats might be exported in various output formats.)

The left of the figure also demonstrates the trade-off between disciplinary skills and digital skills. There is no inherent trade-off, but in practice this tends to be the case. A traditional print outlet in a particular discipline, such as a historical dictionary or a scholarly edition of a book, relies on the conventions of print media, which can be explained further in an electronic interface, but are already familiar to someone with greater disciplinary skills, who is used to those conventions.

The figure also represents different ways of inputting information for a project. Different end-users, if they are supplying the data, will need different methods for producing the data. A student might submit a

TEI/XML document that is then processed by the project's application (as in the Menota text archive at clarino.uib.no/menota); a researcher with more limited digital interests might retrieve and edit the data using web forms or another type of interface; formatted text might be submitted by someone really uncomfortable with anything beyond a Word file, but if it is consistently formatted then it could be transformed into a standard technical format; and, a member of the public might be able to submit data using a more restrictive, but user-friendly, platform. The same project may use some or all these interfaces, depending on the audience and the contributors. The case study outlined below (The Skaldic Project) will illustrate how many of these approaches work.

PROJECT REQUIREMENTS FOR SELECTING INTERFACES

There are a number of practical issues which need to be considered before an interface is chosen. The number and variety of users will have an enormous impact on the solution required, regardless of the project. The first question is therefore about the diversity of users:

1. *Who will be working on the data? Will more than one person be working on similar data at overlapping times?*

If you are the only person working on the data for the duration of the project the solution can be very simple, as it may be a matter of learning the necessary technology. As soon as there is more than one person, there is the problem that users may have different approaches, skills, or interests in technology, and may need to edit the data at the same time.

2. *Where will the users be? At the same workplace? Working internationally? In the field? Do they have access to the same technology (software and hardware)?*

People working at the same workplace will normally have access to shared storage, so they can access the same data simultaneously. This makes it much easier to determine what solution is used, as it is a matter of choosing an application for a particular operating system and storing the data on a network drive. Security is largely taken care of by the institutional infrastructure. Outside of a single organization there are a number of other issues to deal with, including security, and software and hardware support. If data will be created or edited in a fieldwork environment, researchers need to consider whether the users will have network access, the kinds of devices they will be able to use, and how much information they need to support data creation.

3. *What is the nature of the data to be created? Is it, for example, textual, geographical, or visual? Do different types of data or media need to be linked together? Are there external resources that should be linked, such as online gazetteers and registries?*

These issues are dealt with elsewhere in more detail in this book, but some types of data require more graphical or interactive interfaces than others. Information that can be found digitally, in an authoritative form, should link to the source in a way that facilitates updates. The interface needs to be able to handle all the necessary types and sources of data.

Solutions to the problems outlined here (including, multiple users, semantic tagging of information, multiple uses and contexts of the data, simultaneous updating, and so on) have been solved most spectacularly by social media. It is in the nature of a social network to try to bring together those creating information and their audience. Social networking platforms such as Facebook and Twitter incorporate a range of external sources of information provided implicitly or explicitly by the user: geographical information (location, from device or photos), links to external resources (web links shared), semantic tagging (hashtags), networks (friends/followers) and links to networks (tagging friends/handles), and metadata about the users themselves (profiles). These are applied to text, images, videos, links, and other types of resources. This information is used largely to generate targeted advertising, but it is worth considering how such interfaces facilitate the supply, linking, and categorizing of a very broad range of media and data.

INTERFACE SOLUTIONS

There are a variety of interface solutions, which range from simpler to more complex depending on the type of users for the project and the kind of data to be created. The following is a list of user interface solutions depending on the complexity of the project, the number of contributors, the type and complexity of the data, and the storage format for the data.

Single User, Desktop Environment, Data as Files on Computer

If your project has one user working on one type of data at a time, there are several desktop tools with easy to learn interfaces, many of which are free and open source. These solutions do not rely on creating new interfaces or systems. Many of these applications are mentioned elsewhere in this volume: e.g. text encoding (Oxygen), statistics (R, Gephi), geographical data (ArcGIS, QGIS), tabular data (spreadsheet applications), relational data[3] (Access [Windows only], FileMaker). Note that word processors are not considered appropriate solutions in Digital Humanities in themselves, because they do not structure data in a way that can be further processed.

Multiple Users, Desktop Environment, Data as Files on Network

A certain amount of complexity occurs when you have different people working concurrently on the same data or on data that have to work together in some way, such as when it is processed by the same application. If you are all working together in the same location or can otherwise communicate directly, the solution can be as simple as a manual division of labor and manual data management. This might work by using the applications described in the previous section, but storing the files generated in a collaborative repository such as Dropbox or Google Drive. This type of solution is widely used (e.g. projects such as the Menota Handbook [menota.org], Stories for All Time [fasnl.ku.dk]) and requires manual management of file storage, so that the data are retrievable and processable by the project's applications and by other members of the project. Participants in the project should define files naming protocols and the folder arrangement in the drive. This means that an XSLT application, for example, can generate web pages from the contributors' XSML files. Individual files, however, cannot be edited concurrently without the risk of data being overwritten. So, normally, such a project would divide the files and work between different members of the project.

Code repositories such as Sourceforge, Github and Google Code provide interfaces, which allow contributors to safely check out, edit, and check in files as well as other features for managing collaborative projects. This means that files are not overwritten by mistake and changes

---

[3]E. F. Codd, "A Relational Model of Data for Large Shared Data Banks," *Communications of the ACM* 13, no. 6 (1970): 377–387.

can be tracked, particularly if text files are used by the project, such as XML and programming code. Compiling and processing of the files, however, needs to be done off the site, which may require some projects to develop scripts or applications for downloading the files in addition to processing them. A number of Digital Humanities projects use these repositories for managing code, particularly where the code is intended for programming libraries or applications.

Multiple Users, Desktop Environment, Data on Network

When you have multiple users working on the same data or data structures at the same time the normal solution is to use a networked database. Structured Query Language (SQL) is the standard that governs how data is retrieved, stored, and managed in such databases. There are various free and open source SQL databases, which can be used to implement this solution. Some desktop or web applications (such as GATE Teamware [gate.ac.uk/teamware]) will set up a database for you, meaning that there is little extra work except in learning how the application connects to the database, so that other users can access the data. Geographical (GIS) applications (such as ArcGIS and QGIS) work with data in tables that can be stored and shared on various SQL database server applications.

Multiple Users, Web Environment, Data on Network

Where the data used by the project is relatively simple, such as data in tables or geographical data, there may be cloud solutions to edit and store the data using web or mobile applications. Google provides a few free services which allow multiple users to edit tabular data (Sheets, Fusion Tables) or geographical data (My Maps, Fusion Tables) on different devices. There are often web alternatives to desktop research applications, such as RStudio for the R statistics application and GATE Teamware for the GATE language processing application. All these solutions allow for different people to work simultaneously on the same data in different locations and on different devices.

Other applications may require the data to be stored in a networked (SQL) database. There is a powerful web open source application for MySQL and MariaDB called phpMyAdmin, which can be used to set up these databases (the equivalent for PostgreSQL is phpPgAdmin) and enter and edit information online for different users. Most universities provide a MySQL or similar server for staff and students, which can be used for these purposes, although it is increasingly common to use virtual servers for SQL databases.

Multiple Users, Custom Desktop Application, Data on Network

In situations where you are dealing with very complex data, the available software applications may not be able to link together and structure the data adequately for the research purposes of the project. If people are working at the same workplace, where equipment, software, and support are consistent, a desktop application may be the most appropriate interface for entering data. Such systems are often used by larger museums to manage information about their collections, or long-term projects such as dictionaries.

The screenshot in Fig. 15.2 shows an interface to the Dictionary of Old Norse Prose's database.[4] Visual information (here the original citation slip and a scan of the printed edition, which the citation is taken from) is provided to assist the lexicographer in organizing citations within an entry. The interface is a desktop application that connects to an Oracle SQL database server.

Desktop applications tend to be highly responsive to user input, as there is little time lag in connecting to the database and very fast transfer speeds between the application and the data source. Additionally, the code is normally executed natively by the operating system, rather than by an intermediate application such as a browser. This often makes the interface much faster to respond to user input than a web application, but the user needs to have access to the required network and operating system, and to be able to install the software for any device they need to use.

Multiple Users, Custom Web Application

In situations where there are different users in different locations using varying devices, a custom web application is often the most powerful and flexible solution. As mentioned previously, social media sites are examples

---

[4] James Knirk, Helle Degnbol, Bent Chr. Jacobsen, Eva Rode, Christopher Sanders, and þorbjörg Helgadóttir, eds., *A Dictionary of Old Norse Prose/ Ordbog over det norrøne prosasprog* (Copenhagen: The Arnamagnæan Kommission, 1989).

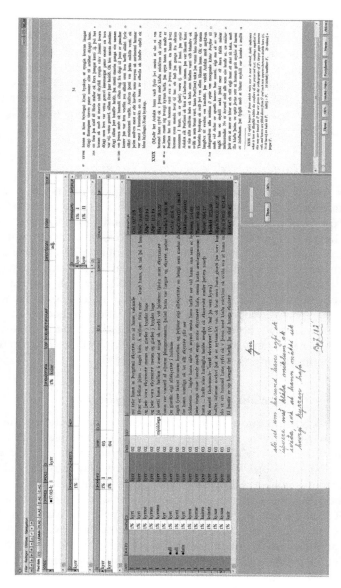

Fig. 15.2   Dictionary of Old Norse Prose: desktop application for constructing entries

of this type of solution, where multiple users are able to access, contribute, and link information. Social media sites represent the enormous **scalability** of the technology, to the extent that hundreds of millions of users can simultaneously edit and link within a single database.

The popularity of this model means that the technologies it uses (database, programming interface and website framework) are free and open source, and are accompanied by a massive amount of support available online. This solution, the custom web application, is discussed at length in the next section.

Crowdsourced, Web Form (No Editing)

Situations where data is collected from non-specialists is often called **crowdsourcing**, but traditionally researchers have often gathered data from the public for research through surveys and forms. Simple digital forms—where the input is in the form of text, yes/no answers, and multiple-choice options—can be created using a variety of free online tools. The information is normally stored in a tabular format such a spreadsheet, which can be used for statistical and qualitative analysis. This type of interface involves single direction information gathering from the end-user's perspective: they submit the information and, once submitted, it cannot normally be edited it. Because the interface is one-way, it is much simpler to create than a system that allows the users to retrieve and edit the information themselves.[5]

Crowdsourced, Custom Web Application

A custom web application may be appropriate in situations where a project is **crowdsourced**, but either requires more complex input than traditional forms (e.g. where images are involved, or linking of data) or a more complex process, where contributors can retrieve and edit their contributions. These interfaces are the most difficult interfaces to develop because they need to be understandable and usable to a very large variety of people with little or no training in the particular discipline. The interface needs to be very clear and simple, with workflows that can be followed by members of the public. Any inconsistencies or faults may put people off from contributing, thus negating the benefits

---

[5] Note that you may require ethics approval before conducting any research that involves gathering any kind of personal information from the public.

of crowdsourcing. The application must be sufficiently flexible to allow complex input, but at the same time there must be systems in place to deal with deliberate misinformation supplied by contributors.

Such projects are normally limited to particular processes that are more reliably or easily done by humans than machines, such as transcribing handwritten documents. Projects such as Zooniverse (zooniverse.org) provide support for developing crowdsourced research projects. At the time of writing all the humanities projects on Zooniverse involve transcribing and annotating manuscripts and other documents, a process that is still easier for humans to do than computers. For example, one project asks users to identify images in historical scientific publications and annotate them according to captions and keywords. Another example of a largely crowdsourced project is the Textual Communities project, which allows signed-up users to contribute XML transcriptions of manuscripts.

This latter type of application gives users much more control over their contributions and credits contributors. It is limited to producing XML code directly (with syntax highlighting to assist) and does not link to detail outside of the page. There are several advantages to giving users this amount of control and credit: they have an incentive to provide more and better-quality input if their responsibility is acknowledged. Additionally, contributions can be included as assessed work in taught courses, or as part of other research projects. There is added complexity in such an interface, because user access and privileges must be carefully managed.

Web Interfaces for Creating and Editing Data

The following is meant as background to creating a web application as a user interface for a Digital Humanities project. A web interface sits at one end of a complete web application providing the necessary information and context to assist input, dealing with the user input, and feeding back information about the input. A user opens a web site by inputting a URL in a browser. The web server executes an application, which produces a web page. The resulting web pages normally have links and/or forms that allow the user to continue the process by opening new pages. The information that is sent may be used to store new information on the server, to retrieve information, or a combination of both.

Web applications can be very complex because they require a knowledge of the structure of the underlying data (e.g. XML, relational data), the ways in which the data can be accessed and transformed (e.g. XSLT, SQL), the programming language used to make the transformation (the

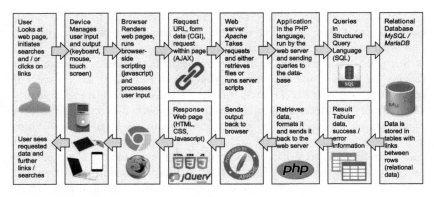

Fig. 15.3 Stages of a web database application and languages used

Application Programming Interface (**API**) language), as well as the web output technologies (normally HTML, CSS and Javascript) used to generate the resulting pages. Fortunately, many of the issues are solved by a range of libraries and plugins, which various projects and initiatives have made public and continue to support.

Figure 15.3 shows the structure of the application from user to database and the various technical languages commonly used at each stage of the process, although the application will tend to focus development on one of the stages (web, API or SQL). There are many libraries and frameworks, which simplify this process. Figure 15.3 represents a configuration widely used by large applications wherein users both contribute and access data. It is the model (with minor variations) used by Facebook, Twitter and Wikipedia, for example, which all specifically use MySQL/MariaDB as the database server and PHP as the API language. Alternatively, an XML-based project might use XLST to read and transform XML data, for example, and there are many other languages which can be used to write the application itself.

EXAMPLE OF A COMPLEX APPLICATION: THE SKALDIC PROJECT

The project Skaldic Poetry of the Scandinavian Middle Ages (or just the Skaldic Project) aims to edit, translate, and annotate a major corpus of poetry from early Northern Europe. It illustrates many of the small-scale solutions that might be implemented in developing a custom interface. It represents some of the limits of what a single researcher-developer can produce over a number of years, or what a small team could create in a shorter period.

There are several complexities to the project's corpus: it is preserved in several hundred manuscripts and is attributed to hundreds of different poets; there is considerable variation between the manuscripts, as well as variation in how previous editors have reconstructed the poems; and, the poetry is largely preserved piecemeal, in prose works, which have their own transmission history. And, not least, the poetry itself is highly complex, requiring a reordering of the syntax to bridge the gap between the verse and the translation, as well as glosses of very complex and variable poetic expressions (known as *kenningar* and *heiti*). The project is led by 5–6 senior scholars, including the author of this chapter, who oversee contributions from over 40 different editors and are assisted by over a dozen researchers funded by various sources. The project leaders and assistants are based in the US, Europe, and Australia, meaning that there is 24-hour use of the project's digital resources. The end-point of the project is both a traditional print publication in the form of a book series as well as an interactive digital edition. The data structure of the resource therefore had to be designed to encompass sufficient information in order to structure and format the edition in the desired forms.

The web interface originally began as a tool to assist contributors in finding contextual information about their texts. As web technologies improved, it became quickly apparent that a web interface could be used for the processes of entering and exporting the edition, as well as searching, browsing, linking, and analyzing it. In order to deal with the level of linking required by the project, the original TEI/XML structure of the text was translated into a relational data model.[6] The resulting structure stores the text as words and lines in tables, rather than as marked-up text. This means that the interface needs to be able to edit the information in tables and output the text in an easily readable form to the user. Web development **frameworks** can effectively create applications that can be used on all devices, such as Bootstrap and (with some modification) JQuery Mobile 1.4.

Figure 15.4 shows the same page adapting for the screen width, using features of JQuery Mobile and some custom CSS and Javascript. The first shows how the page appears in a desktop browser. On a narrower device such as a tablet the left menu is removed and the header

[6] Tarrin Wills, "Relational Data Modelling of Textual Corpora: The Skaldic Project and Its Extensions," *Digital Scholarship in the Humanities* 30, no. 2 (2015): 294–313.

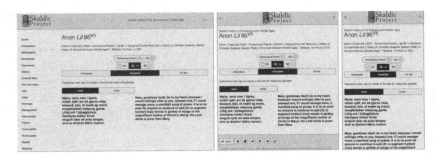

Fig. 15.4   Adaptive web design interface

rearranged, so that the menu is accessed by a button at the top left. On a very narrow device such as a phone the text boxes are **reflowed**, so that they appear above and below each other. Additional information is accessed through pop-ups (e.g. information about each word), and links and buttons are appropriately sized for both mouse and touch interaction.

The advantage of an Adaptive Web Design approach is that the same application can function as a web application for desktops, and a mobile app for tablets and phones. Supplying icons for the two main mobile platforms (iOS and Android) allows users to easily add a link to their phone app list and effectively makes the site function as a mobile app.

The Workflow

Many of the leading researchers in the Skaldic Project were unfamiliar with digital technologies and had previously only worked on projects based on producing word processor files for print publication. Rather than requiring them to learn entirely new processes and systems, the project defined a way in which the data could be submitted as word processor documents using simple but consistent formatting and markup, so that they could be transformed by assistants into the required format for the digital resource. The format for submissions, therefore, had to be structured so that the data could be entered into the digital resource, containing all the information required with some additional formatting and markup. Editors could also choose to use the web interface to enter their editions. The final printed volume is similar to the files provided by most editors, except that the submitted files contain a few additional

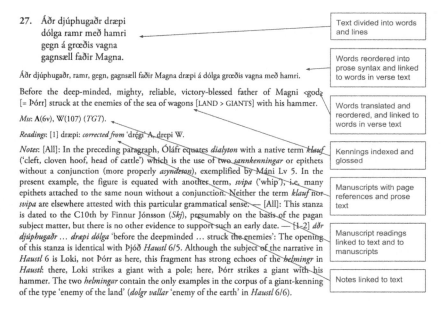

27. Áðr djúphugaðr dræpi
     dólga ramr með hamri
     gegn á grœðis vagna
     gagnsæll faðir Magna.

Áðr djúphugaðr, ramr, gegn, gagnsæll faðir Magna dræpi á dólga grœðis vagna með hamri.

Before the deep-minded, mighty, reliable, victory-blessed father of Magni <god>
[= Þórr] struck at the enemies of the sea of wagons [LAND > GIANTS] with his hammer.

Mss: A(6v), W(107) (*TGT*).

Readings: [1] dræpi: *corrected from* 'drégi' A, drepi W.

Notes: [All]: In the preceding paragraph, Óláfr equates *dialyton* with a native term *klauf* ('cleft, cloven hoof, head of cattle') which is the use of two *sannkenningar* or epithets without a conjunction (more properly *asyndeton*), exemplified by Máni Lv 5. In the present example, the figure is equated with another term, *svipa* ('whip'), i.e. many epithets attached to the same noun without a conjunction. Neither the term *klauf* nor *svipa* are elsewhere attested with this particular grammatical sense. — [All]: This stanza is dated to the C10th by Finnur Jónsson (*Skj*), presumably on the basis of the pagan subject matter, but there is no other evidence to support such an early date. — [1-2] *áðr djúphugaðr ... dræpi dólga* 'before the deepminded ... struck the enemies': The opening of this stanza is identical with Þjóð *Haustl* 6/5. Although the subject of the narrative in *Haustl* 6 is Loki, not Þórr as here, this fragment has strong echoes of the *helmingr* in *Haustl*: there, Loki strikes a giant with a pole; here, Þórr strikes a giant with his hammer. The two *helmingar* contain the only examples in the corpus of a giant-kenning of the type 'enemy of the land' (*dolgr vallar* 'enemy of the earth' in *Haustl* 6/6).

Text divided into words and lines

Words reordered into prose syntax and linked to words in verse text

Words translated and reordered, and linked to words in verse text

Kennings indexed and glossed

Manuscripts with page references and prose text

Manuscript readings linked to text and to manuscripts

Notes linked to text

Fig. 15.5   Example of printed version of the Skaldic Project's editions

simple markup techniques designed to help the application process some of the structured information.

Figure 15.5 shows both a simplified version of the start-point and the exported printed end-point of the process. In the process, a rich digital resource is created as the implied structures of the edition are put into a series of linked tables. There are a series of forms which assist in this process, as described below.

Step 1: Inserting the Text

In the first stage, a form takes plain text in lines and adds it to the database structure as rows in the tables of words and lines, linking each together and numbering them for later ordering and referencing. It processes simple markup representing emendations (where the editor has changed the text from the manuscripts) using angle brackets and asterisks corresponding to the TEI <corr> element.

This method illustrates one way of entering data, where the application takes a simple input and creates a complex data structure. This process is not easily reversible: if the user was able to edit the text the way it was entered, it would risk information loss. For example, if a word's spelling was changed or the word boundaries altered, the data linked to a given word (such as the translation, variants, or notes) may become incorrect. Some other projects use a similar process to allow contributors to create transcriptions with simple markup and transform it into TEI/XML.

Steps 2 and 3: Reordering to Prose Syntax and Linking the Translation
The previous form creates a series of rows in the tables containing lines and words in the database. Once created, the tabular data can be edited using a generic form for editing rows and columns in a table (this form, as with the others in this section, changes format according to the device used). The application includes generic methods for building forms from the tables in the database, giving appropriate inputs for the types of data in each column (e.g. text, numbers, links). The form shown here takes all words linked to a particular stanza and allows the user to adjust the columns which store the information about the prose syntax and order. A Javascript plugin allows drag and drop reordering of the columns. Figure 15.6 shows a word in the process of being moved. Another feature shows the resulting prose word order in the box above the table, giving instant feedback to the user about how the text will appear when outputted. This is very important given that the row/column structure of the data looks very different from the text output, which is in sentences.

The translation is entered using a similar form to the prose word order, allowing the user to reorder the words to form an idiomatic English translation. The words are linked to the original text, so that any

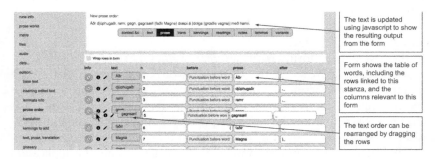

Fig. 15.6 Form for rearranging text into prose syntax

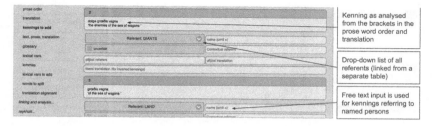

Fig. 15.7 Form for entering kenning analysis

word in the corpus will have a contextual gloss. And, another simple markup convention is used here to indicate the structure of **kennings**, namely, curly brackets. These are processed at a different stage and do not appear in the final edition, but the brackets provide sufficient information to the application to process them (Fig. 15.7).

Step 4: Analyzing the Kennings
Here the application analyzes the inputted brackets to establish which words in the prose order and translation contain kennings. The user is then prompted with a form for each kenning, allowing them to gloss the kenning and provide additional information if necessary. Here the kenning 'sea of wagons' refers to 'land' and 'the enemies of the sea of wagons' (i.e. the enemies of land) are 'giants'. This information is linked, so that an index of kennings is automatically available and an end-user can find these among all kennings for 'land' and 'giant.'

When the form is first used the kennings are generated from the markup in the text and, when updated, the application adds them to a separate table with links to the main text. Subsequent views and updates of the form take the information from the index table rather than from the markup in the inputted text, but they are presented with the same interface (Fig. 15.7).

Step 5: Variant Readings
The variant readings are entered as a separate table where each row links together one or more words in the text to one or more manuscripts, which are witnesses to the text. The manuscripts are entered separately and the user can select each word and each manuscript, which adds the variant reading into a text box. This form uses a generic interface, which

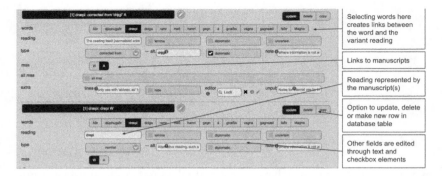

Fig. 15.8 Form for entering manuscript variants

defines how each column in the table is to be edited. The database uses arbitrary numbers to link rows in different tables, so the form defines how the linked data (words and manuscripts) are to be represented in the form based on the information in the linked tables. This information is used to show a traditional variant apparatus in the printed book, as well as an interactive apparatus in the web interface (Fig. 15.8).

Step 6: Annotating the Edition

The notes form links words in the text to annotations. The discursive content of the notes (i.e. sentences) are formatted using a restricted set of HTML tags. This enables simple formatting, but also the identification of bibliographic and internal references, which are later processed so that links and pop-ups can clarify the abbreviated references.

The text is entered using a WYSIWYG Javascript plugin called TinyMCE, which has been set up to restrict the formatting options. The entered text is processed when it is sent to the server to convert the HTML formatting into semantic tags, and to generate links from bibliographic and other references. The same plugin is used to enter other formatted text into the database including introductions to poems and volumes, biographies, and contextual notes.

The WYSIWYG html solution gives quick feedback to the user and leaves the semantic processing to the application. It can be used in a project such as this, because the project uses well-defined conventions about the meaning of formatting styles such as italics (e.g. for references to texts) and superscripts (for references to other poems in the corpus).

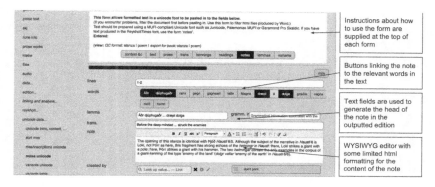

Fig. 15.9 Form for entering notes to the text

While the input (and output) uses simple formatting, simple inputs can be used to create unambiguous and meaningful data for an individual project with clear internal conventions (Fig. 15.9).

Step 7: Linking to Dictionary Headwords and Other Processes
While not part of the printed edition, the process of linking each word to dictionary headwords (lemmatising) allows for lexical and linguistic analysis of the corpus. In a highly inflected language such as Old Norse, there are normally a very large number of grammatical forms and spellings for any dictionary headword. This form (Fig. 15.10) aids the process by remembering previous choices and supplying information about both the word in the text and the dictionary headwords. The form presents each word as a row in a table, attempting to find the possible headwords for each word based on previous input and showing them as a list. Users can click/press various buttons to show pop-ups with information about the word or lemma (in the screenshot above, other words linked to the headword are shown). If the user needs to enter a lemma which is not automatically shown, they can type part of the word into the search box (also shown in the screenshot). These features—the pop-ups and search boxes—are implemented using JavaScript, where smaller pieces of information are fetched from the server. There are other forms (not shown) designed to assist in other processes of altering the table structure of the text, including splitting words (creating two rows out of one in the words table), joining words, and adjusting the alignment of the text and translation.

Fig. 15.10   Form for linking words to dictionary headwords (lemmatizing)

Designing the Interface

The design of user interfaces is the subject of an international standard (ISO 9241), which covers all human-machine interfaces. The standard describes, in great detail, standard ways in which information in the interface should be organized and formatted. These principles of presentation are fairly self-evident and include: clarity, discriminability, conciseness, consistency, detectability, legibility, and comprehensibility. Normally a project will use a pre-existing framework or template and adapt it to its own purposes. Pre-existing frameworks such as Bootstrap and Omeka provide structures for arranging information in a web interface according to these principles, but attention should still be paid to the clarity and conciseness of the specific application's content.

The user interface always involves a **dialogue** between the application and the user, where the application asks the user for input and gives feedback in response to input and information to assist in the input. There are seven principles that outline how the process of interaction should work in relation to the user's knowledge and expectations on one hand, and the required result of the process for research purposes, on the other. These principles are outlined below, with some examples from the Skaldic Project case study.

1. Suitability for the task: the interface should effectively work towards completing the desired outcome of the process. In our case study, the end result is the digital edition with accurate linking of text, translation, and other features.

2. Self-descriptiveness: the input required and the output desired by the user should be understandable at the point it is used, providing immediate feedback automatically (such as through real time updates based on the form input) or as requested by the user (such as through pop-ups).

3. Controllability: the interface should allow the user to determine the speed of the process, as well as go to earlier or later stages in the process. In our case study, this is achieved by separating the stages of entering the edition into separate forms, which can be revisited to modify previously submitted information.

4. Conformity with user expectations: the interface should be consistent; be sensitive to the knowledge, expectations and digital proficiency of the user; and, use conventional terminology and formatting wherever possible.

5. Error tolerance: the interface should prevent users from entering input erroneously, but also where possible it should be able to handle errors from the user, minimizing additional input. Various filters in the Skaldic interface, for example, take the free text input and remove extraneous formatting to ensure the stored data is semantically unambiguous and simple.

6. Suitability for individualization: the interface should be modifiable according to the user's needs, preferences, and knowledge of the system or discipline. The Skaldic interface makes common processes easily available, but allows additional and more complex data to be edited through additional forms. A bookmarking feature also allows users to easily return to pages and forms.

7. Suitability for learning: the interface should guide the user to help them learn the processes and thus improve speed and accuracy of input.

These principles are underpinned by a body of research into user interfaces.[7] By far the easiest way to begin designing a user interface,

[7] Mitchell Whitelaw, "Generous Interfaces for Digital Cultural Collections," *Digital Humanities Quarterly* 9, no. 1 (2015), accessed May 5, 2018, http://www.digitalhumanities.org/dhq/vol/9/1/000205/000205.html; Iwe Muiser, Mariet Theune, Ruud de Jong, Nigel Smink, Rudolf Berend Trieschnigg, Djoerd Hiemstra, and Theo Meder, "Supporting the Exploration of Online Cultural Heritage Collections: The Case of the Dutch Folktale Database," *Digital Humanities Quarterly* 11, no. 4 (2017), accessed May 5, 2018, http://www.digitalhumanities.org/dhq/vol/11/4/000327/000327.html.

however, is to look at other examples which implement processes relevant to your own project. You should consider what makes a particular website or application user-friendly and how it supports complex input.

The technicalities of building the interface are beyond the scope of this handbook, but a certain amount of knowledge can also be gained from existing interfaces. Most research sites will describe how the site is built and additional information can be gleaned from looking at the source code, which will normally reveal what frameworks and libraries are used by the site to structure the interface and create interactive elements.

REFERENCES

Codd, E. F. "A Relational Model of Data for Large Shared Data Banks." *Communications of the ACM* 13, no. 6 (1970): 377–387.

Knirk, James, Helle Degnbol, Bent Chr. Jacobsen, Eva Rode, Christopher Sanders, and þorbjörg Helgadóttir, eds. *A Dictionary of Old Norse Prose/Ordbog over det norrøne prosasprog.* Copenhagen: The Arnamagnæan Kommission, 1989.

Muiser, I., M. Theune, R. de Jong, N. Smink, R. B. Trieschnigg, D. Hiemstra, and T. Meder. "Supporting the Exploration of Online Cultural Heritage Collections: The Case of the Dutch Folktale Database." *Digital Humanities Quarterly* 11, no. 4 (2017). Accessed May 5, 2018. http://www.digitalhumanities.org/dhq/vol/11/4/000327/000327.html.

Whitelaw, Mitchell. "Generous Interfaces for Digital Cultural Collections." *Digital Humanities Quarterly* 9, no. 1 (2015). Accessed May 5, 2018. http://www.digitalhumanities.org/dhq/vol/9/1/000205/000205.html.

Wills, Tarrin. "Relational Data Modelling of Textual Corpora: The Skaldic Project and Its Extensions." *Digital Scholarship in the Humanities* 30, no. 2 (2015): 294–313.

CHAPTER 16

Developing Sustainable Open Heritage Datasets

Henriette Roued-Cunliffe

This chapter will explore issues and methods involved in the development of sustainable open heritage datasets and how these datasets may be used. To do so, it includes discussions of concepts such as openness, crowdsourcing and copyright. The chapter will include a case study based on the collection "Aagaards Photos" from Kolding City Archives (Denmark). The dataset consists of image-files, tables of identified people, and geographical locations for people and places. It is currently stored in three different locations that are openly accessible: Flickr, Google Maps, and Google Sheets. This chapter will present a step-by-step guide to how data is extracted from each of these datasets through readily-available and well-described Application Programming Interfaces (APIs) and how these datasets can be combined for the purpose of analyses or visualization. Open heritage data combines the idea of heritage openness on one hand and working with heritage data on the other. Openness can be understood in broad terms as involving participatory

H. Roued-Cunliffe (✉)
University of Copenhagen, Copenhagen, Denmark
e-mail: roued@hum.ku.dk

l. levenberg et al. (eds.), *Research Methods for the Digital Humanities*,
https://doi.org/10.1007/978-3-319-96713-4_16

287

approaches, community collaborations, crowdsourcing, and audience engagement. Working with heritage data typically falls under the domain of Digital Humanities, archeological computing, heritage informatics, and collection building. The combination of these two ideas constitutes a growing area that is identifiable in a range of initiatives, such as opening-up museum collections to heritage hackathons. Yet, many heritage professionals and humanities students are still seeking concrete methods to deal with open heritage data.

First, I will briefly discuss the concept and practicalities of open heritage data. Then I will illustrate the approach through an example of accessing, transforming, and combining three different types of data. The example is taken from the "Aagaards Photos" digitization and crowdsourcing project, which is conducted through Kolding City Archives in Denmark and incorporates photos, geographical locations, and biographical metadata.[1]

Openness in Heritage Data

There are a lot of things to consider in relation to openness in heritage data. For instance, all Digital Humanities researchers working with heritage data face choices pertaining to formats, platforms, and other technical specifications. When researchers intend to open their data to other users they must also consider issues regarding users, reuse, misuse, commercial use, legal requirements, funding and copyright. Courtney Ruge, et al. identify several issues that make heritage institutions in Australia reluctant or unable to share heritage collections online:

- lack of technological knowledge, resources, and limited funds within the organization;
- questions of ownership (where material has been donated, there are various sources and copyright holders, or where many of the collected texts are **orphaned works**);
- the belief that physical access to the collections meets most needs;
- concerns regarding the unauthorized reuse of images;
- concerns over losing revenue streams (the ability to sell digital copies of images or access to material);

---

[1] See http://aagaardsbilleder.tumblr.com/english.

- concerns regarding infringement of copyright or **privacy** regulation;
- and, the ethics of sharing material about identifiable people.[2]

Although some major heritage institutions around the world have the resources, know-how, and political stamina to rise above these issues, most community groups, as well as smaller and medium-sized institutions share these concerns.

First, the issue of copyright stands out as likely to have the most impact on heritage institutions. It is currently a cause of fear and uncertainty, because many heritage professionals have so little experience with it. Graham Cornish suggests that:

> Copyright law aims to protect [the growth of writing, performing and creating] but, at the same time, tries to ensure that some access to copyright works is allowed as well. Without this access creators would be starved of ideas and information to create more copyright material.[3]

Thus, copyright must balance the protection of current creative work with the support of future creative work. In essence, copyright undermines its stated intention when it suppresses new creative work without a compelling reason. Furthermore, Peter Drahos and John Braithwaite observe that "Copying and imitation are central to our process of learning and the acquisition of skills. [...] The creator of innovation is also always the borrower of ideas and information of others."[4] Fear of copyright is, thus, one of the biggest risks to future innovation because, contrary to the intentions of copyright itself, it can stifle creativity, research, and invention.

[2] Courtney Ruge, Tom Denison, Steve Wright, Graham Willett, and Joanne Evans, "Custodianship and Online Sharing in Australian Community Archives," in *Participatory Heritage*, ed. Henriette Roued-Cunliffe and Andrea J. Copeland (London, UK: Facet Publishing, 2017), 82–83.

[3] Graham Cornish, *Copyright: Interpreting the Law for Libraries, Archives and Information Services* (London, UK: Facet Publishing, 2015), 1, http://public.eblib.com/choice/publicfullrecord.aspx?p=2073251.

[4] Peter Drahos and John Braithwaite, *Information Feudalism: Who Owns the Knowledge Economy?* (Abingdon, UK: Earthscan, 2002), 2.

Open heritage approaches offer an alternative to this fear. The Open Definition project states that: "Open means anyone can freely access, use, modify, and share for any purpose (subject, at most, to requirements that preserve provenance and openness)."[5] In a heritage context the OpenGLAM[6] initiative has developed principles regarding how institutions should engage with the public about the reuse of their open data.

The first OpenGLAM principle is to "release digital information about the artifacts (metadata) into the public domain using an appropriate legal tool such as the Creative Commons Zero Waiver."[7] Releasing metadata can improve the discoverability of your data, whether your data consists of finds, findspots, maps, images, videos, interpretations, official documents, letters, artwork, etc. Institutions have different traditions of metadata. Libraries have always been at the forefront of metadata collection and sharing, mainly due to their fairly homogenous material as well as the obvious value in libraries sharing the metadata for items in their collections. However, when it comes to material that is more unique and scarcer metadata sharing becomes less common. This is an area where initiatives such as the Europeana digital platform for cultural heritage have made a great difference.[8] Europeana has demonstrated the value of sharing metadata, so that cultural heritage material can be discovered and shared across Europe.

The second principle prompts researchers and archivists to "keep digital representations of works for which copyright has expired (so works that are in the public domain) in the public domain by not adding new rights to them" ('OpenGLAM Principles').[9] This principle contains a practical criticism of copyright law and the institutions which use it to maintain control over the material that they digitize. In some countries,

---

[5] Open Definition, "The Open Definition - Open Definition - Defining Open in Open Data, Open Content and Open Knowledge." 2017. Accessed May 10, 2017, http://open-definition.org/.

[6] According to their website, "**OpenGLAM** is an initiative coordinated by Open Knowledge that promotes free and open access to digital cultural heritage held by Galleries, Libraries, Archives and Museums."

[7] "OpenGLAM Principles." OpenGLAM. 2013. Accessed April 8, 2017, https://openglam.org/principles/.

[8] The Europeana.eu platform links thousands of organizations from across the European Union to aggregate digitized cultural heritage works: https://www.europeana.eu/portal/en.

[9] "OpenGLAM Principles." OpenGLAM. 2013. Accessed April 8, 2017, https://openglam.org/principles/.

interpretations of copyright law stipulate that when the process of digitizing analog material constitutes a creative process by a human being (for example, adjusting light, etc.) and is not just an automated machine process (for example, a scanning), then the individual or institution acquires copyright over the digitized version.[10] One could argue that this practice is ethically irresponsible, especially if it is done using public funds or by a public institution. A counter argument is that heritage institutions sometimes rely on the revenue that this practice produces. However, Simon Tanner found that license and service revenue from digital images does not cover the actual costs of digitization practices and services in museums, and concluded that external funding is essential.[11]

The third OpenGLAM principle states: "when publishing data make an explicit and robust statement of your wishes and expectations with respect to reuse and repurposing of the descriptions, the whole data collection, and subsets of the collection."[12] This means that the institution making data available online needs to make sure that they are knowledgeable about the copyright status of the material with which they are working and they are clear about how it can and cannot be reused. Reuse forms a significant part of creative and innovative processes, which are facilitated through the web. Publishing online has, therefore, come to mean that everyone with the technical ability can reuse this material whether they are permitted to or not. Nonetheless, with the movement for openness growing, as it currently is, and the growing availability of heritage material for reuse, the bigger risk is that the material you put online without clear reuse statements is more likely to be passed over and, thus, forgotten. There is also the question of commercial use. It is now generally accepted that commercial use can be anything from posting on a blog with advertising revenue to use by large multibillion-dollar industries. This has the consequence that saying no to commercial reuse not only means saving your material from "big bad corporations", but also stops new creative reuse from artists, bloggers, and others who could potentially use it to make small earnings.

[10] Cornish, 7.

[11] Simon Tanner, *Reproduction Charging Models & Rights Policy for Digital Images in American Art Museums* (KDCS Digital Consultancy, 2004), https://kclpure.kcl.ac.uk/portal/files/48081293/USMuseum_SimonTanner.pdf.

[12] "OpenGLAM Principles."

The fourth principle is "when publishing data use open file formats which are machine-readable."[13] This means avoiding proprietary formats, which can only be accessed by certain computer programs or require special licenses. There are open, machine-readable formats available to suit a myriad of projects and types of material. In essence, a **CSV** file is open and machine-readable, but a webservice using **JSON** or **XML** data format would be even more so. Data documentation is also an important consideration. Without good documentation and a user-friendly interface for accessing the dataset, your well-intended open data is as unlikely to be used as the many boxes in your remote storage.

The last principle states that "opportunities to engage audiences in novel ways on the web should be pursued."[14] This requires funding and an overall strategy for open data. It is a significant aspect of open data and a challenge at which projects most often fail. We put data on the web, we say people can use it, but we do not facilitate and actively engage with the people who would potentially want to use it. This is not only about going to hackathons and encouraging programmers to develop stuff with your datasets. This is also about thinking outside the box and considering who could benefit from your data. School children and teachers, perhaps? In this case, you need to contact some to see how they could use it. University students? Then you will need to reach out to relevant departments or lecturers teaching relevant subjects. Amateur historians? To reach them you can find groups that already exist on social networking platforms that are organized around subjects such as local history or amateur archeology. The likelihood of these groups coming to you is very small if you are just starting out with open data. Further, this is not a task for a temporary student placement. It requires ongoing funding and dedicated staff that have time to reach out and engage people about using your open data. As is exemplified in the Kolding City Archive's Aagaard Photos project, the benefits and outcomes from this approach are many and varied. They include local and national media exposure, interest from scholars and students, app development, new artwork, and a solid network of people interested in heritage (many of whom have contacted the archive and enriched the project with their own funds and time).

[13] Ibid.
[14] Ibid.

Aagaards Photos

The Aagaard Photo project began suddenly after New Year, 2015 when project member Maria Wehde discovered the photographs of Dines Christian Jochum Pontoppidan Aagaard. Aagaard used the early technique of collodion negatives to take portraits of local Kolding citizens, between 1857 and 1880. The early photography technique made the collection historically significant and the name labels on the glass negatives made it particularly useful for family historians in the area.

The project quickly evolved into an ad hoc crowdsourcing project through which family historians helped identify the people in the photos by transcribing the labels, and looking up individuals in the census and parish records. From the beginning, it was a goal of the project to keep all materials, old and new, openly accessible simultaneously with their digitization or collection. This has resulted in a dataset that includes 2103 portraits of which 733 have been identified. All the images are hosted on Flickr and the information about each individual featured in the photographs is hosted in a Google Sheet. Furthermore, all places noted in the customer registry are stored in a custom Google Map. As part of the crowdsourcing effort, volunteers use a simple form to send information they have discovered about the individuals in the photos with references to the sources in which they are found. The archive then checks and approves the information and adds it to the constantly growing list. Like in many other crowdsourcing projects there is also a long-tail distribution of contributors' workloads; a few volunteers contribute most of the information and many contribute only a little.[15] Connection to the genealogy and local, amateur history communities through active Facebook groups has led to various new efforts at the archive, such as ongoing history workshops, a mash-up past and present workshop, and a repair and remake festival with a photographic atelier inspired by Aagaard's photos.

---

[15] Tim Causer and Melissa Terras, "'Many Hands Make Light Work. Many Hands Together Make Merry Work': *Transcribe Bentham* and Crowdsourcing Manuscript Collections," in *Crowdsourcing Our Cultural Heritage*, ed. Mia Ridge (Surrey, UK: Ashgate, 2014), 73.

Why APIs?

Understanding and using APIs is essential to optimize the openness and usefulness of the online publishing methods that researchers and archivists use. I have formulated a list of questions that can be asked about material that is shared online:

1. Is the material published with metadata so that it can be searched and found?
2. Is the material published with an open license or in the public domain, and is this clearly communicated in conjunction with the material?
3. Does the creator actively encourage reuse of the material and provide support for anyone who wishes to reuse it, free of charge?
4. Is a static version of the material available in an open, machine-readable format, that anyone can export/download?
5. Is the material available as a live data stream through a well-described API, that anyone can access?

There are many ways to make heritage material available online and some are more open than others but, currently, the most open method is through an API. An API is, as the name suggests, a set of protocols and tools for building applications. There are many ways to access and use heritage material through APIs. You can download datasets to visualize and analyze in existing software or view it with command line prompts. Another method is to access the live stream of datasets remotely. This method will be described in the following guide.

Many online services (e.g. Twitter, Instagram, Facebook, etc.) provide APIs with the intention that developers around the world can use them to build new applications that complement and support the main service. In this guide we will access two Google APIs and Flickr's API to reuse heritage data stored on these two services. As mentioned previously, one of the most extensive heritage APIs has been built by Europeana, which provides access to 53,455,335[16] artworks, artifacts, books, videos, and sounds from across Europe through different methods and protocols. Europeana labs, which is the hub for apps and app development, includes a strong program for encouraging the use and reuse of this

---

[16]www.europeana.eu, as of October 1, 2017.

enormous heritage dataset. Among other things it showcases 74 API implementations, such as a bulk downloader, new ways of browsing the dataset, host challenges, and in other ways encourage reuse.

GUIDE

This guide will demonstrate how to access and combine heritage data from three linked datasets in order to present and share it online. Additional information and guides on the coding presented in this guide can be found at W3Schools.com (this site is continuously updated to reflect the latest coding uses).[17] The steps will use server-side programming language, **PHP**, web-markup language, **HTML, XML**, and **JSON** data formats. This requires limited technical specifications:

- a browser to view and execute the code;
- a server or localhost that runs **PHP** and has **SimpleXML** and **JSON** installed;
- and, a text-editor and a way of transferring the php files to the server.

Extracting Photos from Flickr

This guide shows how to extract photos from Flickr, which is currently the most comprehensive image sharing site. The biggest advantage of using Flickr for heritage photo sharing as an individual, group, or heritage institution is that it has a built-in and very well-documented API, which is relatively easy to use without signing up. In order to make full use of the API on a different server you will need to apply for an **API-key** from Flickr. The following example will extract the photo URL, title, and id from the identified Aagaard photo album on Flickr.

Step 1: Identify the methods and parameters needed to call the API and retrieve the dataset. In this case, we are using the Flickr method flickr.photosets.getphotos, which will allow us to retrieve data for each photo in the album. When we call this method we include the following parameters (Table 16.1):

---

[17] "W3Schools Online Web Tutorials," W3 Schools. 2017. Accessed May 29, 2017, https://www.w3schools.com.

Table 16.1   API Parameters

Parameter name	Value	Description
photoset_id	72157650969693930	This parameter is required and identifies the photoset/album we want to call. The id can be found at the end of the photoset album url
format	Rest	The format of the data returned (in this case RESTful **XML**)
api_key	[YOUR API-KEY]	The API-key you received from Flickr
extras	url_s	Extra data we need to extract (in this case the url for the small-sized image)

Flickr's API explorer helps us put the method and the parameters together into a URL that can return the dataset as XML:

Flickr.com API

URL: https://api.flickr.com/services/rest/?method=flickr. photosets.getPhotos&api_key=[YOURAPI-KEY]&photoset_ id=72157650969693930&extras=url_s&format=rest

---

Box 16.1: Returned XML

```
<?xml version="1.0" encoding="utf-8"?>
<rsp stat="ok">
 <photoset id="72157650969693930" [...]
title="Identificerede personer">
  <photo id="22297400674" [...] title="0001 Ane
Marie Pedersen, Eltang 73" [...]
url_m="https://farm6.staticflickr.
com/5741/22297400674_97d034a93b.jpg" [...] />
  <photo id="24005467813" [...] title="0002
Andreas Lauritsen, Vejstruprød" [...]
url_m="https://farm2.staticflickr.com/1656/
24005467813_12df393f6d.jpg" [...] />
[...]
</photoset>
</rsp>
```

Step 2: We now have the URL and can use it to call the live dataset for this album. At this point there is the option to save the dataset as a static file on our server or computer and analyze it there. Instead we will manipulate and analyze the data as entities on the server, so that our application is always using the latest dataset updated by the city archive. To do this we need to call the dataset into our PHP file using the simplexml_load_file() function:

Box 16.2: Calling the dataset

```
// URL built with Flickr API
$flickr_api_url =
"https://api.flickr.com/services/
rest/?method=flickr.photosets.
getPhotos&api_key=[YOUR API-KEY]&photoset_
id=72157650969693930&extras=url_s&format=rest";
// Load XML from Flickr URL
$flickr_xml = simplexml_load_file($flickr_api_url);
```

Step 3: We can now treat our dataset like a PHP array, which we can loop through in order to transform id, title, and URL into HTML that can be presented in a browser. The title of the photo in Flickr is made up of the original photo number and the photo title, so we need to use the explode() function to split these two entities. In order to present the image files as actual images in the browser we add the URL to the HTML < *img*> tag.

Box 16.3: Present the image files in a browser

```
// Loop through the photos and add each one to a variable
foreach ($flickr_xml->photoset->photo as $photo){
        // Get title from Flickr
        $flickr_title = $photo->attributes()->title;
        // Split id from title
        $explode_title = explode(" ", $flickr_title, 2);
        // Grab the integer value of the aagaard photo id
        $aagaard_photoid = intval($explode_title[0]);
        // Output photo id:
```

```
echo "<b>Aagaard photo number:</b> " . $aagaard_
photoid . "</br>";
// Grab the title-text of the photo:
$aagaard_title = $explode_title[1];
// Output the title text with a linebreak after:
echo "<b>Title:</b> " . $aagaard_title . "<br/>";
// GRAB URL for photo
$img_url = $photo->attributes()->url_s;
// Output photo-url in a HTML image tag:
echo "<img src='" . $img_url . "'/>";
// Output a horizontal line after each image
echo "<hr/>";
}
```

This enables us to output the image (see Fig. 16.3) below the text: Aagaard photo number: 1, Title: Ane Marie Pedersen, Eltang 73.

EXTRACTING LOCATIONS FROM GOOGLE MAPS

This guide shows how to extract geographical locations from a custom Google map. The archive chose to use a custom Google map to pinpoint the location of individuals in the photos based on the photo registry, because it has a simple interface for doing so. Flickr also allows for geo-locating uploaded photos, however, the level of detail for this geotagging is too low.

Step 1: Build the URL to extract the custom Google map data as a KML XML format. First, we need to find the map id in the map URL. It is located with the parameter mid:

https://www.google.com/maps/d/viewer?mid=1axcGJpqIjtHUfo-MUhKhc3Z-2L74&ll=55.38810642013983%2C9.9925267999999 5&z=8

In this case we are simply requesting the map dataset as KML instead of viewing it through the Google map viewer. An API-key is not necessary for this yet:

https://www.google.com/maps/d/kml?mid=1axcGJpqIjtHUfoMUhKhc3Z-2L74&forcekml=1

Step 2: Again, we use the simplexml_load_file() function to access this dataset as KML, which is a variant of XML.

> **Box 16.4: Accessing the dataset as KML**
> ```
> // Get id for the custom map
> $maps_id = "1axcGJpqIjtHUfoMUhKhc3Z-2L74";
> // Build the URL requesting KML (a form of XML)
> $maps_api = "https://www.google.com/maps/d/kml?mid=" .
> $maps_id . "&forcekml=1";
> // Call the KML as an XML file
> $maps_kml = simplexml_load_file($maps_api);
> ```

Step 3: As with the photos we need to loop through the dataset, but this time we need two loops. Custom Google maps are made up of layers and in this case the archive has made two layers (Fig. 16.1). The first layer contains all the place names found in the photo registry and the second contains all the identified people, which are organized by photo. It is the second layer we want to use here, so first we loop through the layers (stored

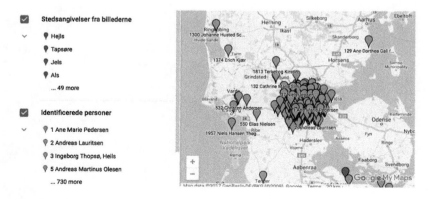

Fig. 16.1   The dataset in Google maps with locations

in *<folder>* tags in the KML) and if the layer has the right name we move on. Then we loop through the placemarks. For each placemark we want the name, which is made up of the original photo id and the title of the photo. This has to be split using the explode() function. The coordinates for each photo are found together in the *<coordinates>* tag and need to be split too.

Box 16.5: Looping the dataset

```
// Loop through map folders
foreach ($maps_kml->Document->Folder as $folder){
    // Retrieve the right map folder
    if ($folder->name == 'Identificerede personer'){
        // Loop through placemarkers
    foreach ($folder->Placemark as $placemark){
        // Get placemarker name
            $map_title = $placemark->name;
            // Split photo id from photo title
            $explode_title = explode(" ", $map_title, 2);
            $map_photoid = intval($explode_title[0]);
            $map_title = $explode_title[1];
            // Output id
            echo "<b>Aagaard photo number:</b> " .
            $map_photoid . "</br>";
            // Output title
            echo "<b>Title:</b> " . $map_title . "<br/>";
            // Get lat/lon
            $coordinates_string =
            $placemark->Point->coordinates;
            $coordinates_explode = explode(",",
            $coordinates_string);
            $longitude =
            ltrim($coordinates_explode[0]);
            $latitude = $coordinates_explode[1];
            // Output coordinates
            echo "<b>Coordinates:</b> " . $latitude .
            " / " . $longitude . "<br/>";
            echo "<hr/>";
        }
    }
}
```

The output for this is:

> Aagaard photo number: 1
> Title: Ane Marie Pedersen
> Coordinates: 55.5277318 /9.5367765

EXTRACTING BIOGRAPHIC METADATA FROM A TABLE

The archive decided to use Google sheets to present the crowdsourced biographic data about the individuals that were identified (Fig. 16.2).

Step 1: Google sheets has a well-documented API and can be used to access the data in the tables in the JSON format. In order to do so we apply for an API-key from the Google API console and enable the API for Google Sheets.

Step 2: Spreadsheets are normally private in terms of access and permission like other Google documents, so to share this sheet through the API we need to publish it to the web. In the sheet go to File > Publish to the web > Publish. Now we need the sheet id, which can be found in the URL:

> https://docs.google.com/spreadsheets/d/1krJlfljyXUY6orNIkgOo8LIH
> lLnYf5NflI81_5GDvEE/edit#gid=681292462.

Then identify the range we want to extract. In this case, the range includes column A to column V (i.e. A:V). Adding the API-key, sheet id, and range as parameters to the URL we can now retrieve this dataset as JSON:

> https://sheets.googleapis.com/v4/spreadsheets/
> 1krJlfljyXUY6orNIkgOo8LIHlLnYf5NflI81_5GDvEE/values/
> A:V?key=[GOOGLEAPI-KEY].

	A	B	C	D	E	F	G	H	I
1		Photoid	Firstname	Lastname	Title/job	Born	Birth place	Death	Death place
2	02/08/2016 10.01.04	1	Ane Marie	Pedersen		12/08/1852	Gudsø Mark, Eltang		
3	02/08/2016 10.54.27	2	Andreas	Lauridsen		25/09/1863	Vejstruprød, Vejstrup		
4	10/04/2015 11.01.48	3	Ingeborg Margrethe	Topsøe		21/05/1869	Store Heddinge Sogn	18/02/1953	Vallekilde
5	02/08/2016 10.57.56	5	Andreas	Olesen		24/06/1843	Fredericia		
6	10/04/2015 11.10.01	9	Poul Jepsen	Bekker	Kludesamler	20/09/1828	Øster Starup		
7	10/04/2015 11.12.21	9	Else Marie	Jepsen		05/09/1829	Bøgvad, Egtved		

Fig. 16.2 The dataset in Google sheets

Step 3: As with the photos from Flickr and the coordinates from the custom Google map, we request the data from the API. However, this time we use the get_file_contents() and json_decode() functions to pull the dataset into a PHP array.

Box 16.6: Requesting data from the API

```
// API key - apply to Google, remember to enable
Google Sheets API:
https://console.developers.google.com/apis
$sheets_api_key =
"AIzaSyAZXM3NNUF_zVBEncYzVNU4byo3cOVrqvw";
// Sheet id - remember to publish sheet: File >
Publish to the web >
Publish
$sheet_id = "1krJlfljyXUY6orNIkgOo8LIHlLnYf5NflI81_5GDvEE";
// Range to extract from sheets - use spreadsheet
syntax, fx. A:D or A2:B32
$range = "A:V";
// Combine URL to call sheet
$sheets_api = "https://sheets.googleapis.com/v4/
spreadsheets/" . $sheet_id . "/values/" . $range .
"?key=" . $sheets_api_key;
// Call the JSON file
$sheets_json = file_get_contents($sheets_api);
// Decode JSON file into a PHP array
$sheets_array = json_decode($sheets_json);
```

Step 4: Because this data originated as a table where the first row consists of headers for each column, we begin by setting a counter before the loop and start the output after the first row in the dataset. Unlike the XML data, this data is not contained in meaningful tags and therefore we need to consult the original table to find the right column. For example, the original photo number is in column B and the equivalent of this in the $rows array is index number 1 (array indices always begin at 0). Note how this dataset is built up around individuals in the photos, rather than the photo themselves. This is why this dataset contains more than one row of information with the same photo id number (Fig. 16.2).

Box 16.7: Setting a counter and starting the loop

```
$counter = 0;
foreach ($sheets_array->values as $rows){
    // Add a counter to skip first row of labels
    if ($counter++ == 0) continue;
    // Find photo number in column B (array value 1)
    $sheets_photoid = $rows[1];
    // Output photo number
    echo "<b>Aagaard photo number:</b> " . $sheets_photoid
    . "</br>";
    // Find other information in the columns C=2, D=3,
    F=5, G=6
    $firstname = $rows[2];
    $lastname = $rows[3];
    $born = $rows[5];
    $born_place = $rows[6];
    // Output information
    echo "Full name: " . $firstname . " " . $lastname. "";
    echo "Born: " . $born . ", " . $born_place. "";
    // Add line after each individual
    echo "<hr/>";
}
```

The output from this is a list of photos with the id, full name, and birth date and place:

> Aagaard photo number: 1
> Full name: Ane Marie Pedersen
> Born: 12/08/1852, Gudsø Mark, Eltang

COMBINING DATASETS

The datasets have two components: identified individuals and photographs. The two components have a many-to-many relationship; identified individuals can be in more than one photo and each photo can have more than one identified individual. Because only photographs have an id number, we will use them as the basis to combine the three datasets.

Step 1: The first step is to extract data from each dataset and loop through the data. Instead of outputting the data, we add it to one array called *$photographs*. To do this we use the photo id from the flickr dataset (*aagaard_Photoid*), *themapdataset* (map_photoid), and the sheets table ($sheets_photoid) as the key to combine the information from the three datasets into one array.

Box 16.8: Extracting Data

```
$photographs[$aagaard_photoid]['img'] = "<img src='" .
$img_url . "'/>";
                $photographs[$map_photoid]['latitude'] = $latitude;
                $photographs[$map_photoid]['longitude'] = $longitude;
$photographs[$sheets_photoid]['people'][$name] = $birth;
```

Step 2: Loop through the array and output the information about the two components as HTML in the form of a single listing for each photo (Fig. 16.3).

Box 16.9: Loop through the array

```
// Loop photographs array
foreach ($photographs as $photoid=>$photoinfo){
        // Output photo id:
        echo "<b>Aagaard photo number:</b> " . $pho-
        toid . "</br>";
        // Output coordinates
        echo "<b>Coordinates:</b> " . $photoinfo['lat-
itude'] . " / " . $photoinfo['longitude'] . "<br/>";
        // Loop people in photo
        foreach          ($photoinfo['people']          as
$name=>$birth){echo $name . ", " . $birth .
"<br/>";
        }
        // Output image
        echo $photoinfo['img'] . "<br/>";
        // Add line after each photograph
        echo "<hr/>";
    }
```

Aagaard photo number: 5
Coordinates: 55.4890425 / 9.4724867
Andreas Olesen, 24/06/1843, Fredericia

Aagaard photo number: 9
Coordinates: 55.5856339 / 9.422493
Poul Jepsen Bekker , 20/09/1828, Øster Starup
Else Marie Jepsen, 05/09/1829, Bøgvad, Egtved

Fig. 16.3 The final output of the combined datasets

CONCLUSION

The Aagaards Photos archive and the step-by-step guide to use Flickr's API in a Digital Humanities project demonstrate opportunities for open heritage datasets. Researcher working with open heritage data still face a number of questions related to ownership, copyright, and data protection. However, other important and often neglected considerations involve the risks of losing data and failing to have social impact.

Even though we spend enormous funds digitizing and structuring heritage data, it is still as vulnerable to being lost or falling into disuse in our digital archives. In other words, digitization and online publishing do not ensure that heritage material will have a broader or long-lasting social impact. The motivation of this chapter is to reduce this risk through open data and APIs. It is still not as simple as building an API and sitting back to wait for the public to use it. As with any dissemination of a heritage project, it still requires facilitation. Good examples, which involve the public in open heritage data include heritage hacks and data sprints. The main goal is often to explain and motivate the use of heritage datasets to programmers and interface designers and encourage participation. Furthermore, teaching new generations of humanities students the basics of programming and data management will go a long way towards promoting deeper understandings of humanities materials through new digital platforms.

Acknowledgements I want to thank Maria Wehde for pushing the open agenda and including me in the Aagaard Project in the first place and City Archivist, Lene Wul, for continuing down this path with me. I also want to thank the students at University of Copenhagen for their willingness to learn to program with open data and for enabling me to develop my tutorials.

REFERENCES

Causer, Tim, and Melissa Terras. "'Many Hands Make Light Work. Many Hands Together Make Merry Work': *Transcribe Bentham* and Crowdsourcing Manuscript Collections." In *Crowdsourcing Our Cultural Heritage*, edited by Mia Ridge, 57–88. Surrey, UK: Ashgate, 2014.

Cornish, Graham P. *Copyright: Interpreting the Law for Libraries, Archives and Information Services*. London, UK: Facet Publishing, 2015. http://public. eblib.com/choice/publicfullrecord.aspx?p=2073251.

Drahos, Peter, and John Braithwaite. *Information Feudalism: Who Owns the Knowledge Economy?* Abingdon, UK: Earthscan, 2002.

Open Definition. "The Open Definition—Open Definition—Defining Open in Open Data, Open Content and Open Knowledge." 2017. Accessed May 10, 2017. http://opendefinition.org/.

"OpenGLAM Principles." OpenGLAM. 2013. Accessed April 8, 2017. https://openglam.org/principles/.

Ruge, Courtney, Tom Denison, Steve Wright, Graham Willett, and Joanne Evans. "Custodianship and Online Sharing in Australian Community Archives." In *Participatory Heritage*, edited by Henriette Roued-Cunliffe and Andrea J. Copeland, 79–86. London, UK: Facet Publishing, 2017.

Tanner, Simon. *Reproduction Charging Models & Rights Policy for Digital Images in American Art Museums.* KDCS Digital Consultancy, 2004. https://kclpure.kcl.ac.uk/portal/files/48081293/USMuseum_SimonTanner.pdf.

"W3Schools Online Web Tutorials." W3 Schools. 2017. Accessed May 29, 2017. https://www.w3schools.com.

CHAPTER 17

Telling Untold Stories:
Digital Textual Recovery Methods

Roopika Risam

Digital environments are increasingly becoming the spaces where the cultural memory of humanity is produced, disseminated, and consumed. At the same time, these spaces are increasingly being colonized by corporations like Sage and ProQuest, which are creating and paywalling knowledge.[1] As a result, digital cultural memory is in danger of becoming a product of corporate interests, which favor canonical texts and writers. This risks a critical lack of representation for writers outside of the dominant cultures of the Global North.[2] However, the affordances of Digital Humanities and availability of Web 2.0 tools create possibilities for intervening in these gaps in representation.

---

[1] Stephan Bottomore, "Scholarly Research, Then and Now," *Early Popular Visual Culture* 14, no. 4 (2016): 317.

[2] Roopika Risam, "Other Worlds, Other DHs: Notes Towards a DH Accent," *Digital Scholarship in the Humanities* 32, no. 2 (2017): 380.

R. Risam (✉)
Salem State University, Salem, MA, USA
e-mail: rrisam@salemstate.edu

© The Author(s) 2018
l. levenberg et al. (eds.), *Research Methods for the Digital Humanities*,
https://doi.org/10.1007/978-3-319-96713-4_17

Literature of the African diaspora is one such area where digital textual recovery has a long history. As Amy Earhart notes, scholars of African American literature embraced the emerging internet culture of the early 1990s to recover texts by African American writers.[3] While some of these digital projects like *The Charles Chesnutt Archive* (http://www.chesnuttarchive.org) still exist, many of these early projects have been lost because they were not preserved and sustained.[4] With the advent of new methods, however, a number of older projects have been revived, such as Maryemma Graham's *Project on the History of Black Writing* (https://hbw.ku.edu), while new initiatives have emerged, such as Kim Gallon's *Black Press Research Collective* (http://blackpressresearchcollective.org).

Exploring interventions in digital textual recovery, I begin this chapter by discussing *The Harlem Shadows Project*, a Digital Humanities project I created with Chris Forster. I examine our work developing a critical digital edition of Claude McKay's poetry using TEI, the approach we took, and the decisions we made in the process. Further, I consider alternatives to creating TEI editions. Finally, I discuss using TEI Boilerplate as a way of getting started with TEI.

THE HARLEM SHADOWS PROJECT

One approach to digital textual recovery is using the Text Encoding Initiative (TEI) guidelines for digitizing texts to create digital editions of public domain texts.[5] According to copyright laws in the United States, texts published before 1923 are in the public domain and are thus available for use for digital editions. This facet of copyright law is why digital libraries like Project Gutenberg are able to provide full-text versions of texts online. Taking advantage of these copyright dates, we created *The Harlem Shadows Project* (http://harlemshadows.org), a digital edition of Claude McKay's *Harlem Shadows* (1922), using TEI. Forster conceived of the idea for the project as a teaching assistant at the

---

[3] Amy Earhart, *Traces of the Old, Uses of the New: The Emergence of Digital Literary Studies* (Ann Arbor: University of Michigan Press, 2015), 65.

[4] Ibid., 77.

[5] "TEI: Text Encoding Initiative," Text Encoding Initiative, last modified July 19, 2016, http://www.tei-c.org/index.xml.

University of Virginia when he discovered that Amazon.com was selling cheap reproductions of public domain versions of McKay's *Harlem Shadows*. This led Forster to wonder how Digital Humanities methods might be used to make public domain texts more useful, particularly for teaching.[6] Around the same time, as a teaching assistant at Emory University, I assigned James Weldon Johnson's *The Autobiography of an Ex-Colored Man* (1912), and my students bought the cheapest versions they could find on Amazon.com. While discussing the novel in class, we realized that one of the versions was missing more than a chapter of the text. Subsequently, we discovered that a print-on-demand publishing operation was simply reproducing extant public domain copies of texts without any quality control. The great tragedy of these editions is that writers of the Harlem Renaissance, like Claude McKay, were writing to claim their humanity and make the case for their incorporation into the democratic space of the nation. Yet, less than 100 years later, this invaluable work is circulating through poor-quality editions produced purely for profit. Looking into whether scholars were using Digital Humanities methods to intervene, I learned about Forster's work and joined *The Harlem Shadows Project* as co-director.

To begin, Forster and I sourced the original periodical appearances of the poems in McKay's *Harlem Shadows*. We relied on bibliographies of McKay's work and found microfilm versions of the periodicals where McKay published to find the original versions. As we did so, we discovered that there were variations between the originally published versions of the poems and those that appeared in the published version with an introduction by writer and political activist Max Eastman. Given our interest in including these variants in the digital edition, we used the TEI guidelines to digitize *Harlem Shadows*. The TEI, founded in 1987, develops guidelines for marking up texts with tags that make them machine readable.[7] TEI tags look similar to HTML tags, set off by open tags (<) and close tags (>) that enclose elements that indicate features of texts, such as stanza breaks, underlining, italics, deletions, and additions. The difference between TEI and HTML elements, however, is that TEI elements are descriptive and do not function as operators. Conversely, a

[6]Chris Forster, "Public Domain Editions," Chris Forster, last modified June 21, 2012, http://cforster.com/2012/06/drill-baby-drill/.

[7]"TEI: Text Encoding Initiative."

```
<TEI xmlns="http://www.tei-c.org/ns/1.0">
 <teiHeader>
  <fileDesc>
   <titleStmt>
    <title>
     "The Tropics in New York", from
     <ref target="http://harlemshadows.org">Harlem Shadows:
A Digital Edition</ref>
    </title>
   </titleStmt>
   <publicationStmt>
    <publisher>
     This file is produced from the material at
     <ref target="http://harlemshadows.org">Harlem Shadows: A Digital
Edition</ref>
    </publisher>
    <date>December 6, 2015</date>
    <availability>
     <licence target="https://creativecommons.org/licenses/by-nc/4.0/">
Creative Commons Attribution-NonCommerical 4.0 International
</licence>
    </availability>
   </publicationStmt>
   <sourceDesc>
    <bibl>
     <note>
This file is generated from a master file containing the text of Claude
McKay's 1922 collection of poems
<title level="m">Harlem Shadows</title>
and related documents (other appearances of McKay's poems, reviews, and
related material). The base text for this file is drawn from the item listed
below.
     </note>
     <author>Claude McKay</author>
     <title level="a">The Tropics in New York</title>
     <title level="m">Harlem Shadows</title>
     <pubPlace>New York</pubPlace>
     <publisher>Harcourt, Brace, and Company</publisher>
     <date when="1922">1922</date>
     <biblScope unit="pg">8</biblScope>
    </bibl>
   </sourceDesc>
  </fileDesc>
 </teiHeader>
```

Fig. 17.1   TEI header markup of Claude McKay's "The Tropics in New York"

bold (<b>) HTML element renders text in boldface print. TEI markup
uses a tree-like structure, where the document itself functions as the
root, while the divisions and features of the text function as branches
(see Fig. 17.1). This facilitates the machine-readability of the text.

Using TEI allowed us to not only create an edition grounded in
existing practices of digital textual editing but also encode the differences between the textual variants. To transform TEI into an edition
that would be available online, we used XSLT stylesheets to render the

Fig. 17.2 HTML edition of Claude McKay's "The Tropics in New York" with highlighted variants

Fig. 17.3 HTML edition of Claude McKay's "The Tropics in New York" with editorial notes

TEI file in HTML for web browsers. Because we were using XSLT, we were also able to build features into the edition to allow users to toggle the textual variants on and off (see Fig. 17.2). Given our interest in the pedagogical value of such an edition, we also drew on the affordances of XSLT to include editorial notes glossing terms with which student readers may be unfamiliar (see Fig. 17.3). These choices were made through collaborative decision-making, considering each poem through the perspective of a college student reader. As the left-hand sidebars in Figs. 17.2 and 17.3 also indicate, we included the textual history of the poems' periodical appearances and have also generated PDF and plain text versions of the poems to download along with a downloadable TEI version.

ALTERNATIVE EDITIONS

The primary challenge of the project was the time- and labor-intensive nature of the work. We had originally anticipated that we could design a workflow to efficiently create digital editions of public domain texts, but discovered that this was not a quick process. This raises the important question of what kinds of alternative approaches to creating editions are possible. One such example is *Harlem Echoes*, a class project directed by Amardeep Singh and Ed Whitely of Lehigh University and "little sister" project of Forster's and my edition.[8] Singh and Whitely encouraged their students to explore and reimagine *The Harlem Shadows Project* with student readers in mind. In response, they created their own edition through a WordPress website. Unlike *The Harlem Shadows Project*, *Harlem Echoes* tags poems thematically to offer users points of entry into McKay's poems through themes that may interest them, such as sexuality, gender, and race. The site also includes short contextual essays that facilitate readings of the poems ("'If We Must Die' – In America," "'If We Must Die' – In England") as well as interpretive pieces ("The Birds of Harlem Shadows," "Claude McKay's Relationship with His Craft"). While *Harlem Echoes* lacks the machine readability provided by the TEI edition in *The Harlem Shadows Project*, it offers an alternative approach to reading McKay's poetry beyond digital reproduction of the print text.

An alternative approach to creating digital editions is the "minimal edition." Edward Vanhoutte defines the minimal edition as "a cultural product that is produced by the scholarly editor acting as a curator or guardian of the text."[9] The minimal edition stands in contrast to the "maximal edition," or, "an academic product in which the scholarly editor demonstrates his/her scholarly accuracy and scrutiny."[10] One approach the minimal edition is Alex Gil's Jekyll theme "Ed." Ed. is a theme for the Jekyll static-site generator. Built using minimal computing principles, Ed. is "focused on legibility, durability, ease and flexibility" with the goal of producing "beautifully rendered scholarly or reading

---

[8] Amardeep Singh and Ed Whitely, "Harlem Echoes," last modified November 11, 2016, https://harlemshadows.wordpress.com.

[9] Edward Vanhoutte, "Every Reader His Own Bibliographer—An Absurdity?," in *Text Editing, Print and Digital World*, eds. Kathryn Sutherland and Marilyn Deegan (London: Routledge, 2016), 100.

[10] Ibid.

editions of texts meant to last."[11] By making Ed. available for public use, Gil raises an important question for those editing texts to consider: when and under what conditions are maximal editions, such as those that use TEI or include critical apparatuses, beneficial for producing an edition of a text, and when is a minimal edition the appropriate choice?[12]

GETTING STARTED WITH TEI EDITIONS

For those interested in learning to use TEI to create an edition, a relatively easy way to get started is to use TEI Boilerplate, designed by John Walsh, Grant Simpson, and Saeed Moaddeli of Indiana University.[13] TEI Boilerplate allows users to publish text that has been marked up with TEI to the web. TEI Boilerplate intervenes in challenges faced by users who wish to publish TEI documents online, such as dimensions of the text that HTML will not render or having to use CSS (cascading style sheets) to style the TEI document.[14] As the creators note, "TEI Boilerplate is not intended to be a replacement for the many excellent XSLT solutions for publishing and displaying TEI/XML on the web. It is intended to be a *simple and lightweight* alternative to more complex XSLT solutions."[15] For the purposes of those wishing to try out TEI, however, TEI Boilerplate is a logical starting point.

To get started, download the TEI Boilerplate files (https://github.com/GrantLS/TEI-Boilerplate). Working with these files requires working within a plain text editor, such as Textwrangler (https://www.barebones.com/products/textwrangler/), Sublime Text (https://www.sublimetext.com/), or Vim (http://www.vim.org/download.php), which are freely available online for download. Open the sample text for Thomas Hardy's "A Singer Asleep" (hardy_a_singer_asleep.xml) by opening the "Dist" and "Content" folders. If a plain text editor is already installed, the file will open automatically in your editor. This file

---

[11] Alex Gil, "Ed.: A Jekyll Theme for Minimal Editions," *Ed.*, last modified July 12, 2017, https://elotroalex.github.io/ed/.

[12] Alex Gil, Facebook Message to Author, July 17, 2017.

[13] "About TEI Boilerplate," *TEI Boilerplate*, accessed July 17, 2017, http://dcl.ils.indiana.edu/teibp/.

[14] Ibid.

[15] Ibid.

is a TEI marked up version of a poem that uses TEI Boilerplate and thus renders the TEI version of the poem in a web browser.

TEI Boilerplate is a useful place to begin for those who are new to TEI because the essential components of the TEI document are built into the TEI Boilerplate files. For example, the Hardy poem begins with "TEI xmlns" tags that indicate that the document is in TEI. The next important element of the document is the TEI Header (<teiHeader>), which includes metadata elements for the text being digitized, such as title, author, editor, place of publication, publisher, and availability of the text, as well as licensing for TEI Boilerplate. There are alternative schemas provided for metadata for born-digital documents, as well as documents transcribed from another source. The next section of the file, which is still part of the TEI header, outlines the encoding scheme for the file (<encodingDesc>) as well as the tags that render styled text in browsers (<tagsDecl>). These tags, which begin "rendition xml: id=" are the ones that can be incorporated into the text itself to style it.

Beneath the TEI Header is the body, which is where the poem itself can be found. There, rendition tags are in use to indicate and render features of the text, such as alignment, indents, and small caps. The Hardy poem is a relatively simple sample, so it does not make use of a significant number of the rendition tag elements. However, these tags can be used for documents where they are appropriate. With this basic look at the key features of the TEI document in TEI Boilerplate, getting started with creating a TEI document is fairly straightforward.

The easiest way to begin is to rename the hardy_a_singer_asleep.xml file to reflect the title of the document to be marked up. Those more experienced or comfortable with TEI and TEI Boilerplate may wish to work from the dedication.xml file. However, for those new to TEI, working through the renamed hardy_a_singer_asleep.xml file involves simply replacing the information relevant to the Hardy poem with information for the text being marked up. Begin by leaving the TEI namespace (<TEI xmlns>) section as is, because this information is not unique to the text being marked-up. Make sure that the TEI Header remains in place and change the relevant information (title, author, editor, publisher, and availability) for the text being digitized. Leave the TEI Boilerplate licensing information in place, to properly credit use of TEI Boilerplate for creating the digitized text. If the text is born-digital (originally published as a digital document, rather than a print one), use the suggested language: "This TEI/XML document is the original." If the document is transcribed from another source, use the <biblStruct> tags outlined in the XML file.

The next step is to take a look at the encoding tags that are listed. Identify the ones that are features of the text to be digitized. It may be easiest to copy these tags into a separate file to facilitate easier cutting and pasting, rather than having to scroll back up to the encoding tag section to retrieve them. Then, in the body section, replace the material from Hardy's poem with the text to be digitized. This is best done line-by-line, rather than cutting and pasting the entire document because cutting and pasting will strip existing formatting. Line-by-line replacement preserves the formatting and allows the user to identify where tags need to be adjusted to account for the features of the text being digitized. Once the substitutions have been made, go over the original text again to ensure that the features of the text have been marked with the relevant rendition tags. Thus, the TEI document is complete.

As noted, the clear affordance of TEI Boilerplate is the ease with which it transforms the TEI document so it can be rendered in a web browser. Simply upload the TEI Boilerplate directory (the folder containing the downloaded files) to a webserver, and the TEI document will be viewable online. For those who do not have access to server space, it can be purchased from a hosting service. Reclaim Hosting is a useful option for academics and students because it was designed for higher education and has swift and helpful customer service. Further, for those who are not comfortable working in the command line, Reclaim Hosting has a control panel, where uploading files and directories is simple.

While working with students, in particular, TEI Boilerplate has provided a way of introducing the concept of digitizing texts using TEI without the significant learning curve of beginning with TEI from scratch. This allows those who are new to TEI to experiment with its affordances and challenges before committing to deeper exploration of the method. For example, Jennifer Petz, a student in the Digital Scholars Program at Salem State University, used TEI Boilerplate to digitize an excerpt from a memoir of Walter George Whitman, a Salem Normal School professor who traveled to China in the 1920s.[16] Using TEI Boilerplate, she was able to depict the handwritten emendations that

---

[16]Walter G. Whitman, "Glimpses of Life in China," Excerpt, *Digital Salem*, accessed July 17, 2017, http://di.salemstate.edu/omeka/exhibits/show/walter-george-whitman/item/33.

Whitman made on the manuscript for his memoir. Petz's work on this edition has brought to light the untold story of Whitman's travels, illuminating the colonialist perspective through which he viewed the people he met in Nanking.

With the developments of TEI and solutions such as TEI Boilerplate, the possibilities for digital textual recovery are clear. As the digital cultural record continues to be developed, it is critical to ensure that writers who are elided from literary canons are not simultaneously omitted from digital cultures. The process of marking-up a text to create an edition and making it available online can bring new attention to texts from writers who have previously received little attention or have disappeared from readership. Greater availability of these texts increases the chance that they will be subject to critical inquiry and scholarship, thus, adding new stories and voices to the digital cultural record. Engaging in the work of digital textual recovery is, therefore, an ethical and political intervention in digital humanities that is essential to cultural survival for marginalized voices.

References

"About TEI Boilerplate." *TEI Boilerplate*. Accessed July 17, 2017. http://dcl. ils.indiana.edu/teibp/.

Bottomore, Stephan. "Scholarly Research, Then and Now." *Early Popular Visual Culture* 14, no. 4 (2016): 302–318.

Earhart, Amy. *Traces of the Old, Uses of the New: The Emergence of Digital Literary Studies*. Ann Arbor: University of Michigan Press, 2015.

Forster, Chris. "Public Domain Editions." *Chris Forster*. Last modified June 21, 2012. http://cforster.com/2012/06/drill-baby-drill/.

Gil, Alex. "Ed.: A Jekyll Theme for Minimal Editions." *Ed.* Last modified July 12, 2017. https://elotroalex.github.io/ed/.

Risam, Roopika. "Other Worlds, Other DHs: Notes Towards a DH Accent." *Digital Scholarship in the Humanities* 32, no. 2 (2017): 377–384.

"TEI: Text Encoding Initiative." *Text Encoding Initiative*. Last modified July 19, 2016. http://www.tei-c.org/index.xml.

Vanhoutte, Edward. "Every Reader His Own Bibliographer—An Absurdity?" In *Text Editing, Print and Digital World*, edited by Kathryn Sutherland and Marilyn Deegan, 99–112. London: Routledge, 2016.

Whitman, Walter G. "Glimpses of Life in China" Excerpt. *Digital Salem*. Accessed July 17, 2017. http://di.salemstate.edu/omeka/exhibits/show/walter-george-whitman/item/33.

GLOSSARY

Algorithms The underlying evolutionary principle of the survival of the fittest is applied to an algorithm in order to create a solution to the proposed problem. Based on the first iteration: "some of the better candidates are chosen to seed the next generation by applying a recombination and/or mutation to them. Recombination is an operator applied to two or more selected candidates (the so-called parents) and results one or more new candidates (the children). Mutation is applied to one candidate and results in one new candidate. Executing recombination and mutation leads to a set of new candidates (the offspring) that compete—based on their fitness (and possibly age)—with the old ones for a place in the next generation," (Eiben and Smith 2003, p. 15).

Arrays Arrays are special variables that can contain more than one value. The index inside of square brackets for the array indicates which value is being used. `variableName[0]` is the first value, `variableName[1]` is the second value, etc.

Big data Most simply, big data is a collection of very large amounts of information that might include a variety of media such as text, images, video, and metadata (data about the data, such as the location and time it was collected). More formally, though still vaguely, big data has been defined in terms of its three "Vs": "Volume – large amounts of data 2. Variety – the data comes in different forms including traditional databases, images, documents, and complex records 3. Velocity – the content of the data is constantly changing, through

319

l. levenberg et al. (eds.), *Research Methods for the Digital Humanities*, https://doi.org/10.1007/978-3-319-96713-4

the absorption of complementary data collections, and from streamed data arriving from multiple sources" (Berman 2013, p. xx).

Data visualization Attempting to understand data by placing it in a visual context. Historically this process has focused on charts and graphs, but may include any type of visual element. Programs such as Microsoft Excel and Tableau are frequently used for creating such visualizations.

For loop A for loop is a procedure that facilitates iteration by looping through the code that is contained in it multiple times. Variables in the opening line of the loop tell it how many times to run. In this case, it starts at 0 (i = 0) and runs until i is equal to rowCount, which has been previously defined as the number of rows of data in the CSV file. i is increased by one (i++) each time the loop runs through one iteration.

Generative design A type of design approach that is based on the combination of repetition and variation.

Information aesthetics An approach developed by Lev Manovich (2001) that studies aesthetic approaches in context of the larger cultural forms that are specific to the contemporary information society.

Iteration A form of repetition, used here in the context of computer code. This can be created using a variety of approaches such as loops, addressed later.

Media studies The academic study of the history, content, and effects of media.

Modulation Modulation is a change or variation, and works particularly well in combination with repetition. For example, the lines in Image 1 were created by varying, or modulating, their location on the screen using a simple algebraic algorithm that alters each line's location slightly.

Parameterization A parameter is a value that sets the conditions of an operation and impacts the output. For example, the budget for a project is a parameter that places constraints on the possibilities for design. Reas and McWilliams (2010) explain this in relation to code: "Thinking about parameters provides a bridge between repetition and transformation... While transformation describes a parameter's effect on form, repetition offers a way to explore a field of possible designs for favorable variations," (p. 95).

Repetition Coding is particularly well-suited for repetition, or the repeating of particular design elements such as lines, text, images, or sounds, because these repetitions can be created with only a few lines of code as part of a "for loop" (see below). Repetitions can create a sense of rhythm, depth, and/or motion depending on how they are used (Reas and McWilliams 2010). Image 1 Generative Design in this text is an example of the repetition of lines.

Transformation Transformation is, most simply, the moving of an object, but when done digitally can include shearing, stretching, reflecting, warping, and distorting (Reas and McWilliams 2010). Such transformation can be used in computer graphics and animation to create movement.

Variables Variables are named placeholders that can hold any value, much like the variables you may be familiar with from algebra. For example, x can be a variable that is assigned a numerical value. It can also be set to contain a string, which is a series of numbers and letters. Numeric variables can be used in calculations, while those containing strings cannot.

INDEX

© The Editor(s) (if applicable) and The Author(s) 2018
I. levenberg et al. (eds.), *Research Methods for the Digital Humanities*,
https://doi.org/10.1007/978-3-319-96713-4